by Jackie Greer

life
ALWAYS BEGINS

To Joan Steinhoff
With special love in
Christ —
Jackie M. Greer
10/28/03

life

ALWAYS BEGINS

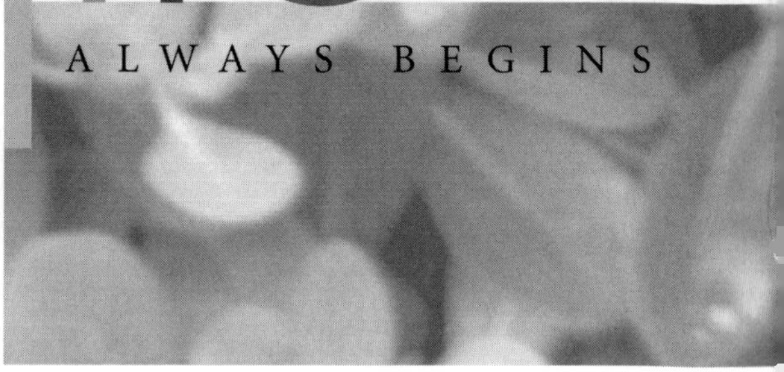

ISBN # 0-9637324-8-X

Published by:
Silver Grace Hope Foundation
P.O. Box 55709
Houston, Texas 77255-5709
713.681.0524

For questions contact:
Jackie Hall 713.520.9600
hallj@thehallgroup.com

Design and Layout by: Limb Design, www.limbdesign.com
Photographs by: Kara Matheny

No one event, or series of events, in your life has to define your life—even if it is filled with difficulties. There are as many ways to heal from broken bodies, dreams, or relationships as there are ways to be wounded in these areas. We have an innate capacity to rebound from the blows life may throw our way. I know about trauma, and I know about rebounds. And I know that life always begins . . . again.

The purpose of *Life Always Begins* is to let you know that, if you allow it, God will be present in all your life's activities. Without His guidance I would never have made it to ninety-four as a happy person. Often I have been reminded that I am never alone and God will not leave me with something I cannot handle if I will just let Him take control. If I can help one person realize that all things are possible with Christ, then I have been a successful author and friend. I want you to close this book realizing that no matter what life deals you, "life always begins again" and Christ will give you "a crown of beauty instead of ashes, the oil of gladness instead of mourning, and a garment of praise instead of a spirit of despair."

May you profit from every new beginning as you give thanks to God for each opportunity.

Jackie
Matthews Greer 2003

Foreword

Jackie Greer is without question one of the most amazing persons and one of the most joyful Christians I have ever known. Despite a life of much disappointment and pain, she was a trailblazer for women in banking and is an influential witness for Christ.

"The Energizer Bunny" must have been patterned after Jackie or someone like her. She is full of life and zest and energy. Her life is filled with achievements, purpose, and a checklist of things to do. She is tireless in her love for life and unwavering in her commitment to God, her community, and her friends. This is all the more amazing since on March 23, 2003, she celebrated her ninety-fourth birthday.

Life for Jackie has not been a "bed of roses." She has experienced much heartache. She lost her dad tragically when she was quite young. Her husband died in the war effort not long after they were married. She has known rejection and sadness and disappointment, but she has never wavered in her love for God, her love for people, and her love for life. After each tragedy she has just looked for a new opportunity to serve God and help people.

Why? Because she is so grateful to God for what He has done for her in Jesus Christ! She is so thankful to God for all the hope and help He has given her that she can't sit still. Motivated daily by that gratitude to God, she wants to share God's love with everybody she meets. She hopes her autobiography is yet another way to encourage people, even those she may never meet. The title, Life Always Begins, means that whatever may come our way, God will love us through it and heal us and give us a new start and a new life. God, through His love, always has a new beginning for us.

Jackie Greer's life has shown us this over and over again.

In February, 2003 Jackie was the guest of honor at the annual Women's Ministry Tea of St. Luke's United Methodist Church in Houston, Texas. She was honored for her incredible record of service to our church and for her compassionate "can-do" spirit. Jackie has been an exemplary servant of every church to which she has belonged. Teacher, counselor, choir member, mentor, stand-in mother and grandmother, advocate, leader of workshops and seminars, and caller of first-time visitors . . . Jackie is all of those and much, much more.

The Women's Tea honoring her was held on a Sunday afternoon. The following Wednesday morning she checked into the hospital for surgery. The procedure went well, and she was back in her hospital room by early that afternoon. I called Jackie's room. The line was busy. I tried again. Busy again. Finally after about thirty minutes, I got through and Jackie answered the phone. She sounded great. We celebrated her good results and had a prayer of thanksgiving.

Then I said, "Jackie, I've been trying to reach you for some time, but the line has been busy."

She laughed, "Yes, I know. I've been on the phone calling our first-time visitors. One family said they are going to join this coming Sunday."

She went on to relate that she had reached the man at his office and told him that she was ninety-four years old and the great-grandmother of St. Luke's. She told him that we have a great church and the one thing that would make it better is if this man and his family would come back and join.

The man reacted as many do who visit with Jackie. "Now let me get this straight. You are ninety-four years old and you are making phone calls for your church? That's unbelievable."

"Well," Jackie answered, "if you think that's unbelievable, guess where I am right now? I'm in the hospital."

"As a patient?" the man asked.

"Yes, I had surgery," Jackie explained.

"Surgery? When?" the man asked incredulously.

Jackie responded simply, "This morning."

"This morning!" the man exclaimed.

"Yes, but I'm back in my room now and I'm doing just fine," she assured him.

The man said, "Jackie, my family and I will be there to join the church next Sunday in the 11:00 service. If anybody loves the church the way you do, it must be some kind of church!"

Every organization Jackie has participated in and every person Jackie has befriended could add, "It's not that I'm so great; it's that Jackie is some kind of person and friend—and she has changed me for the better with her talents, her energy, her example, and her love!"

Dr. James W. Moore, Senior Minister, St. Luke's United Methodist Church
Houston, Texas

Dedication

This book is dedicated to my pastor, my friend, and my shepherd, Dr. James W. Moore at St. Luke's United Methodist Church in Houston, Texas, for encouraging me to write my story. The wisdom of his suggestion has been evident as I have been able to release ten decades of animosity towards my mother and grandmother through this work. I praise God that I am finally at peace with Him and with myself and can be a better citizen for Christ as I reach out to touch the lives of others through a cleansed heart.

Also, I dedicate this book to my precious friends, Sylvia Pennywell, Judy King, Jackie Hall, Clyde Petterson, the Women of Texas Executive Women, and the Aldine Mentoring Programs and my girls, who enabled me to bring this book to life, and to my friend and student, David Thomas.

To my father, Robert Coleman Matthews, and my beloved husband, Kenneth Sidney Greer, I express my eternal gratitude for teaching me the meaning of unconditional love and showing it at every turn in our lives together. These two precious ones remain a focal part of my life that brings smiles and joys even today. They were always my steady support when new beginnings were difficult.

I thank Tommie Jones, my guardian angel, without whom I would not be alive today and would not be capable of all the things I schedule for my days. A well-known banker, Tommie has been my mainstay for 32 years. She manages my home and provides me with a way of life I would not have but for her. I could never pay her or do enough for her to compensate for the life she makes for me. Her daughters, their families, and her sisters are all as much a part of me as anyone could be. There are no words to express my deep appreciation of her, so I hope this public recognition will reflect just a little of all I feel about Tommie and her family.

Last, but by no means least, I am grateful for the love and support of my extended family which paved the way for me to see the beautiful in what used to seem so ugly. My transformed memories now enhance my opportunities to serve my fellow man and my God. Often the difficulties of life become the bridges of strength that help us move forward as we experience accomplishment in spite of pain and disappointment. Because of this, I give thanks to God, who led me through the difficulties into a family circle of immeasurable richness.

Jackie
Matthews Greer 2003

table OF CONTENTS

one

chapter 1
PLANTING SEEDS FOR LIFE

The strong, mellow notes of Beethoven burst through the open window into the backyard like gusts before a thunderstorm. However, they did not brighten my four-year-old heart. With each chord I pounded the wet sand in my sandbox as I shaped the next structure in my sand village. Mother liked tidiness and order. Well, my village had three tidy castles and would soon have a church in the same row. She'd like them if she would just come outside long enough to look at them. Maybe if this steeple were just a little taller like the one at First Methodist Church of Palestine where she spent so much time, she'd like it better.

Slapping my hands together around the steeple, I lost my balance and sat down hard right on top of the church and two of the castles. Not one to cry easily, I jumped back on my feet, dusted the sand off my black cotton dress, jabbed my hands onto my hips, and surveyed the damage. I could use the metal tractor Dad had bought me and smooth out the ruined mounds of sand to begin again, but I was tired of working on creations no one would admire except myself. By the time Dad got home from his job as postmaster, it would be dark and the night rains would probably wash away my efforts.

I didn't want Dad to think I was ungrateful for the new sandbox and the clean white sand he had had shipped 190 miles from the Gulf Coast at Galveston to our tiny town of Palestine, deep in the heart of East Texas. I had had fun with the tractor, shovel, and other digging equipment he had supplied and taught me how to use, but now I needed a project that would rival Mother's piano students for her attention.

My eyes ran around the backyard for inspiration. No idea came to me as I glanced around at the woodshed, the garage, and the back porch where the icebox preserved the lemon pies Grandmother made for her catering business. Of course! I thought as my eyes landed on the plot of land in the corner of the yard from which sprouted several varieties of leafy green plants. I'll make a garden just like Grandmother's. Mother likes to look at pretty gardens. She'll be proud of me.

Grabbing my metal bucket and shovel, I ran to the well-tended garden and scanned the rows for the tallest plants. My garden had to be the best if it were to please Mother. Gingerly, I stepped onto the rich soil and bent over a flourishing tomato plant. Down went the shovel. Up came the plant, roots and all, and into my bucket. When I had harvested several tomato, lettuce, and string bean plants, I lugged them back to the sandbox, carefully dug holes in a row, and replanted them. When I had three rows of the healthiest plants, I stood back to admire my work.

For some reason I was not satisfied. What was missing? Again I scanned my surroundings for the solution. There it was! Running all around the house! Grandmother's other gardens had color—peach-colored roses, purple hyacinths, blue geraniums, and multicolored hollyhocks. Avoiding thorns, I concentrated on every flower except the roses. One by one, I transported samples from the front and side flowerbeds to the perimeter of my sandbox. I made sure I got the ones with the biggest blossoms. Oh, yes, Mother would love my garden.

So absorbed in my work was I that I did not hear the back screen door open and slam shut. I was not aware that my efforts had been noticed until I heard Mother's shriek, "Alice Cornelia! What have you done now?!"

Happy that she had come to play with me, I whirled around with a proud grin on my face. My grin melted at the sight of her stern countenance. Her eyes crackled like fireworks and her face was as red as the roses in the front flowerbed. The wispy blonde curls that surrounded her pale face shook as she stalked towards me. Without giving me a chance to explain myself, she yanked me by the arm, marched me into my bedroom, and declared, "Just wait until your father gets home, young lady. You have gone too far this time!"

She slammed the bedroom door just as the door bell rang. I heard her steps quickly move down the hall and her composed voice sing out, "Well, good afternoon, Heather. No, you are not too early. Did you get in all your practice time this week? Well, I'm so proud of you. . . ."

Heather was the last pupil before supper, and I hoped Dad would be home before Heather left. He would listen to me. I pulled out my suitcase of paper dolls and half-heartedly searched for Jo and Meg, my favorites from the Little Women family.

At last I heard Dad's voice booming. I had fallen asleep. He usually was not so boisterous when he came home from work. Listening carefully, I realized he was out in the backyard. He must have seen my garden! I hid behind the curtain and peeked out my window. Dad was wagging his index finger over my remaining castle while he faced Mother and Grandmother. I could see his neck muscles bulging and his forehead wrinkled as he shouted most uncharacteristically, "Of course, I see very clearly what has happened! You have neglected my daughter again to concentrate on your businesses. What is she supposed to do? She's not old enough for school yet. You won't let her have friends over to play. All day you . . . ," he snapped, gesturing towards Grandmother, "you are in the kitchen with Tildie and your cooking, and you . . . ," he swung his hand towards my mother, "are preoccupied with your music career. She's only four! She needs guidance . . . and attention. Why couldn't you see how she loves to follow you around and dig in the dirt and give her her own seeds to plant? I see she has quite an eye for design," he smiled, glancing up and down my ragged rows of drooping plants. "Every one of your precious plants will be replaced. That is the end of this discussion."

I jumped back into my room as he turned and stomped toward the house. Shortly afterwards there was a soft knock on my door and Dad's voice sang out,

"Tootsie?" He had nicknamed me that after a doll he had seen. "It's time to eat."

As he tucked me in bed that night, he asked, "Tomorrow will you help me build two more gardens?"

The next day we carefully returned Grandmother's plants and flowers to their original places. Then Dad tilled a large area of the side yard and, with strips of burlap tied between two poles, divided it into his garden and my garden. He let me select which vegetables and flowers to plant, and for years we worked side by side tending our gardens. What fun it was that first year when mine produced tomatoes before his and I sold some to a neighbor for a quarter. I kept that quarter for years—my first personal income! Little did I know that sale was the seed of my life's work as a banker and that Dad's example paved the way for me to mentor hundreds of girls who, like me, had emotional issues to deal with and grow beyond.

Dad outpaced me when he began experimenting with grafting. Once he brought an expert over from Texas A&M College at College Station to teach him how to graft pecans, berries, and plums. I was surprised that he never tried to patent his outstanding results. He also tried his hand at raising chickens, ducks, and turkeys, but I did not join him in these pursuits nor did Mother. She refused to gather eggs or kill a chicken. In fact, she would not help with weeding or planting. Picking flowers was the extent of her contribution to the gardening efforts at our house.

The garden incident was also the seed of my coping with what life threw at me: finding sunshine behind the clouds and learning that life always begins—not just once, but over and over as new experiences come our way and circumstances change. The promise of a new beginning carried me through my childhood with a mother who seemed to blame me for not being the son she wanted. The surprise of new beginnings, pleasant as well as unwelcome, marked most of my adulthood. Just knowing that new beginnings would show up, and I could survive them and be happy, helped temper their impact.

For Retha and Robert Coleman Matthews of Palestine, Texas, their lives began as parents on March 23, 1909, when a little red-haired baby girl came to make her home with them. I was named Alice Cornelia Matthews for my two grandmothers—Alice for my mother's mother, Alice Wagner, and Cornelia for my paternal grandmother, Cornelia Matthews. It was a big name for a little girl.

My mother always addressed me by my full name. My father called me any endearing term that came to mind. An uncle called me Little One. Father Lee, the local priest and good friend of my family, dubbed me Colleen because, at three, he said I looked like an Irish lassie. He was right. My reddish-blonde hair trumpeted my father's Scotch-Irish heritage.

Because I was always popping up on top of the house or high in a tree, neighbors Homer and Emma Murphy, who owned City Drug Store on the square, nicknamed me Jack-in-the-Box. When I went to college, the girls in my dorm shortened that to Jackie, the name that has stuck with me the rest of my life. My college friends even dubbed my mother Mama Jack. When she died in 1957, I ran her obituary under Retha Wagner Matthews. Later friends chastised me for omitting "Mama Jack" from the name. They didn't even recognize who she was and missed the funeral.

My birth highlighted two major issues in my family: religion and ambition.

The religious question arose after my dad went to live with a foster family. His mother died when he was 13. The next year his father died, so he moved in with the wonderful Mr. and Mrs. Hugh McKernan, whom I called Granny and Paw-Paw. Their two boys and two girls were grown, and they opened not only their home but their hearts to my father. These good folks were Catholic. Because Dad's family had lived in the country outside of Palestine, they attended a community church, which welcomed preachers of all denominations to fill its pulpit. They liked the Methodist doctrine best.

Religion was not a topic of concern in my father's new home. The McKernans felt in due time he would declare a religious preference, and they left the matter up to him. However, through the years Granny told Dad that while he might never join the church with them, she expected any children he had to be raised Catholic. Dad dismissed the subject, saying that only time would tell. As a youth he attended First Methodist Church in Palestine, where he met my mother. They were married there March 4, 1901, and continued to be active in that congregation throughout their lives as long as they lived in Palestine.

My mother had a long, difficult labor with me. When finally my lusty cry rose over her groans, she fell into a stupor from the medication she had been given. My father gently washed her face with a clean rag and smiled at the tiny baby girl in the doctor's arms. He didn't care about the baby's gender although he knew that a son would make his wife happier. He must have hoped that somehow this tiny new life could restore to him the woman he loved and had lost to music.

Kissing my mother gently on the forehead, he left the room to call the McKernans and announce my arrival. He returned to our the bedroom to be sure the doctor and Grandmother Wagner, in whose house we lived, had everything under control. Mother groggily opened her eyes and couldn't push out her words. Dad guessed what her question was and leaned down close to her ear to say, "It's a sweet little girl."

Mother grimaced and replied thickly, "Are you sure?"

Dad nodded. Mother closed her eyes, turned her head toward the wall, and slept for another twelve hours. Before Dad could escape to his bedroom for much needed rest, the doorbell sounded. He was surprised to see not only the McKernans but Father Lee as well. He invited them in and led them to the bedroom where Mother and I were sleeping. Mother did not stir at the sound of their voices and footsteps. When Granny could not get a response from her, she nodded to Father Lee, "Retha is still out and who knows when she might wake up. We need to go ahead."

Father Lee dutifully drew two vials of blessed sand and blessed oil from his pocket and set them reverently on the bedside table. He motioned to Granny to take me from Mother's arms, and he gently laid his hand on my head. "Parents, what name have you given your child?" he intoned. Grandmother Wagner realized immediately what was about to take place and excused herself to go to her room. Before my weary Dad could consider what was happening, Father Lee was making the sign of the cross on my forehead with chrism oil and I had been baptized. Later when my mother awoke and learned what had happened, she merely said, "Well, bless his heart. He tried."

After some refreshments Granny and Paw-Paw took their leave, but not before reminding Dad that I should start my first catechism when I was four. Dad replied nonchalantly, "I'll keep that in mind."

He did act on the advice. When I was about five, my parents, Granny, and I began attending once-a-month Saturday afternoon classes at the Catholic church. Father Lee taught us such Bible basics as the Beatitudes, the Ten Commandments, and the Lord's Prayer. The year I was nine, I attended a Communion service at the Methodist church. I sat with Dad while Mother played the organ. Although the procedure was the same that I had seen in that church all my life, this particular Sunday I noticed that only the adults and some of the older children approached the Communion railing. The smaller children and a few others were the only ones who did not go forward to receive the sacrament of the grape juice and bread.

I leaned over and whispered my concern to Dad. "Why can't we children go kneel at the railing?"

He explained that only members of the church were allowed to receive the Communion elements. "Let's talk about this later, honey," he whispered back.

Later that day we were out swinging when Dad opened the subject again. "You know, Tootsie," he began, "when people join our church, they are asked some questions like 'Do you believe that Jesus is the son of God?' and 'Do you promise to be faithful to the Methodist Church and uphold it with your prayers, your presence, your gifts, and your service?'"

He paused while I thought about what he had said. Then he asked, "Are you ready to join the church?"

After a moment, I said, "I think so. I believe in Jesus and I'll do what I can to help the church." Dad hugged me tight and said, "Then next Sunday at the end of the service you can walk down the aisle to join. I'll go with you."

So one Sunday in the spring I made my profession of faith with Dad at my side. For years we had an informal Bible study when Dad would tell me the stories of the Bible and explain to me the ways of God as he understood them. One thing Dad told me that didn't make sense until I was much older was that when we pray, we don't always get what we pray for. "Instead," Dad said, "God does what is best for us." My child's mind could not grasp how what was best for us could be different from what we prayed for. I would come to see, however, that God always answered my prayers, but often in ways that I never would have predicted—or even wanted. Some answers I honestly still do not understand, but that's where Dad told me that faith comes in—faith that God is aware of all that is happening in our life, that He is always right beside us in the hard times as well as the happy times, and that He will bring good out of sorrow and suffering. "You can count on that," Dad assured me.

When I was ten, I began to attend services at Easter, Christmas, and other special times with the McKernans at the Catholic church, and I did have a catechism which Dad faithfully taught me. The first part of the prologue explained, "God, infinitely perfect and blessed in himself, in a plan of sheer goodness freely created man to make him share in his own blessed life. For this reason, at every time and in every place, God draws close to man." Although I did not then fully understand the promise contained in this amazing fact, I smiled every time I heard it—inside and out. God wanted me and made me so I could stay near Him. He was never absent from me while He attended to someone else. No wonder everyone called him "Father." He reminded me of my Dad.

My parents and I lived with my maternal grandmother, who, like Mother, didn't want me around. When Grandfather Wagner failed in the grocery business and died, my parents moved into my grandmother's house to help support her. I lived there until I went off to college. Both my mother and grandmother had expected to marry only once and have one child, a son. Their disappointment over not having a son, no doubt, is what prompted all kinds of restrictive rules for their daughters so the women would not continually have to find a place for them in their life. My grandmother had provided the example which my mother chose to follow. Just like Mother as a child, I could not eat between meals, have friends over, go over to a friend's house, or ever mention boys. Both focused on their careers as paramount to their happiness—not, in either case, their child or their husband.

The truth about these two talented women is that neither of them should ever have married or had children for their husbands suffered from their professional commitments the same as I did. My dad was my trump, and we had nothing but fun when time permitted our doing things together. Those who knew my maternal grandfather, Charles George Wagner from Gruenberg, Germany, said he was gentle and would have adored me as he did my mother. Grandfather died three months to the day before I was born. I will ever regret not knowing him.

Fortunately Granny and Paw-Paw McKernan were wonderful to me, and their children loved me as a little sister. I reveled in this love and always felt so wanted by their family. It was a sad day in 1918 when Paw-Paw died and an even sadder one in 1920 when Granny was gone. That meant that at eleven I had lost a haven I had come to depend upon. Sometimes Granny would see me playing by myself in the yard and invite me to her house. There we made doll clothes or played paper dolls. She filled in for the companions I was not allowed to have. With their deaths I began to adjust to life at its best and worst.

While Mother was always busy with her varied interests, our cook, Tildie, which was short for Matilda, was delighted a little girl had come into the family. She looked forward to teaching me to cook, bake, and play in the kitchen, and she fretted that Mother would not allow her to give me a cookie when I came home from school. The day before I turned four, Tildie asked me what I would like to do for my birthday. I answered, "Cook breakfast." So the next morning she stood me on a stool in front of the stove while she and I scrambled eggs and she showed me how to make toast and hot chocolate. From then on, I was Tildie's shadow. The attention Tildie gave me and the love I developed for her did not bother my mother. She was busy teaching piano and organ lessons, and no doubt realized that Dad was my focal point in life anyhow.

In spite of all her faults, my mother was a woman before her time. She graduated from high school at fifteen, then graduated from Kidd Key Music University in Sherman, Texas, college at eighteen and started a kindergarten and music school before she was 20. Also in her teens she became organist and choir director of First Methodist Church, Palestine. She wrote much of the Sunday school material for our Junior Department, which consisted of twelve and thirteen-year-old children, and worked with the MYF, Methodist Youth Fellowship. Before she was twenty, she started a kindergarten and music school.

In addition she was a fund raiser extraordinaire. Largely through her efforts, the Palestine Operatic Hall was erected in about 1915 on a triangle between Main and Elm Streets. It could seat more people than would fit in First Methodist Church. That church could hold 300, so the opera house could hold approximately 400. Through Mother's connections at Southern Methodist University in Dallas, where we spent our summers while she studied pipe organ under a fine teacher, she brought many wonderful programs to the citizens of our little city. She engaged speakers on religion, economics, or other current subjects and scheduled musicians of all kinds.

Often performers would swing by Palestine after their performance in Dallas, so our community enjoyed nationally known musicians. Once we heard the entire score of Aida. Another time the program was a full orchestra. Still another time the opera house offered a whole concert of only Beethoven's works.

My mother may also have mimicked my grandmother's ambition. My grandmother was a caterer before that was even recognized as a legitimate business. Her business started one Christmas after her husband had died. She invited friends over for dinner and decorated a cake with holiday motifs. Someone suggested that she go into business offering her creations. Another friend whose daughter was soon to be married asked her to make the wedding cake—and she was in business. She furnished refreshments for weddings, teas, and other special occasions. Her customers came from all around the area. She finally stopped her business when she lost one eye to glaucoma. My grandmother too was ahead of her time.

Both my mother and grandmother were too focused on their respective careers to have room for anyone in their lives. Their husbands no doubt were deprived of many facets of married life because the women's time was their own and to be shared only when they wanted a time of sharing. I felt, and I feel sure that Dad and my grandfather agreed, that we never lived in a home but in a house. Mother taught her music classes in this house; Grandmother ran her catering business from this house. I was lonely in this house.

While neither my father nor grandfather approved of the restrictions their wives placed on their daughters, in that society child care was the prerogative of the wife and the men had to settle for circumventing the rules when they could. Largely because of my mother's and grandmother's business connections, we had lots of company at our house, both local and out-of-town visitors. Dad always saw to it that I was included in all the activities with our guests. However, when Mother was the only parent at home, she would allow me to eat with the guests, then would send me off to another room with a book or paper dolls or to the bedroom to take a nap.

Everyone seemed to realize who my guardian angel was. I often heard visitors comment, "Bob, you have a real pal in that little girl." He would smile down at me and squeeze my hand or pat my head or make some gesture of love that evidenced his caring attitude.

I learned my people skills from my father, who often had long talks with me. He let me know in little ways that there was a way of life that was better than the one I had and gave me hope that eventually I would enjoy it. His fawning over me helped me to understand Father Lee's teaching that God was like a father who would always be there for me. Somehow, I knew that to rebel against my mother would be disastrous so, feeling secure in God's and my father's love, I bided my time.

Although too little to understand all the ramifications of my upbringing, I learned that someday the cocoon would break and freedom would come. Life would have new beginnings. What preparation did I have to meet adult life when I had had virtually no childhood and little training in relationships? Time would tell—the new beginnings were yet to come.

two

chapter 2

THE UNEXPECTED NEWS

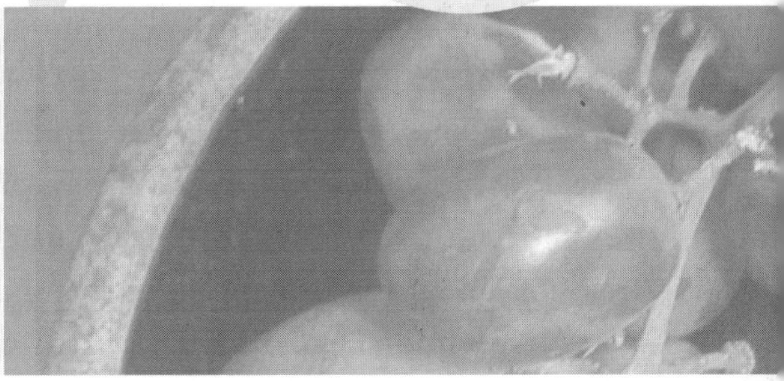

At seven I had not yet started school. My birthday was in March, so I had to wait until September to enroll in the first grade. The May before I was to start school, my family was eating dinner one evening when Mother blurted out, "Bob, I am going to Chicago in September and will be taking Alice Cornelia."

My father paused with his fork in midair and cocked his head forward as if he had been struck by the unexpected words. "I see," he replied quietly. "How long will you be gone?"

"Three to four months," my mother answered tersely, staring down at the slice of roast beef she was cutting. To take her mind off the uneasy silence, she took an exaggerated sip of iced tea and dabbed her mouth with her starched white napkin. I held my breath and pleaded with my eyes that my dad not allow me to go so far from home for so long a period without him.

Mother glanced up warily at my father, who remained in his same pose as if frozen, and she quickly reached for more mashed potatoes. Dad's jaw tightened and his eyes stared past his wife at the antique china cabinet behind her. Finally he spoke, "What do you plan to do there?"

Relieved to have a response, even if an icy one, my mother answered with forced cheerfulness, "I have been in correspondence with a fine musical group from Germany that my father knew. They are sending an outstanding organist to America for several months, and I have been accepted to study under him."

My eyes grew large with apprehension, but I dared not look at my father. I recognized the hard tones of my parents' conversation, and I knew my role was to be a silent table guest. I swung my leg against the carved leg of the dining room table to divert my attention from the frightening possibility of several months without my dad's intervention in my life.

"Exactly how long will you be gone?" he pressed.

"I don't know exactly. That will be determined after I get there," Mother responded defensively as she fingered her napkin.

"And who will care for our daughter while you study?" Dad continued.

"I . . . I haven't worked that out yet," Mother replied simply.

Dad's voice rose along with the color in his cheeks. "And how much will this . . . study . . . cost?"

Mother set her fork down and looked Dad in the eye as she said, "I haven't figured what everything will cost, but I have made enough money to pay for my lessons."

"Lessons?" Dad retorted, restraining his anger. "What about housing, clothing for a cold country, food, and care of my child?"

Mother swallowed hard and stammered, "I'll find all that out. Just give me a little more time. Now if you will excuse me. . . ." She abruptly pushed back her chair and walked from the room with her head held erect.

I opened my mouth to beg Dad not to allow this, but he held up his hand as if to ward off my protest. We finished our dinner without mentioning the trip again.

Several days later when Dad came home for the noon meal, he announced after saying grace, "I will be taking a four months' leave of absence from work. I will arrange travel, housing, schooling, and all else for the three of us."

Mother's knife clattered against her plate and fell to the floor. She just sat and stared at her husband. Even at my young age, I realized that Mother had had no thought of Dad going with us on this venture. I will always wonder what her plans were for me and the other essentials like lodging.

When the three of us arrived in Chicago, a taxi drove us to an apartment house the local postmaster had assisted Dad in renting. Our apartment was a modest, but tidy one-bedroom with a tiny kitchen and furniture that had seen its peak years. Mother didn't even help unpack the bags. Instead she waited in the taxi while the driver and Dad wrestled the suitcases and trunks up the stairs and into our little dwelling. Then she had the driver take her to the Institute of Music to enroll. She returned home late that evening after I was already in bed. This became her pattern. I didn't mind because I had Dad all to myself until school started.

What the building lacked in style was compensated for by the pleasant, short, German landlady. The first morning after we arrived, someone knocked on our door midmorning. Dad opened the door and greeted a fidgety Mrs. Mudgett, dressed in sensible black with a dark green apron tied around her ample waist. "I hope you are finding everything satisfactory," she smiled.

"Oh, yes," Dad responded politely. "Everything is just as I expected. Thank you. Won't you come in?"

"Thank you," Mrs. Mudgett replied as she bustled into our living room. "Would you allow me to speak with Alice? Please excuse my attire. I am expecting special company and am baking this morning."

"Don't mention it," Dad said, turning toward the back of the apartment. "Tootsie, you have a visitor."

Shyly I stepped into the room and extended my hand to the landlady as Mother had taught me to do. Mrs. Mudgett took my hand and gently pulled me into her soft frame in a big hug. "Alice, I am so glad you have come to live here for a few months. Will you do me the honor of having tea with me and a few friends this afternoon?" She winked at Dad, then glanced back down at me. I was sure I had not heard her correctly. Grown ladies did not have children over for tea—at least in Palestine they didn't. I glanced at Dad for an explanation.

“Well, of course, she would be delighted to join you for tea, Mrs. Mudgett. What time would you like her to arrive?”

“That’s wonderful!” Mrs. Mudgett cried and hugged me again. “I’ll expect you about two then. Oh, if you have a favorite doll, please bring her.” She wiped her hands on her flour-stained apron before shaking Dad’s hand. “Thank you, Mr. Matthews. I’ll see Alice at two.”

My apprehension grew as the hour for my visit neared. I changed dresses twice and finally decided on a yellow, princess-style dress with a large white lace collar. I donned socks with lace around the top and my white patent Sunday shoes. I had never been to a party before and wasn’t sure what to expect, but Dad insisted that I go. “You’ll have fun, honey,” he assured me.

At five minutes to two, Dad and I headed out the door for Mrs. Mudgett’s apartment, which was on the first floor. I clutched my baby doll tightly. On the stairs we were joined by three other children about my age and their mother. “Oh, hello,” said the mother with excitement. “You must be the new tenants.” She nodded at Dad and grinned, “You know, I guess, that parents are not invited to Mrs. Mudgett’s parties.”

Dad raised his eyebrows and listened as she went on. “Every couple of weeks Mrs. Mudgett has these parties for the children. You know she wanted children and was not able to have any, so she enjoys our children as much as her time permits.”

By then we had arrived at Mrs. Mudgett’s door. Dad knocked. The door swung open to reveal a living room lively with children from toddlers to youth. They were crowded around a coffee table in the center of the room that held three plates piled high with several kinds of homemade cookies. On one corner of the table was a glass pitcher of lemonade. In the center were a half dozen dolls of every kind. Mrs. Mudgett scurried to the door and said to the young lady who had answered the knock, “Thank you, Patricia.” Turning to the new arrivals, she exclaimed, “Well, I’m so glad you Andersons got back from the store in time to come. And, Alice, I’m delighted that you chose to join us. Patricia, this is Alice Matthews. Will you introduce her around? Oh, and I forgot to tell you that you didn’t have to dress up. My parties are very casual.”

Patricia, who looked to be a few years older than I was, motioned for me to follow her. For the next three hours we six girls and four boys played games, sang silly songs, and ate our fill of cookies and homemade divinity candy. I had never eaten cookies except for dessert after a meal, so at first I hesitated to indulge. Finally I succumbed to the temptation and relished every bite of the forbidden food. Even if Mother found out, I at least would have had a snack between meals one day.

By the time the party was over, I had made friends with all the children and promised to ask Dad if one of them could come over to play the next day. Mrs.

Mudgett repeated her parties for the children about every two weeks. When the weather turned cold, she substituted hot chocolate for the lemonade, but she always had more than enough cookies for her guests.

Several times she asked Dad and two of the mothers to help chaperone the group as we took a picnic to Lake Michigan, three blocks away. Since the weather was chilly, we ran along the beach to keep warm and heartily gulped down a lunch of ham sandwiches, pickles, apples, and a homemade buttermilk cake. Even on the weekends when I would have thought she would want to rest like the other adults, she concocted activities for the children in the apartment house. Because of her and my new friends, I did not miss Granny as much as I would have otherwise and I did not miss Mother at all.

Mother was quite happy with her new professor and stayed at the Institute of Music from early morning until almost eight each night to practice. Dad and I usually cooked simple meals as we had seen Tilde do and ate our meals alone. Sometimes Mrs. Mudgett invited us to her apartment for dinner along with other parts of families from the apartment house or we went to the cafeteria, which was a real treat since we did not have a cafeteria in Palestine. Many nights Mother did not arrive home before I went to bed, but I did not mind. Dad would tuck me carefully into bed and say my prayers with me. After just a few weeks my nightly prayer went something like this, "Dear God, thank you for giving me friends to play with and time to play with them. Help Mother with her lessons and Dad with cooking dinner. Amen."

We arrived in Chicago in mid-August, and school started right after Labor Day. Dad enrolled me in a private school which Mrs. Mudgett recommended for all her resident children. Each day Dad, along with other parents, walked me to the school campus and watched me go inside before he returned home or began whatever he had planned for the day.

A week after school started, I came home crying. "What's the matter, Tootsie?" Dad asked with concern.

"My shoulder hurts!" I whimpered, holding my left shoulder gingerly. Mother, of course, was not home.

Dad looked helplessly at me and sighed, "Well, let's see what Mrs. Mudgett says about this."

He walked to the phone and briefly relayed my complaint to Mrs. Mudgett. Shortly thereafter she arrived at our door with a hot water bottle and some Sloan's Liniment.

She gave me a sympathetic smile and turned to Dad. "Here, Mr. Matthews. Sit in this big chair and hold Alice Cornelia on your lap."

Dad obligingly picked me up and held me tenderly on his lap. Mrs. Mudgett rolled up the sleeve of my dress and gently began rubbing my shoulder with the ointment. I cried out,"It hurts! It hurts!" and tried to wriggle away as she continued massaging my shoulder.

Finally she laid the hot water bottle against Dad's chest and positioned me so my shoulder would rest against the warmth. Soon I was asleep, but only for a moment. I cried off and on all night with pain.

The next morning Mrs. Mudgett made an appointment for us to see a doctor. However he could not examine me because I hurt so bad I would not let him touch me. He suggested we continue the treatment Mrs. Mudgett had recommended and come back if I was not better in a couple of days. I was not, so Dad decided to take me to school and talk to the principal. The principal could not shed any light on what had happened to me, so he suggested he and Dad go talk to my teacher.

I followed behind, knowing what Dad would learn and wondering what his reaction would be. The principal knocked on the classroom door. Shortly the teacher opened the door with a look of surprise on her face. No sooner had the door been opened than my dad boomed out,"What is this?!"

Four of my unlucky classmates were seated in chairs at the back of the room with their left arms tied behind them with large cotton ropes, just as I had been the first week.

The teacher explained weakly that children who insisted on using their left hands for writing had to be persuaded to write the correct way. Before she could say more, Dad boomed,"But . . . but . . . this is not acceptable! Alice Cornelia is no longer a student at this school!"

He turned to me and asked,"Baby, which is your desk?" I led him to my desk where he promptly gathered up my things. He took my hand firmly as we marched from the room.

When Mrs. Mudgett found out what had happened, she called the president of my school's board and told him he had best do something about the atrocious situation.

Two days later I was enrolled in an Episcopal school close to our home. It was a fine school, complete with a beautiful, old, stone building and unusually appointed classrooms for children of various sizes and abilities. The teachers were highly skilled and very sensitive to their wards. I finished the semester there although most of my friends from our complex went to the first school I had gone to. When school was out, I hated to say goodbye because we would be returning to Palestine before Christmas and I would not see my new friends again.

The day we turned our keys over to Mrs. Mudgett, we all cried for she had been the most wonderful friend any family could ever have. For years we kept up with her, and then one day a birthday card was returned "Addressee Unknown." Dad and I cried and wished her a happy landing in a place where there is the greatest of all new beginnings.

Mother's stay at the institute was very rewarding. To share her musical experiences, soon after we arrived back in Palestine, she gave a brilliant organ recital that was attended by people from all over our little town. She was an exceptional musician, and I felt proud when the newspaper wrote a glowing article about her. Dad went back to work at the post office. Preparations were made for me to enter Alamo Elementary School, where I would spend the next five years. All three of us were back in our home territory just as if we had not been away. However, Mother had learned new organ techniques and I had had a taste of friendship that I would continue to miss.

three

chapter 3

LESSONS FOR LIFE

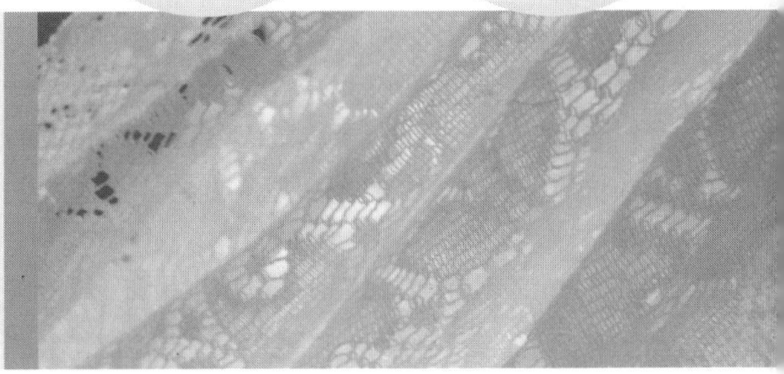

Returning to Palestine at mid-semester made it necessary for me to enroll in a new school, new to me since I had been in Chicago, but it was the school I was scheduled to attend all along.

To prepare for school, my daddy saw to it that Auntie Bess, Mother's dearest friend, made me a new dress for Mother was too busy with scheduling her students to take me shopping for clothes. I called many family friends "aunt" and "uncle" although we were not related because I had no "real" relatives. Mother was an only child and Dad's foster family did not live near us, so friends graciously filled in for nonexistent relatives.

My new dress was a Scotch plaid with a pleated skirt. Dad bought me a pair of the popular, black Buster Brown shoes. Buster Brown was a midget about sixty years old with white hair, who toured the country with his dog, Tige, promoting his Oxford tie shoes. He even came to Palestine several times. Everyone wanted to wear his style shoe. Mother protested that the shoes were not necessary since I had a perfectly good pair of button shoes that still fit. Dad overruled her and also bought me a new yellow lunch pail. The excitement of my new outfit relieved some of my anxiety about starting a new school.

The first day of school Mother braided my hair like hers, although she left the braids hanging rather than wrap them in a bun like she wore hers. Dad walked me to Alamo Elementary School, which was housed in a stately-looking building on a large plot of beautifully kept grounds. It served as a school for two generations before ultimately being converted into the library of the city of Palestine. A slender lady with a no-nonsense bun at the nape of her neck was standing just outside the front door of the school. She bent down to be at eye level with me when I stepped up. "Ah, Miss Alice. It is good to have you home again and in our school at last," she smiled.

I glanced at Dad, who squeezed my hand. "Tootsie, this is Miss Gertie Phool, the principal. If you ever have any problem, just go to her and she will help you." I nodded. She did not seem as ferocious as I had feared after hearing about her from the town gossips. I remembered hearing a client of Mother's say, "No wonder Miss Phool is not married. What man would put up with such a leaning toward perfection?"

Most of the faculty were unmarried and were referred to unkindly in our town as "old maid school teachers." They were made to sound rigid and unimaginative. Shame on us, for these were women dedicated to being good teachers and fair players. I look back and realize that Miss Pearl, my first-grade teacher, never made it to the altar, but Miss Gertie did on her sixtieth birthday. What an adorable man she married too. They had ten marvelous years together, and everybody loved Mr. and Mrs. Howard. Miss Gertie was accessible to her students, standing at the door each morning to greet us and each afternoon to bid us good-bye. Although an only child, she had an uncanny sensitivity to children and a great sense of responsibility for them. Even when she had to discipline a child, she gave him a chance to say, "I'm sorry." Because of the respect she showed children by her love and the standards she imposed upon them, she was loved and respected by the students.

After introducing me to Miss Gertie that first day, Dad led me to my first-grade classroom, where Miss Pearl Moore, my teacher, assigned me a desk near the back of the room. Each desk seat, which was a bench open on both sides, had a desk table attached behind it, facing so that it became the writing surface for the pupil behind. Each pupil was issued a speller, a reader, a writing manual, a drawing book, and a numbers pad. After we put our names in our books, it was time to adjourn for recess.

Because Palestine was so small, I knew most of the children in my class. I was enjoying playing with children I had not seen since returning from Chicago when I looked up and was surprised to see Elizabeth Naylor, a friend who was a half year younger than I and therefore not eligible to enroll until the following January. Elizabeth's pale face lit up when she saw me. Her blonde braids swung energetically as she came running, calling my name. When she reached me, she grabbed my hand and said excitedly, "Alice, I am going to school with you!"

While I, like everyone else, truly enjoyed Elizabeth, her presence at school confused me, so I corrected her, "Oh, no, Elizabeth, you are too young, so you have to wait until January."

She tilted her head and stepped back as if she had been hit. Big tears formed in her eyes and spilled down her cheeks. Regretting that I had said anything, I patted her sympathetically on the shoulder and shifted from one foot to the other, not knowing how to comfort her. She jerked her shoulders away from me, turned abruptly toward the building, and stalked away. She had come to go to school, and to school she was going.

When the class got seated after recess, there were two of us in my desk seat. One was Elizabeth, who had picked up one of my pencils and a notepad I had and had begun to write her name. I opened my mouth to say something, but no words came to mind. I just shrugged, shoved a piece of paper to her side of the desk, and began copying the words from my speller as we had been instructed. Wanting to share as Father Lee had often encouraged us to do, I tilted the book so we both could see the assigned page.

It was well into the last period before lunch when Miss Pearl discovered Elizabeth. She said nothing until the bell rang for lunch. Then, she calmly called the two of us up to her desk.

"Alice, I see you have a friend with you today," she began. "Did you know that Elizabeth is not old enough to come to school yet?"

"I know that, Miss Pearl. I didn't ask her. She just showed up," I answered with a quiver in my voice.

Realizing I had no control over the visitor, Miss Pearl turned to Elizabeth and said kindly, "Elizabeth, it's wonderful that you are eager to go to school. I look forward to having you in my class next year. However, you are too young to come this year. I'll have to ask you to go home now and not come back until next January."

Elizabeth pulled herself up to her full height and, shaking her head so that her long braids flopped back and forth, replied politely but firmly, "No, Miss Pearl. I will be coming to school to learn, and I will sit with Alice Cornelia until you assign me my own desk."

Taken aback at being talked to so directly by a child, Miss Pearl bent down until she could look Elizabeth in the eye and said gently, "Elizabeth. Please listen to me. In school there are rules we must follow. One rule says you are not old enough to attend class. I will ask you again to obey that rule. However, if you do not, I will have to call your mother to pick you up immediately. Do you understand?"

Elizabeth gave a half nod of her head and left the room. I breathed a sign of relief and headed home for lunch, or "dinner" as our big noon meal was called.

Coming back from dinner that day, I kept wondering if Elizabeth would come back. I hoped not because I hated to see the scene that might develop. Suddenly, I saw the little girl carefully tucked behind a big bush and I cringed. I sped up my steps, acted as if I did not see her, and headed through the main door of the school. The bell was ringing as I opened the door to my classroom and when I sat down, so did Elizabeth. There beside me was this determined little girl at work with her pencil and pad as if she belonged. What could I do? I would draw and give her a piece of paper to copy what I had done until finally Miss Pearl discovered our visitor was back. She took Elizabeth by the hand to the principal's office with Elizabeth complaining all the way.They called her mother, who thought she was taking a nap. Right away Miss Beulah (Mrs. Frank Naylor) came to school and took her daughter back home, but that was not the end of Elizabeth and school. The next morning while her mother was ordering groceries over the phone, Elizabeth slipped out of the house, climbed over the fence, and dashed to school and right into the room and told Miss Pearl she was there to stay.

Another visit to Miss Gertie's office reinforced the banishment. Elizabeth did not come back until her eligibility date the forthcoming January. All through school though she never got over not being in our class. She attended all our parties and was in all our class pictures for she felt that was where she actually belonged. She graduated a half semester after my class, but through the many years we shared, she was a best friend, to whom we all said goodbye in the middle of 1999 when she died from a heart attack. She was beloved by all, never married, and was always in a good humor and generous to a fault. Elizabeth had a shyness that was refreshing, and it gave her a charm like no other person had. I often wondered why she did not melt the heart of every boy who dated her. Her mother, however, told me one day that if Elizabeth ever had a proposal, she would likely faint and that would be her end. Miss Beulah said instinctively Elizabeth was scared to death of boys.

Along with my school lessons, Mother decided I needed to learn to play the piano when I turned ten. Fortunately, she did not have time in her schedule to teach me, so I took lessons from Miss Louise Stephens. Having another teacher did not stop Mother from evaluating my playing, however. As I practiced, she continually scolded, "Alice Cornelia, you are using the wrong finger to hit that high note. Stretch your hand like this" or "Alice Cornelia, play like you mean it! Start over again and do it right this time."

"But that's the way Miss Stephens told me to do it!" I would protest.

Mother would fume as she approached the piano, "Well, no matter. That's not right. Here is what you should do."

Whatever enjoyment others found in piano escaped me. Often my practice session ended with me in tears and Mother calling out as I ran to my room, "What is the matter this time? I would think you would appreciate knowing the right way to play."

After two years I begged Dad, "Please don't make me take any more! I'll never play to her satisfaction."

"You're probably right," he agreed sadly. "Music should be for pleasure, and neither of you is enjoying your piano playing." He allowed me to stop taking lessons. Perhaps in retaliation, Mother never allowed me to play her organ.

One morning when I was twelve, Mother announced at breakfast, "Alice, your father is going to Dallas on business today. I have instructed him to place an order for a very fine violin to be made for you. When it comes in a few weeks, you will take violin lessons from Allie Crozier."

"Yes, ma'am," I mumbled, knowing it was pointless to argue. Maybe the violin would not spark the arguments the piano had. I enjoyed music and thought maybe learning the violin was not such a bad idea.

"And you will resume your piano lessons with her sister, Hattie," Mother added. "Tilde, please bring us more toast."

I tightened my jaw and stabbed the sausage on my plate with my fork. I sliced through the link with one swift pull of my knife. Piano again?! I didn't think I could stand Mother's constant correction.

With no fanfare Dad became my mediator for my practice sessions. The evening after my first violin lesson, I stood in the living room trying to place the instrument under my chin the way Miss Allie had shown me. It kept slipping as I struggled to arch my fingers and rest them on the strings in the proper places. Finally I managed to hold the correct position and pull the bow smoothly across the strings. I jumped as applause broke out behind me. I whirled around to find that Dad had slipped into the room and had been watching me struggle. "You got it, Tootsie! Just keep doing that and you'll be playing a concert before you know it," he cheered me on.

I blushed and turned around to try to play three clear notes in succession. Hum, squeak, squeak. I heard Mother's rapid footsteps approaching and held my breath. When no tirade of criticism broke the silence, I cautiously turned my head towards the door. Dad had parked his six-foot frame in the doorway with his arms crossed in front of his chest and his back to me. Mother was trying unsuccessfully to squeeze her five-foot, four-inch body around him. Finally Dad's whisper filled the vacuum, "She is doing just fine, Retha, and I have this practice session under control. If we need your assistance, we will come find you."

Mother hesitated a moment, then spun around and stalked away. Dad then turned to me and said quietly, "Alice, will you please follow me to my library? I would like you to practice in there from now on if you do not object."

Knowing that Mother did not enter his library without an invitation, I eagerly gathered up the music stand, sheet music, instrument, and violin case and deposited them in Dad's private room. From then on, Dad sat as guard by the door while I practiced the violin in his library. A few times Mother tried to intervene, and he just looked at her and shook his head. As I lost interest in climbing peach trees and raising vegetables, I substituted playing the violin for my special activity with Dad. He loved great music and encouraged me to learn the masterpieces. Because he applauded my attempts, successful or not, I tried extra hard to play well and please him. Besides recitals, the only places to show off my skills were ladies' clubs or churches. While I never was invited to play at my church, where Mother was choir director, the Baptist church and a few local clubs asked me to play for occasional social events. I didn't mind sharing my musical accomplishments, but my favorite audience was always Dad.

He was a constant support to me, even when the skills I showed off were not music to his ears.

four

chapter 4

THE ANTIC KID

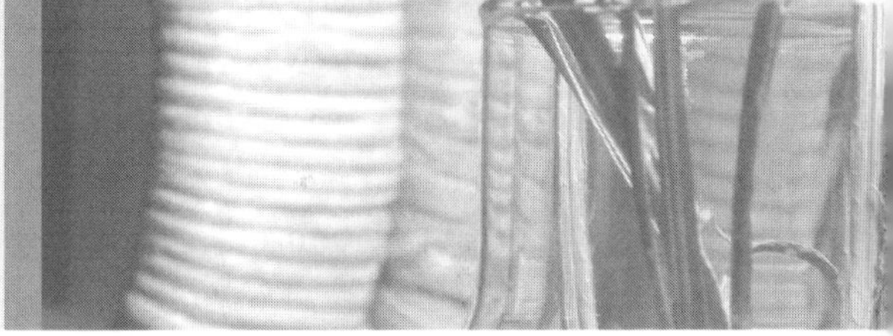

Today I know only too well what prompted the antics I pulled during my childhood: rebellion. My behavior speaks to the need I had to be accepted, recognized, or given some form of personal identity—or more realistically, visible evidence of love from other family members besides my dad and his foster parents. While I never repeated an antic, I always thought of something else of a greater magnitude the next time. It is hard to believe that a child would not be privileged to have a snack when arriving home from school, to visit or have friends over except for a birthday party, or to climb a tree. These were my mother and my maternal grandmother's house rules. My father had as much difficulty coping with these restrictions as I did.

Dad did not discuss the house rules with me because when he came home, I was his shadow and we had "our rules." We climbed a few trees and ate peaches we had just picked in our orchard. Frequently, when Mother was teaching, we went for walks and visited neighbors who had children to play with. I loved these times.

Although Dad understood the way my life was and sought out things that would give me pleasure, my behavior did not always live up to his expectations. The spring when I was eight, my grandmother received a gorgeous handmade lace umbrella from her family in Germany. The material was black Chantilly lace, and the handle was handmade Bentwood. A few days before its arrival, I had gone to the movie with some neighborhood friends and their mother to see Pearl Buck jump from a high cliff with a parachute. A movie was a rare treat for me, especially going with friends. It was so exciting to see the actress flying through the air—and the stunt looked so easy.

Sitting alone in the peach tree a few days later while Mother and Grandmother were at a meeting at church, I suddenly thought of my grandmother's lovely umbrella. While Tildie was busy fixing supper, I slipped into Grandmother's room, took the umbrella, and climbed up on the woodshed via a small ladder. I opened the umbrella, held it high over my head, and took a deep breath. Without a moment's hesitation, I ran and jumped off the roof and landed in a bed of beautiful hollyhocks and an adjoining pile of broken bricks. Staggering up on my feet, I first noticed that what had been colorful hollyhocks looked like a short-pile rug. I saw blood all over my legs and hands almost before I felt the sting of the cuts. Then my eyes fell on the jumble of lace, wire, and wood that had been the umbrella. It took a long time before I understood why the umbrella did not work for me as the parachute had worked for Pearl.

Even Tildie took little pity on me. She cleaned the cuts with soap and water and then led me back to the woodshed where she firmly applied the peach tree switch on top of my bruises and cuts. When Daddy came home, Mother made me tell him what I had done. He looked at both Mother and Grandmother and said with the sweetest, forced smile, "I think she has talents to think of such a parallel. Getting a new umbrella will be my pleasure. It will be just like the one that no longer exists, so this topic will not come up again."

Dad led me into his special library room for a never-to-be-forgotten lesson. He put me on his lap and asked, "Baby girl, if you had to do this all over again, what would you do?"

I hurt so much from the crash landing that I began to cry, "I would not do it!"

"Good," he replied as he hugged me. "Always think twice before you act and you will not get hurt as often and you will make better decisions." What a genius he was in helping me to grow to be a better person. I would love Dad to know that I am still growing and I hope I never quit.

That was not, however, the end to my antics. One morning when I was ten, Mother called me in to take a bottle of freshly churned buttermilk to a sick neighbor across the street. "Alice Cornelia, you are not to stop for anyone or anything before you hand this bottle to Mrs. Rose. Is that clear?"

I nodded obediently; picked up the cold, white glass jar; and started across the street. As I looked both ways before crossing, I recognized the car at another neighbor's house down the street. The Firebaugh family from California had arrived during the night! They were the daughter and grandchildren of Mrs. Doyle, another neighbor. It had been so long since they had been to Palestine I couldn't wait to see them. I ran across the street, put the milk jar down on Mrs. Doyle's sidewalk, and hurried into her backyard. I hugged Mattie Belle, Albert, and Frances and then ran with them to the climbing tree.

After some time Mrs. Doyle asked if we would like some milk and cookies. Milk!! "I'll be back in a minute!" I told my playmates breathlessly. I ran to pick up the jar and dash to Mrs. Rose's door to deliver the milk. As soon as I picked up the jar, it slipped from my sweaty hands and shattered into a jillion pieces. I gulped and stared at the glass shower as if I could will the jar back to a whole. Knowing what was ahead as a result of my disobedience, I had to think fast where I could retreat.

As I crossed the street back to my house, I noticed a tall ladder leaning against the house. The roofer was at work. What a fortunate coincidence! Knowing my mother was afraid of heights more than an inch off the ground, I felt I would be secure and in a strong bargaining position if I climbed on top of our fifty-foot chimney. Up the ladder I scampered, up the gable, and then up to the top of the chimney. I perched there with my feet dangling carelessly down toward the ground, wishing the whole town could see me on my throne. There I sat with a glib look, knowing that sooner or later I would not be accounted for and the search would be on.

Sure enough, it was not long before I heard the front door open and saw my mother march out in the yard looking toward Auntie Rose's house. Nobody was in sight, and I watched the scene with a gleam in my eyes. Mother looked up and down the street. She even went to the edge of our yard to have a better view. After a few minutes she began calling my name, but I did not answer. "Alice Cornelia!" she would yell, then cock her head to listen for my answer. "Alice Cornelia!" she repeated. "Where are you?" I laughed to myself, but not very loud, for I was not yet ready to be found.

Mother vanished inside the house, and I heard her calling over to the Roses' house to determine if I were there, only to learn I had not ever been there that morning. The next thing I knew both my mother and my grandmother were outside calling my name. I loved my silence! I still was not ready to be found. I was surprised to learn that my mother and grandmother had such lusty voices; they could have won hog-calling contests!

Suddenly the evidence was discovered. I heard Mother exclaim, "Look, Mama, at that broken jar on Mrs. Doyle's sidewalk. So this is why we cannot find that child!" Oh, ho! Now was the hour—now it was my time.

With a smile in my voice, knowing the fright I would cause, I called out, "Ladies! Here I am!" These ladies had never fainted, but we had a close call that morning. They jerked their heads up, scanning the heavens looking for me. I could hear them catch their breaths when they spotted me, well aware that one false move would be the end of me. Danger was not in my thoughts; being in control crowded out even common sense. I was having the time of my life with no thoughts of the future. I was in control and was this a new experience for me!! I was going to play this episode to the hilt!

For the first time in my life I thought, "Well, they are glad to see me." Truthfully they were, and they knew that getting me down safely was another matter. Mother began pleading with me, "Please come down, but please be careful."

I heard a real panic in her voice, but I was not giving an inch until I had carried out my plan. I answered, "OK, I will be careful, but are you going to whip me or punish me in any way after I get down?"

Mother shook her head and promised, "I will do nothing. We just want you to be safe."

That tactic had worked, so I tried another part of my plan. "Are you going to tell my daddy?"

"No, darling, we will not tell your father," she sighed as she gazed intently at me, shading her eyes from the sun with one hand. That was what I wanted to hear. Now it was review time. Assurance is mighty important when you are in control for the first time and you don't want to step out of that experience, so I repeated the questions. To my surprise, my mother's answers were more emphatic and seemingly more tender than the first ones, so I began my descent. Actually I came down with fear and trembling. It is a wonder I did not fall into the chimney or down to the ground for I could not remember exactly how I had gotten up there. I backed down the roof, bending over and balancing myself with my hands. I gingerly stepped onto the top rung of the ladder and slowly made my way to the ground.

Luck was on my side except for one thing: I was about halfway down the ladder when I felt two strong arms grab me. I had forgotten about the cook. Tilde grabbed me and off we raced to the woodshed, where she brought the switch down again and again on my bare legs. I never forgot that whipping, and I often wondered where my mother and grandmother were when this bit of history was made.

"Stop, Tilde!" I cried. "Ouch! Ohhhhh," I yelled as I tried to wriggle out of Tilde's grasp.

"Shame on you, Alice, for scaring us half out of our wits!" Tilde scolded as she brought the switch down again on my reddening legs. "Don't you ever do that again, do you hear, girl?"

When Dad came home that night, I was waiting at the gate. After my usual hug and kiss I suggested timidly, "Let's sit in the swing for a minute, OK? I have something to tell you."

He took my hand, followed me to the porch swing, and said gently, "Tell me." I guess the word pictures of me up high with the ladies on the ground turned on his laughing mechanism for he grabbed me up as the story unfolded and when I had spilled it all, he exclaimed, "You are safe! The rest is history!"

"History" sounded good, so I guessed all was well. I got in bed early that night in case there was a discussion about the day's activities. Before I went to sleep, however, Dad came to my bed and asked, "Sweetheart, what did you learn from today's experience?"

"I learned how to keep the peach tree switch hidden behind the pictures," I replied honestly. That was not the answer he wanted, but it had merit and so we agreed I had had another growing experience. If I could have made money as easily as I could think up situations that upset the family and neighbors, none of us would ever have had to work. As Dad leaned over to kiss me good night, he whispered, "Little girl, Dad would be glad if you did not make such dangerous efforts to avoid the switch and get control." That message was clear and worth listening to. Maybe I was getting too big to be so daring. Only time would tell.

Dad told me years later that one of the neighbors had called him at work that morning to tell him I was up on top of the chimney and Mother and Grandmother were frantic about my safety. He said he laughed and replied, "She will surely make the most of this effort, but I have confidence she will come down safely." We had a good laugh. The years after this antic were not uneventful. My antics were a little less dangerous but no less foolhardy.

The real lesson I learned from my day on the chimney was that it is not wise to flash danger in the face of assurance. To be truthful, being in control was so important to me that safety was not even a remote concern. As I was growing up, I remembered a saying I had heard somewhere that really applied to me: "The Lord takes care of fools and little children." While I was not grown, I was not really a "little child" either. One day when I was in college, I saw the children of our college president climbing up on their roof. As I watched, I wondered if they were looking to be in control and were not concerned for a moment about personal safety.

Before I fell asleep the evening of my chimney escapade, I heard Dad pray, "Thank you, God, for keeping my baby safe. Help her to be more careful and her mother and grandmother more understanding." Then he sang as he laughed out loud, "That's my baby now!" Years later that was the title of a popular song, but at the time there was no such song.

It was after this stunt that I acquired my nickname, Jack-in-the-Box. With each antic, no doubt my dad sighed with relief that I had survived and hoped I had learned something useful I could apply as I continued to experience new beginnings.

I see now that these antics were a necessary part of growing up. While the attention they brought me was painful, the climax to each experience was the joy I had in waiting for Dad to come home so I could tell how I had misbehaved. I knew beyond a doubt that he would pick me up, hug me, kiss me, and say, "Darling, Daddy wishes you would not do such dangerous things. I understand, but please for my sake don't do this again. I love you and don't want to see you hurt." It was through such repeated assurances of Dad's love and concern for me that I learned to trust in the forgiveness and guidance of my heavenly father.

Maybe my close call on the chimney is why I was allowed to have a birthday party on my ninth birthday, the only birthday party I had as a child. I always suspected that Dad was behind the festivities. Mother invited a distant cousin who lived nearby, Auntie Bess's daughter, and a neighborhood girl over to play in our yard. We entertained ourselves, then Grandmother brought out a cake she had decorated. Dad completed the celebration when he came home early enough to serve the ice cream. I delighted in the presents I received—some books, a frilly flannel gown, a gaudy necklace, and a set of watercolors and crayons. Mother, of course, gave me a doll like she did almost every birthday. She desperately wanted me to play with dolls, but I much preferred trains, Indian suits, and guns. Changing my focus to girly things was a new beginning I was determined not to have. Dolls were boring and, besides, it would have meant a victory for Mother. I did not want to encourage her in her reign over my life.

five

chapter 5
A CHANGE THAT LINGERS

When my class finished Alamo Elementary, we went to the Palestine Grammar School for three years. Clint Wylie, the principal, took a personal interest in each student, to the point of knowing our favorite subjects and asking us about them when he would pass us on campus. We had different teachers for each of our classes. Our math teacher was Miss Edna McDonald, whom we loved for her patience. One morning when I was in the seventh grade, Mr. Wylie stood up in assembly and told us he had a very important announcement to make. "Miss Edna, will you join me up here please?"

Miss Edna dutifully rose and climbed the steps to stand beside him on the platform. The other teachers probably noticed her flushed cheeks, but we students were so naïve we did not read anything into this scenario.

"Children," Mr. Wylie began, then cleared his throat. "I am happy to announce that Miss Edna and I will be married tomorrow. We will be gone for a week, then when she comes back to class, you are to call her Mrs. Wylie."

The quiet hall erupted in laughter and wild applause. Mr. Wylie and Miss Edna exchanged glances. She blushed and turned demurely to face the assembly with a big smile. We had never had a wedding between two teachers, so we all rushed for the steps of the platform to embrace our beloved teacher and principal. In a few minutes the bell rang and we returned to our classrooms, but it was hard to concentrate on lessons that day. I couldn't help but wonder if any boy would ever ask me on a date, much less to marry him. Mr. Wylie and Miss Edna seemed so happy. Were Mother and Dad ever that happy with each other? I tried to imagine them in that blissful state, but my mind would conjure up only half of such a picture. I could see Dad teasing Mother to make her smile and Mother scolding him for being "impractical."

Several mothers in our class took up a collection and bought a nice piece of silver for the bride and groom. The only regret we children had was that we did not get to be present when the gift was presented nor did any of the students get invited to the wedding. Probably it was a simple affair in someone's home and there would not have been room for many more than family.

The first day Miss Edna and Mr. Wylie were back at school, someone unexpectedly opened her classroom door and asked, "Are you Mrs. Wylie?"

Without thinking, she replied, "No, I am Miss McDonald."

We all howled and she turned so red it was almost sad. We promised not to tell Mr. Wylie. That experience helped all of us remember to call Miss McDonald by her new name. Those two were loved by everybody I knew. The day we left grammar school, both of them stood at the door and shook the hands of each of us who would be going on to a new beginning—the ninth grade and high school.

Going to high school held no charm for me for the things all the other girls participated in were off limits for me. I was allowed only to go to school and return home to practice the piano and violin and study. No one invited me to after-school clubs or weekend parties because they knew I would not be allowed to attend. I would listen longingly to conversations between classes at school and try to imagine talking to a friend on the telephone or sharing secrets in my bedroom after the lights were out.

Even worse than missing school social activities was facing myself in the mirror. My long hair was braided like ropes used to tie prisoners and piled high on my head, similar to the braids Mother looped into a bun on the back of her head. My clothes were whatever "sensible" garb Mother found on sale at the store in town. Seldom was I privileged to wear a fad because "it won't last long enough to pay for itself," Mother would remind me.

Studying in my room one evening when I was thirteen, I heard raised voices. A shudder ran through me. While my parents disagreed on quite a few topics, they usually restrained themselves in their discussions, and arguments were rare. I quickly reviewed my day to see if I could be the topic of this animated conversation. Suddenly I remembered a similar argument near the beginning of school two years before and couldn't suppress a wish that this one was on a related topic and would be resolved the same way.

I remembered hearing Mother protest loudly the last time, "But that makes no sense! Her clothes are perfectly suitable. It is impractical to buy more outfits just because she wants to look like everyone else. And her high-top shoes still fit, so she does not need another pair."

Dad's response had boomed down the hall and penetrated my door, "The point is not the cost. We can afford clothes for our daughter! She feels odd enough, not being able to participate in school activities or go to her classmates' parties. The least we can do is help her feel a part by dressing like everyone else. I'll hear no more about this, except that you have called Auntie Bess and ordered three dresses."

I had heard Dad's footsteps approach my door, and I timidly opened it after he knocked. "May I come in?" he smiled.

"Sure," I shrugged and opened the door to let him pass.

"Tomorrow your mother will take you to Auntie Bess's to be measured for some new clothes. Be thinking what style you want so you can tell her."

I let out a squeal and wrapped my arms around his neck. "Oh, thank you, Daddy! Thank you!"

The next day Auntie Bess had measured me and a week later presented me with three adorable outfits. Jumpers were popular that year, so two were jumpers, in different shades of red plaid. The third was a mint-colored linen with a white tatted collar, which I wore to church. At least two schooldays a week I could feel good about myself.

However, the argument at the beginning of my freshman year did not turn out the same. I waited expectantly for Dad's knock, and it never came. So I continued wearing the shapeless, long-sleeved dresses Mother picked out for me. She insisted that I wear union suits, long ribbed-cotton underwear. My first stop at school would be the girls' restroom where I would roll up the legs until they were hidden under my unfashionable skirt. The high-top shoes did not even resemble the saddle oxfords my classmates wore, and there was no way I could hide them.

Unfortunately my academic standing did not compensate for my embarrassment over my clothing. Classes the first year of high school were very difficult for me, and I had to have tutors in science and math. Gradually the subjects began making sense, and my self-esteem rose with my grades. However just when my grades were rebounding that spring, a change took place that would effect my life forever.

Dad had lost the election for postmaster in 1923. In a town of ten thousand, there was little hope for finding other employment at his age. Nevertheless, Dad sported a smile all the time and never showed signs of defeat although he did seem distracted much of the time. One Friday night in April, Dad and I were swinging on the front porch and he said to me suddenly, "Tootsie, tomorrow you and I are going to get Tilde to fix us a nice fried chicken lunch and we are going down to Uncle George's and spend the day on the creek. It should be full of water now with the spring rains behind us. We will go to bed early so we can get up and take off—just the two of us." I was thrilled that Dad's playfulness seemed to be returning and conquering his recent concerns over not having full-time employment.

When we got to the farm, Uncle George Matthews, Dad's stepbrother, and his wife, Aunt Mode, were sitting on their porch sipping cups of coffee. My first question to Aunt Mode was, "Are you making vegetable soup today?" She laughed and nodded her head. I grinned back, knowing I would go home with a big jar of the best vegetable soup I had ever eaten in all my life. Even up until now I have never tasted such a subtle blend of flavors and fresh vegetables.

When Dad and I got to the creek, the water lapped to the top of the banks, the wild flowers sprinkled color over the pasture, and the trees were as green as the new grass. It all smelled so good and so fresh. We put our picnic baskets and blanket under a tree, pulled off our shoes and socks, and began climbing up the big oak next to the creek. Our favorite stunt was to climb out on its main branch, jump into the cold water, wade across to a hanging grapevine, swing back to the tree, drop to the ground, and repeat the feat. What fun it was. We waded and swung until we were panting for breath. Finally Dad looked at his watch and suggested that we check out our lunch.

After a most delicious lunch of fried chicken, homemade potato chips, pickles, bread and butter sandwiches, and tea cakes, we cleaned up our mess, put the baskets back in the car, and then dashed up the hill to roll down through soft beds of red and white clover. Sometimes I reached the bottom of the hill first, and sometimes Dad did, but we just laughed like a couple of kids.

Suddenly Dad looked at me and said seriously, "Now, baby girl, Daddy needs to have a long talk with you."

I looked up into a face I had never seen—troubled, wrinkled, and ashen.

I gasped, "Daddy, what's wrong?"

He did not answer but took my hand and led me to the shade of a towering oak and motioned for me to sit down. I lowered myself mechanically to the ground, and he laboriously plopped down beside me and leaned heavily against the tree trunk. I followed his lead. He began to speak words I had never heard come from him. My heart felt heavy in my chest and ready to break.

He began, "You know, Tootsie, that sometimes we have to grow up overnight, and I . . . I . . . feel this is about to be your lot in life."

I could not ask him what he meant. I felt as if I were being strangled, but I dared not cry. Somehow I knew he did not want me to do that, upset though I was.

He continued with a sad, weary look on his face, "I realize, baby girl, that you do not really have a family . . . and you might not ever have one of your own . . . but I feel sure that God will give you a blessed family that will be extensive and lasting."

I opened my mouth to tell him he was frightening me, but he shook his head and plowed on as if the words were burning his throat and he had to spit them out or be choked himself.

"You will be loved by this extended family," he reassured me with a weak smile. "And you will also be very secure."

He told me many more things, so much until I felt something terrible was going to happen that I would never get over. Finally he reached out and drew me close to him. He gently kissed the top of my head, then held me at arm's length as if he were studying me to form a picture that would last him a long time.

"Tootsie, you are such a treasure to me, the best thing that ever happened in my life. I am so proud of you—I want you to know that."

The weight of the moment became too heavy for me, and I dropped my head to avoid meeting his sad eyes. "Whatever happens," he continued, "I want you to go to college and be married. I hope you will someday—and I hope to live to see you a happy, happy child."

I thought I heard his voice crack, and I looked up quickly to see a tear trickle down his cheek. He gazed into my eyes a moment, then whispered, "It's time to go."

In silence we walked back to the car and drove back to the farm house.

Aunt Mode had my soup ready in a Mason jar, and I could hardly wait to get home so we could heat it and relish every bite. As I recalled Dad's strange words, the warm soup soothed my churning stomach. After supper that night Daddy sat with me in the swing only a few minutes and then I was off to bed. He came out to the sleeping porch, tucked me in, and gave me a big kiss. Moments later I opened my eyes and realized he was still standing by my bed. Before I could say anything, he turned and walked back into the house.

The next morning, April 25, 1923, I was awakened to the screams of my mother yelling, "Bob has killed himself!"

As Mother dashed by me into the house where my grandmother and Tilde were, I heard my grandmother utter the most callous words I could have imagined at such a time, "Retha, I hope you will be happy now that you have what you want." I thought I would choke to death.

About that time Tilde realized that Mother had awakened me. She hurried out onto the porch, put her arms around me, and held me close to her while I sobbed and screamed. When I was weak from my sobbing, Tilde took me into the kitchen and fixed some breakfast. I have no idea what she fixed or whether I ate it or not. I do remember dashing out of the kitchen to my room, pulling a jumper over my head, putting some shoes on my feet, and running down the street to the home of Aunt Clara, who was a special friend of our family. As soon as I saw her, I relayed the awful news and asked if I could stay all day and the night. She merely put her arms around me and let me sit by her and cry and cry. After I quieted down a little, she said gently, "Stay right here. I'll be back in a minute."

I heard her talking to my grandmother. "Alice, Alice Cornelia is at my house. She'll be staying the night." What a relief! I could not face my mother or grandmother ever again—or at least not this soon.

Ever so often this scenario intrudes into my memory, and I cringe as I realize my mother never spoke to me about my dad's death, then or ever. The gap between us had been great, and now there was a chasm. I later learned that he had taken his life with his favorite pistol.

Later that day Aunt Lucy and Uncle Ernest Douthitt, my parents' best friends from Dallas, arrived, and Grandmother called to ask Aunt Clara to bring me home. I was so glad the Douthitts were at the house for both of them understood the life my father and I were living. With them at the house I was willing to stay home and even sleep there.

The funeral was the very next afternoon at the First Methodist Church. Still in shock, I did not notice that Mother did not walk with the rest of our relatives to the reserved family pews in the front of the sanctuary. I sat staring with disbelief at the mahogany casket at the front of the church and did not even notice a single straight chair at the head of the casket. Just as the organist was finishing the last hymn before the minister began the service, I heard a gasp ripple through the gathered friends and looked up to watch, horrified, as my mother sat heavily into the chair, flung her arm over the casket, and laid her head against the polished wood. I could see the minister looking uncomfortably at the organist, who played another hymn to give the grieving wife time to compose herself. However Mother never moved except to dab her eyes occasionally with her embroidered linen handkerchief.

The congregation fidgeted as it was time for the service to begin. The minister cleared his throat, yet Mother remained draped over the casket. Uncle George approached her and gingerly laid a hand on her shoulder. She threw back her shoulder as if to brush off a wasp and continued in her pose without saying a word or acknowledging his presence. Uncle George made eye contact with the minister, shrugged his shoulders, and nodded his head.

The minister slowly rose from his seat and approached the pulpit. There was still no movement or sound from Mother. He tentatively began, "Friends, we are gathered here today to offer our condolences to the Matthews family in the tragic loss of Bob Matthews, a dear friend to everyone." He hesitated. We could see Mother's torso heaving from her silent tears.

I dared not look around the church to see people's reactions. Anger competed with the numbness inside me. How could Mother make such a spectacle of herself, of us? If she cared that much, why hadn't she shown Dad so this would not have happened? I buried my head in my hands and sobbed. Daddy! Why did you leave me alone with her?

At home after the services I retreated to Dad's library, crawled up on his couch, and cried myself to sleep. A host of people had come to the house, and I knew I could not face one of them. Taking a nap was my escape.

The next few days are a fog in my memory. I do remember that a week later I returned to school. I dreaded that first day, knowing everyone would stare at me and avoid me, not knowing what to say. I was surprised when several girls who usually did not acknowledge my existence came up to me as soon as I stepped onto the campus. One by one they gently hugged me and said, "Alice, I'm so sorry. Truly I am." When I burst into tears, they formed a circle of protection around me to keep curious passersby from staring. For several weeks my friends as well as mere acquaintances made a special effort to include me in casual conversations. I wondered if this were the extended family Dad had prophesied for me. Regardless I was grateful for their genuine sympathy.

Mother stepped back into her routine almost as if Dad had never existed. She cancelled only a week of piano lessons. The second week after Dad's death she suddenly appeared in my bedroom door and announced, "It's time for your violin lesson, Alice Cornelia. You're late."

Instinctively I snapped my head up from the textbook I was studying and retorted, "No, I'm not late, Mother. I'm through with the violin. I will never play it again if I can't play it for Daddy."

Stunned, she opened her mouth and hardened her eyes as she stared at me. Then as suddenly as she had appeared, she was gone. She never mentioned violin lessons to me again although she did insist that I continue piano lessons. After a few months even she grew tired of hounding me about my practice. She could tell my heart was not in music any more, and she let me drop my piano lessons.

Three years later a friend begged me to play "Meditation" on the violin at her wedding. "Alice, it's been so long and you were so good at it. Maybe you'll find you can enjoy it again if you just give it a try. Will you consider it—for me?"

Out of friendship I reluctantly agreed. As I reached to lift the instrument out of the case for my first practice, I burst into wrenching sobs. "Daddy! Why did you abandon me? How can I go on without you?"

I heard him say, "Tootsie, there is a better way of life than you know and it's waiting for you. Someday you'll be a happy child."

Wanting to believe him, I stoically placed the violin against my shoulder and ran my fingers along the cold strings. I faithfully practiced the song my friend had requested and performed adequately at the marriage ceremony. When I returned home after the wedding, I stowed my violin case in my closet and never opened it again. I have no idea what eventually happened to it.

At special milestones in my life I missed Dad so much I could hardly stand it. For instance, before the fog of sleep left me as I woke the morning of my sixteenth birthday, I briefly anticipated what Dad would give me for this special occasion. As soon as I opened my eyes, I remembered that Dad would never give me another present. I turned my head and stared at the white wall as if trying to conjure up an image of his kind face. Throwing back the covers in rage, I jumped out of bed and raced to my dresser. Jerking open the top drawer, I grabbed a long black box out of a corner and ripped off the top. I gingerly fingered the smooth white pearls of a necklace Dad had given me the Christmas before he died. I lifted it reverently out of the box and slid it around my neck. Somehow the cool feel of the smooth stones on my skin gave me the feeling that Dad was near. I wore it to school that day under my dowdy brown dress and felt like a princess.

My remaining days in high school have no highlights, except one that I created and got away with for reasons still unknown to me. One very hot May afternoon I was in study hall under the watchful eye of Miss Marie McDonald, my history teacher. Suddenly I not only felt so hot I thought I would expire, but I also realized I needed to go to the ladies room. Hands were popping up all around the room, and Miss Marie was denying everyone's requests to go for water and the restroom. I finally decided I had to act, so I scribbled a note and passed it to the girl in front of me without attracting attention.

The outside of the note read, "Read this and pass it up to the front." Inside the note said, "When Miss Marie is not looking, signal me. I'm going to slip out of the room. Alice." In preparation I slid out of my seat, scrunched down on my hands and knees, and began crawling down the aisle toward the main door of the auditorium, which was inconveniently at the front of the room. My row was nearest to the door.

Fortunately everyone cooperated and nobody got the giggles. The boy in the front seat suddenly dropped his arm down beside him and brushed his hand toward the door. I stood up and made a dash for the entrance. Breathing a sigh of relief, I opened the door and ran smack into our principal, Mr. Rickman, and our superintendent, Mr. Frizzell.

Frozen with fear, I just looked at them. One said simply, "Young lady, do you have a destination?"

I quickly responded as my face turned red, "Miss Marie is not letting anyone be excused for water or the lounge. I couldn't wait, and I sure cannot wait now." Without giving them a chance to answer, I brushed past the men and disappeared into the ladies room.

As I think back on the expression on those two gentlemen's faces, I know they were ready to burst into laughter that would have rocked the building. I always thought maybe they let me go unpunished because they thought I was clever to take the chance I did.

After I finished in the lounge and got a drink of water, I reported to the principal's office. I hadn't planned far enough ahead to know how to get readmitted to study hall. As I walked in, I saw, seated in the waiting room of Mr. Rickman's office, my best friend's mother, Mrs. Margsue Hodges. She had come to get her daughter, Margaret, for a dental appointment. When she saw me, she asked sharply, "Alice, what are you doing out of class this time of day?"

Just then Mr. Rickman walked in and gruffly asked me to tell my story. As soon as I finished, I turned to Mrs. Hodges and pleaded, "Miss Margsue, please don't tell my mother for she will kill me." My friend's mother hesitated and gulped. Finally, she looked at Mr. Rickman and Mr. Frizzell, who had also entered the waiting area, and said, "I am going to ask you not to call Mrs. Matthews but allow me a few minutes with this young lady by myself."

Her request was granted, and she motioned for me to follow her to a corner of the room. Looking me straight in the eye, she began, "Alice, do you know that what you have done is a very serious infraction of the school rules?"

I nodded gravely, "Yes, I'm sorry. I just . . . ."

She shook her head and continued, reaching out and taking hold of my hands, "I understand your dilemma. However, it is unbecoming for a young lady to act as you have acted."

I could feel the tears stinging my eyes as I replied, "I know. I'm sorry. Please don't tell Mother, okay? Please?"

She shifted uncomfortably from one foot to the other, then squeezed my hands. "Alice, I do understand . . . I mean, I know . . . how . . . things are for you with your mother. I see no need for her to know of this incident. That is . . . if you assure me that you will never, ever do such a thing again. Will you make that commitment?"

I sobbed in relief, "Oh, yes. I promise. I'll never do such a thing again. Thank you. Thank you!"

Mrs. Hodges hugged me roughly and walked over to Mr. Rickman and Mr. Frizzell.

"Gentlemen," she reported with dignity, "Alice and I have discussed the situation and determined there is no need for her mother to be bothered with this incident because it will surely never happen again."

Mr. Rickman looked over at me and said, "Alice, shouldn't you be getting back to class? Here is a permit for Miss McDonald."

Sighing with relief, I smiled and grabbed the paper out of his hand, "Thank you, Mr. Rickman. Thank you. I'm so sorry . . . I . . . ."

"You'd better hurry if you are to have any study hall left," he said quietly.

I nodded, swallowed hard, and headed back to class.

Miss Margsue was my heroine once again in my senior year. When all the graduation parties started, she knew that even if I were invited to one, I would not be allowed to go. Nevertheless she quietly engaged Auntie Bess to make a pretty dress for me. She was determined that I would attend the party she was planning for Margaret and her niece, Louise, and she knew I did not have the proper clothing. After Miss Margsue realized Auntie Bess was delighted to make the outfit, she went to see my mother.

When Mother invited her friend in to visit, she declined, "No, Retha. I have just one thing on my mind. I'll say it and go on home. I am giving a tea for Margaret and Louise in two weeks. I will be inviting Alice, and I expect her to come. Bess is making her a dress, so there is nothing you have to do except see that she gets there. Do you understand?" Mother was too stunned to respond or to disobey.

My party dress was beautiful. It was a pale lavender, accordion-pleated chiffon. Auntie Bess got a milliner to make me a hat the same color. Then she took me to Mr. Hodges's store and bought me some white dress shoes. This was too much for Mother. "They are not practical!" she complained loudly. My reaction to her tirade was softened somewhat by the knowledge that Dad would have applauded everything that was being done to enable me to go to one party with the girls in my graduating class.

The party was great fun, and many complimented me on my looks. I had never been that happy over material things and appearances. At last I felt I belonged with my peers. However, this was not a new beginning for me. When I got home from the party, Mother was sitting in the living room embroidering a tea towel. She looked up at me over her glasses and did not say a word. Forgetting myself, I launched into a description of the wonderful afternoon. "Oh, Mother, everything was just divine. You should have seen all the food—at least a dozen kinds of cookies, three cakes decorated in the school colors, a lemon punch, and chocolate candies in the shape of roses."

I continued telling about the other guests and what they wore as I walked into my room. Mother followed me quietly. Still caught up in my once-in-a-lifetime experience, I unzipped my dress, stepped out of it, and placed it carefully on the bed while I plopped down to remove my shoes. Quicker than a lizard darting across the sidewalk, Mother grabbed the dress. "We will put that dress up for there will likely not be any more occasions for that outfit to be worn," she said tersely.

Feeling as if all the air had suddenly been sucked out of the room, I watched helplessly as she carried the lovely dress from my room. I never saw the dress again.

I cried many a night during graduation week for there were dances, swim parties, and others events I did not even get invited to because everyone knew such festivities were off limits for me. Of course I was permitted—required, actually—to participate in a recital of the town's piano students. In the spring of my senior year Mother had suddenly insisted that I resume my piano lessons. I took from Miss Kate Hunter, a very fine and exacting teacher. Mother resumed her criticism of my playing, so preparing for the recital was excruciating, not only during my practice sessions but also in our discussions of the recital itself.

No amount of pleading would convince Mother to bring forth my purple party dress to wear that evening or to relax her plan for my hair. Mother had never allowed me to cut my hair once in my life. While my peers wore short, perky hair-dos, I carried around sixteen years of growth on my head, unimaginatively plaited then wound four times around the crown of my head. The ends of the braids touched my face just by my ears. Not only was the arrangement terribly out of style, it was a pain to take care of. Of course, there were no hair dryers, so shampooing depended largely on the weather. If the sun was likely to shine for three or four hours, then it was safe to wash my hair. A breeze shortened the process even more. In the winter I would sit by the window in my bedroom and take advantage of the warming effect of the sunshine through the glass to hasten the drying of my strands. If the sun snuck behind a cloud and refused to reappear, then I went to bed with a wet head.

The day of my senior recital Mother uncharacteristically had taken up the entire day curling my long locks for the evening event. She did not even allow me time to practice my pieces. When it was my turn on the program, I walked self-consciously to the piano bench and lightly took my seat. I gritted my teeth when I heard a gasp echo through the audience. Although I was not looking at my mother, I knew she had a smug smile on her face. She had accomplished another of her goals for me. My hair hung down my back and pooled in a soft pile on the floor. I doubt anyone heard the results of years of agonizing piano practice because of their watching my locks gyrate as I slid my fingers gracefully along the keys.

Graduation Friday afternoon was routine for me, but for many it was a very exciting and festive time. I remember walking across the stage and hearing polite applause as I received my diploma from Mr. Rickman. I imagined the admirer was Dad. How I missed him that day! Not even the events of the day before could dispel the grief and loneliness I felt.

The day before graduation Mother had surprised me at supper by asking abruptly, "Would you like to drive the car to school tomorrow?"

I couldn't believe what I was hearing. "Why, yes!" I answered.

"Well, you have my permission—provided you take nobody in the car with you. You are to go to school and come straight home." Of course I readily agreed. I could hardly wait until morning to drive up in our Model T Ford and park beside all the other cars that belonged to the graduates. When lunchtime came, one of my classmates asked if I would like to go to the hamburger stand close to the school and eat our lunch there instead of going home for the meal. I wanted desperately to go, yet I knew Mother would never approve. I was tempted to risk going anyway and hope I would not get caught, but I dared not with graduation just the next day. Would she forbid me to attend the graduation ceremony as punishment? I could not take the chance.

Finally I went into the counselor's office, got permission to call home, and announced to Tilde, "I will be going with some of my classmates to the hamburger place, so I won't be home for dinner." Tilde laughed and clapped her hands, "Honey, do be careful." The short trip was a successful venture, and I felt like I had conquered the world.

As I drove home that day, I realized I had been in the high-school building for the last time and the next school building I would be entering would be at a college that had not yet been chosen. I wondered if all of us graduates would ever see each other again as a class.

Twenty-five years later my class had a reunion. How glorious it was, especially when several people came up to me to ask if I was Alice Matthews. You see, my hair was short, and I wore an exquisitely tailored plum suit, matching spike heels, and a set of matching gold bracelet, earrings, and necklace.

six

chapter 6
THE COCOON BREAKS

The summer after my high-school graduation held no charm for me. After long hours of trying to decide what college I would attend, Mother finally settled on Texas Woman's University in Denton, Texas, then known as the College of Industrial Arts (CIA). It was the only all-girl's college in the United States and the second largest of its kind in the world. It was small, fairly inexpensive, and only about 300 miles from home.

The preparations that had to be made for me to go to college were very simple since I would be wearing uniforms. All CIA students had three selections of dress—and specific rules on when to wear each outfit. For classes and around town we wore a long-sleeved, sky-blue chambray dress with a sailor collar and a dark blue tie. For Saturday dinner and for church we all wore long, white poplin dresses with long sleeves and two bands of white ribbon around the cuffs. In thc winter our Sunday attire was a heavily starched blue serge dress from the same pattern as the poplin.

The uniforms identified us as CIA students with the purpose of keeping us in line when we were away from the watchful eyes of the school staff. They also simplified my wardrobe needs, so I concentrated over the summer on gathering book covers, school supplies, and the like. I furnished my own bath and bed linens, but those took no time to acquire since Mother would not approve of anything other than plain white, "sensible" linens.

My roommate was to be Evelyn Davis, a longtime friend with whom I had gone to school most of my life. Within a couple of weeks after graduation, my preparations were complete. While most of my high-school friends were enjoying farewell parties and visiting relatives out of the city throughout the summer, my life was confined to the house where I was born. I read, talked with Tilde, and occasionally even fingered the piano keys.

I did get two breaks from the monotony. Once I was allowed to spend the night at Edith Eilenberger's house, where everyone was known to my mother. Mother lectured me before I went, "If any boys come by and the other girls go out to the cars or get in the cars, you are to stay in the house. You are not to go outside for any reason, do you understand?"

I would have agreed to anything to get to attend a party with my friends. Sure enough, about nine o'clock we heard the toot of a horn. Several of the girls squealed and ran to pull the curtains back from the front windows. "It's Horace and Robert and some of their friends," they giggled and rushed to open the door.

Edith ran to find her parents and told them, "Some of us are going to the Root Beer Drive-In, and a few are staying here. We'll be back by eleven."

All but three of the girls stampeded out to the waiting convertibles and climbed into the cars without even bothering to open the car doors. A few others had similar instructions to mine and hung back. "I don't like joy riding," one lied. "I'd rather stay here and talk." So we carried on bravely about our college plans and life in general until the rest of the girls returned.

Besides the thrill of attending a party with my friends, I was astounded when Mr. Eilenberger interrupted our chattering at three in the morning to present fresh donuts he had just made!

The second change in my routine came when Mother allowed me to invite two friends to spend the night with me two days before we were to leave for college. Ruth Miller and Helen DePree were both going to the University of Texas at Austin.

"Where will you be staying?" Ruth asked Helen.

"Littlefield Dormitory. How about you?"

"I'll be in a private boarding house for the first year, and Reed will be rooming just down the street! Isn't that fine?"

I fidgeted with my pillow and stared at the ceiling. It was fine enough to have a boyfriend, and to have him going to the same university was unimaginable.

"I'm jealous," Helen replied. "Myron will be at A&M, so I won't get to see him until Thanksgiving—that is, unless he finds a friend with a car and comes to visit." She giggled and looked over at me as if she had forgotten about my existence.

"Are you all ready for school, Jackie?" she inquired, trying to include me in the conversation.

"Oh, sure," I yawned.

Turning back to Ruth, Helen teased, "Hey, didn't I see you and Reed at the lake Saturday night? You didn't seem to notice anyone else around."

Ruth blushed. "Where were you? I didn't see you. We were making plans for the civic club dance."

"Yeah, right," said Helen, wrinkling her nose.

I fell asleep while their chatter continued. I had nothing to add.

Finally the day came when I was to leave for school. Evelyn and I were going to ride a bus to Denton, Texas, as the train went only to Dallas and our parents did not want us changing trains by ourselves. The bus went straight through to Denton. When the bus arrived at my house, Evelyn had already been picked up with her load of things. I shall never forget that day. An hour before leaving, my mother and grandmother took me into the parlor, a place I went only when company came or when I was to polish Grandmother's antique furniture.

"Alice Cornelia," Mother began in her best teacher voice, "even though you will be away from home, there are certain things I expect you to do—and not do. You are not to leave campus without my permission or to ride in a car with anyone I have not approved. I expect you to write every week and keep me informed of your grades.

Do remember that I am sending you to Denton to study and that we do not have the funds to subsidize socializing. You, of course, will obey the rules of the school and attend church every Sunday."

I listened politely and was glad the lecture was cut short by the blast of the bus horn. I picked up my purse and hesitated. Passing by Mother and Grandmother to leave the room, I gave each a cursory hug that was not returned. Then I stopped at the door and announced, choosing my words carefully, "I want you both to know that ... so long as I live ... I will never darken the door of any church nor give one dime to a church." I had gone to our church since I was born and was there, it seemed, every time the doors opened and left when they closed. My family lived at the church because of my mother's involvement, especially after Dad died. I had nothing really against the church and certainly appreciated the friends we had there. It was just the symbol of my mother's emotional absence from my life. Perhaps that was my way of saying, "I survived your unreasonable parenting, and now I'm free. You can't control me any more."

Both women were speechless. Mother's face contorted momentarily, then resumed its stern, dispassionate look. She retorted, crossing her arms across her chest as if to ward off the repercussions of my defiance, "Well, that is between you and your God." If she ever understood what I meant, she never let on.

Neither Mother nor Grandmother made a move to follow me to the door and bid me good-bye and good luck. The bus driver toted my suitcase and trunks to the bus and loaded them while I boarded and sat down heavily next to Evelyn. She had a puzzled expression on her face, but she did not say a word about my solitary exit. I exhaled loudly and forced a smile, "Are you ready? I am!"

The trip to Denton was uneventful, in fact so boring that Evelyn and I slept a good part of the way. With each town we passed through, I figured I was that much farther away from oppression and that much closer to freedom. Those thoughts buoyed me the first few hours between naps.

As we passed through Dallas and had only an hour to go before reaching Denton, reality began to take up residence inside my heart. Besides Evelyn, I knew no one on campus. I had to swallow away a lump in my throat remembering Dad's introducing me to Miss Gertie my first day at school in Palestine. I wondered whom I could call on if I had trouble in Denton. Evelyn also remained quiet as we neared our destination, and I saw her reach surreptitiously into her purse, pull out a clean linen handkerchief, and dab her eyes.

Eventually the bus turned onto a tree-lined street between unimaginative stone buildings. This was to be my home for the next four years. My mind froze and refused to take in the names on the signs identifying each building. When the bus pulled up to a two-story white frame and stopped, neither of us made a move to leave our seats. The sidewalk outside the dorm buzzed with families and students lugging their gear. Everyone else was waving to friends and hugging classmates they had not seen all summer. What were we doing here among strangers? Freedom felt very lonely.

The bus driver called from the door of the bus, "Ladies, come show me where to put your things."

We looked at each other for support and walked down the aisle with legs trembling. Not knowing what the etiquette was for entering a dorm, I climbed the front steps and reached for the doorbell. Before I could press it, the screen door flew open and a tall, slender lady with graying hair gathered neatly in a French twist greeted us with a warm smile. "You must be the girls from Palestine," she said. "I'm Mrs. Maria Knause, your housemother. The bus company informed me when you would be arriving. Your room is on the second floor. Here are your keys. Take a right at the top of the stairs. It's the corner room. If you need anything, let me know." Later I learned that she had been the housemother at Oakland Annex for twenty years, and her daughter, who grew up on the campus, was head of the Violin Department at the college.

When Evelyn and I reached our room, neither of us wanted to open the door. It was as if that gesture would seal our fate. As long as it stayed closed, we could change our minds and take the bus back home to the familiar. Finally we heard the bus driver say impatiently, "Ladies, do you have the key? I really need to get back on the road."

Startled out of our apprehension, we both extended our keys toward the doorknob at the same time. We laughed and I jammed my key into the lock, turned the knob, and pushed open the heavy wooden door. Until that moment I had not really thought about what my room would look like, so I was not disappointed. Even if I had known any of the details, Mother would not have agreed to spend anything on decorations, so what did they matter? On each side of the small room a metal Army cot with spongy springs and a sagging mattress and a three-drawer oak dresser lined up like soldiers along the bare grey wall. On the wall opposite the door was a large wooden table that would serve as our joint desk and a roomy closet, which we would share. I instinctively walked over to two large windows which touched in the corner and peered out. Because of the corner location we had two nice views of the tree-lined campus. I sighed happily. I liked my new home already.

After the bus driver had deposited our belongings inside the room and left, we set about unpacking. Soon we were finished and began to notice the drone of voices in the hall. Gradually the sounds became distinct words. "Hey! Did you take that trip you had planned?" "It's great to see you again!" "Ohh, goodie! We're going to be neighbors again." "Our last year! I thought it would never come!"

Evelyn and I realized at the same time that we were the only freshmen in the dorm. She jumped up and closed the door as if to ward off some evil spirit. What that closed door did I don't know, but it gave us some sense of protection against an experienced crowd whom we had yet to meet. We did not open our door all afternoon until the assistant housemother, Julia Kemper, came to tell us where to go for our evening meal. As we descended the stairs, several of the older girls were waiting for their friends to come down, and they introduced themselves, "Hi. I don't remember seeing you before. I'm Jeanne Leslie and this is Grace Rae Palmer. Are you new?"

"Yes," we mumbled. Another group of three girls joined us and told us their names. I had already forgotten the names of the first two and worried that I would never remember anyone in the morning. The churning in my stomach was fear, not hunger pangs. I had never expected to wish for home, but I almost did that evening.

"Come on," one of the girls motioned to us. "We'll show you where we eat. It's in a different building." The dorm with the dining room was on top of the hill where most of the buildings were located, and it was a long way from our dorm especially when the weather was bad. As we walked that first evening, I scoped out the buildings we passed so I would not get so lost tomorrow.

We had arrived at CIA on a Thursday and spent all day Friday getting registered, buying our books, and getting our meal cards from the head of the dorm where our meals would be served. I got registered before Evelyn, came home with my books, and began putting covers on them when I heard a knock on my door. Overcome by panic, I froze in my chair. The knock came again and I slowly rose from my chair and approached the door as if I expected a robber to confront me.

When I opened the door, a tall blonde and a shorter brunette greeted me. "Hi," they said. "We're Eula Pierson and Polly Patrick, and we wanted to welcome you to CIA." I awkwardly invited them into our room and offered them a seat on my bed. "Where are you from?" Eula asked, accepting my invitation.

"Palestine," I answered. "And you?"

"We're both from McKinney. Are you a freshman?"

"Yeah," I admitted with a shy smile. "It's all pretty new to me."

"Hey, we remember what it was like our first year here," Polly assured me, crossing her legs under her on the bed. "We're juniors and have known each other all our lives. It takes awhile to get used to everything, but everyone's friendly. You'll see and you'll like it here."

We visited a while and I envied their excitement about graduating the next year and probably getting married. Both those goals seemed out of my reach.

"There are a couple of things that aren't in the catalog that you'll want to know," Polly informed me. "Every Saturday night the school shows a movie at the auditorium. Tickets cost twenty-five cents, and it's a great place to see everyone. Then Sunday morning a bus comes at nine and delivers us to whatever church we want to go to. Sunday dinner begins at one. Don't be late or you won't get to eat. Then supper is a sack lunch at 6:30. We can take it onto the front steps or to one of the areas with benches on campus if the weather is nice. If you have any questions about anything, please come ask us. We're down in room 215."

All of this was important to me except the information about the church bus. I would not be going to church on Sunday. I had been careful not to mention this for I did not want to start a controversy right away. I had made up my mind to divorce myself from everything to do with church now that I was on my own.

Saturday morning was warm. I pulled on my blue sailor dress for the first time and walked to the drug store across the street from my dorm to buy some notebook paper. As I passed through the door, my eyes fell on a box of big red apples. I hesitated a moment before reaching out and feeling several of the luscious fruit. Suddenly I grabbed one fiercely, marched to the cash register, and paid for my trophy. I hurried back to the dorm, triumphantly drew the apple out of its paper bag, and washed it quickly over the sink. Then I spun around with a gleam in my eye and a smile on my lips and announced loudly to the confused dorm mates who were visiting, "Folks, I am going to eat an apple with the peel on it!"

Amid the puzzled looks of my new friends, I slowly raised the apple to my mouth and purposefully sank my teeth into the red flesh. I relished every bite and then explained that this was my first time to eat an entire apple with the peel on. I told them about my visiting a neighbor who gave me an apple with the peel on it when I was eight. My mother became irate when she heard about it and stormed over to the neighbor's house and shouted, "Alice Cornelia is not to eat any fruit with the peel on it, and you have deliberately broken my rule. You are no longer welcome in our home!"

Such harsh rules set the stage for my life that was yet to come, but it also opened the way for me to prove that a person can survive—and survive well—anything life offers if she will turn the problem over to God. I am so grateful to my precious dad for having taught me this lesson and having helped me keep all the misfortunes of my childhood in perspective through being my friend and understanding my plight. Love and understanding are great healers and great catalysts for overcoming difficulties.

The first Sunday morning in Denton I awoke and looked at the clock. It was seven, and the sun was streaming in through the curtains. Evelyn was already up and dressing. Thoughts of my leaving home a few days earlier hit me with full force. I had been pretty rough on my mother when I left home and had not repented of my attitude, understandable though it might have been. I knew Dad would have been unhappy with me, and I was quite sure that my heavenly Father was also unhappy with me. I tossed in bed and could not get comfortable. Finally, I folded my hands on top of my chest and squeezed my eyes to keep out the morning light. "Father," I prayed hesitantly, "I know I was wrong to speak to Mother like I did. You know how she exasperates me, but that was no excuse. You have told me to honor my father and my mother. I'll try harder, I promise. Will you please forgive me? If you will, I'll do something to make it up to you. Just show me what you want me to do. Thank you, Father. Amen."

Feeling a weight lifted off my mind, I swung my legs over the side of the bed and sat up wide awake. Evelyn and I trudged to Brackenridge Hall for a quick breakfast and hurried back to don our white Sunday uniforms. Evelyn was taking an inordinate amount of time with her hair, and I became impatient. "I'll see you downstairs," I called as I headed out the door. No one else was in the lobby when I arrived. Before I could sit down, I heard the bus approach and screech to a stop. Without even a hesitation, I boarded the bus and sat in the front row. The driver asked which church I wanted to go to. "The Methodist," I answered. I laughed ruefully as Evelyn joined me and the bus drove to the First Methodist Church of Denton. So much for independence.

At First Methodist, Evelyn and I took a seat safely in the middle of the sanctuary. Soon a middle-aged couple sat down beside me. "Hello, dear," said the wife. "Are you new here?"

"Yes," I said, with more confidence than I felt.

"I didn't think I had seen you before," she smiled. "Are you a freshman?"

I frowned slightly, thinking how transparent the uniform made me. I nodded and fell into a conversation until the minister, Dr. Edward Barcus Sr., stood up to begin the worship service.

During the sermon Dr. Barcus spoke about depending on God. He said, "God provides for us in so many ways—food, friends, and opportunities. Today I am praying that He will provide a teacher for us. We have a lovely class of thirteen-year-old girls that still lacks a teacher. I know God will provide someone to open the Word of God for these delightful young ladies."

His request caught my attention. For two years I had been teaching a class of thirteen-year-olds in Palestine. It was not an easy task. Mother was always after me to teach them the way she would, not the way I was comfortable. Also the girls confronted me weekly with situations I had not experienced and looked to me, the older one, for answers. I wondered if the girls in the Denton class might not be more sophisticated than the girls in Palestine since they were living in a university town and if I would be able to relate to them.

During the sermon the Holy Spirit whispered to me that I should answer the minister's plea. He brought to mind a part of the catechism Dad had faithfully taught me, "The dignity of the human person is rooted in his creation in the image and likeness of God . . . By his deliberate actions, the human person does, or does not, conform to the good promised by God and attested by moral conscience." I saw clearly that I had a responsibility to make the most of my new freedom. I didn't know all the answers to the questions the young girls might ask, but I did know my Bible and could share with them God's promises.

At the end of the sermon Dr. Barcus prayed, "Heavenly Father, lead us now into the world to spread your love and to serve you. Father, I know you have prepared the heart of someone to come to the altar today and rededicate his or her life by accepting the position of teacher to our thirteen-year-old girls. Thank you, Lord, in advance for answering my petition. You are a faithful God. Amen."

As the organist pounded out "A Mighty Fortress Is Our God," I looked shyly around the sanctuary. All eyes were trained on the words in the hymn books. As the last verse began, I felt as if a hand were touching my elbow and gently pulling me out into the aisle. Without fully realizing what I was doing, I found myself standing at the altar whispering to Dr. Barcus, "I . . . I'm a new student at CIA and would like an associate membership at First Methodist while I'm in college."

Dr. Barcus smiled warmly as he extended his hand, "Well, I'm so happy to have you join us. . . . ah . . . ?"

"Jackie," I said. "Jackie Matthews. And I'll . . . I'll take that class you mentioned. I was teaching that age back in Palestine."

He hesitated as if he had not heard me, then beamed and pumped my hand vigorously up and down. "Oh, yes. . . yes. . . The Lord is good. Stay after the service and we'll talk, okay, Jackie?"

Teaching this class opened the doors for me to meet Dr. Barcus's children and become close personal friends with the entire family. What a glorious relationship this was through the years. The church was also a training ground in my journey of independence. In teaching the class and other activities I participated in, I had the freedom of making decisions and going about church life in a way that meant most to me. And when I made poor decisions, there was always another member to support me and show me a graceful way out of any predicament. As often happens, I as the teacher derived the most from the lessons.

The first Easter I taught the girls, one of the students arrived at our room accompanied by her father and carrying a cardboard box with a lid on it. Curious, the other girls gathered around as I asked, "What do you have there?"

"A rabbit," Mary Louise replied.

Her father quickly added, "Mary Louise received the rabbit as an Easter present and wanted to show him off to her friends." He raised his eyebrows and turned to look at his daughter, who was busy fending impatient hands off her box. "Mary Louise has promised that the rabbit will stay in the box. I will come back in 20 minutes to take the animal to the car."

"Well, that's very nice of you to want to share your pet with us," I smiled rather weakly at Mary Louise. "Please put the box on the table and let us all see him."

Relieved to have permission to show off the furry creature, Mary Louise pushed through the giggling crowd and set the box on the table. She pried the lid open a few inches and let the other girls take turns eyeing the white ball of fur. Her father frowned slightly and left.

Realizing that no one could really see the rabbit, I quietly closed the door and told Mary Louise, "You can open the lid a little more if you will hold on to the rabbit."

She squealed and tossed away the lid. Not yet adept at handling the animal, she didn't grab him in time. As if he had been fired from a cannon, the frightened rabbit hopped onto the table and over the screaming girls and found refuge in a corner under a chair. While several of the girls ran in the opposite direction, others pursued the pet with great gaiety.

But the little bunny was not to be caught. As one girl would reach under whatever piece of furniture he had hidden under, the bunny would dart out and find another obscure space to try to hide in. The chase went on for fifteen minutes. Finally someone succeeded in capturing him and deposited him back in his box. Just moments later Mary Louise's father returned to carry the rabbit to the car. The class groaned in unison when they saw him. In a weak moment I persuaded him to leave the rabbit for the remainder of the class. The girls cheered. The father returned in a few minutes and placed some grass in the box. The rabbit hungrily nibbled while the father placed the box on a desk beside me. "Are you sure you don't want me to take him out?" he asked.

I assured him that the rabbit was no trouble. I didn't tell him about the escape or that I realized that my lesson for the day would have to wait for another time. After he left, I talked to the class about how sometimes we feel as if God's will is a box and we want to escape its limitations, so we act outside of God's will and find ourselves in a corner, shaking with fright. Back in our "box" of God's will, God takes care of us the way Mary Louise's father had fed the rabbit and we are content.

All in all, it was a memorable Easter. I realized weeks later that the rabbit had served another purpose besides being an object lesson. Pursuing the rabbit around the room, the shy girls forgot their inhibition and interacted with the others with an ease they had not shown before. After that rabbit visit, the class was a more cohesive whole.

It was several months before I wrote home and stated casually that I was teaching a Sunday school class of thirteen-year-old girls and finding it very rewarding and challenging. Most of the girls were daughters of faculty families, so came from an educated, inquisitive environment. They were smart and mature beyond their years. Mother never mentioned the class to me.

One event I did not write home about involved my hair. One weekend early in the semester Auntie Bess and Uncle George Saunders, close friends from Palestine, came visiting at CIA with their daughter. I was taught to call her Sister since neither of us had a sibling. When I saw Sister, I exclaimed, "Your hair! It's adorable!" Sister blushed and quickly grabbed my elbow and steered me away from her parents.

"Don't make a big deal about it," she whispered to me. "Mother's still mad. Dad agreed to take me to have it cut one day when Mother was away. I love it, don't you?"

Suddenly my four plaits seemed a heavy burden to continue carrying around.

"Sister," I asked rashly, "will you cut my hair like yours?"

She looked at me horrified. "You can't do that! What would your mother say?"

"I don't care," I answered defiantly. "Go ask your parents if you can come to the dorm with me for an hour or so. It shouldn't take longer than that."

"Well, I don't know. . . ," she hesitated. "Don't you want to think about this?"

"I have," I declared, "and I'm ready to look like everyone else. Go on. Ask your folks." I pushed her gently towards her parents, who agreed to let her visit me in the dorm until dinnertime.

Giggling, we ran up the stairs and into my room. "What shall we use to cut it?" Sister asked.

"I don't know," I replied, frantically opening drawers. I was afraid I would lose my nerve before the deed was done.

"Here!" I cried. "Here are my scissors for home economics. Use them."

"Well, okay," Sister grinned. "Sit here in the desk chair."

I sat in the straight, oak chair. We draped a towel around my shoulders and another one on the floor to catch the strands as they fell from my head. "How short do you want it?"

"Just like yours," I stated firmly.

"Above the ears?" she asked for clarification.

"Sure. Why not?"

"Okay. Here goes. This is your last chance to change your mind." She bent down and peered at me around my shoulders.

"Onward!" I cried, waving a fist into the air for emphasis.

Clip. Clip. Snip. Little by little my head became lighter as strand after strand of hair more than five feet long fell heavily to the floor. I hardly recognized the girl in the mirror. Not only did I have short hair, I had a big smile across my face. I was away from home and at last I could make my own decisions.

As soon as Sister finished cutting and shaping, I angled a hand mirror so I could see my likeness in the mirror over the sink. I stared critically, then cocked my head to one side, and laughed, "It's gorgeous! I love it, don't you?"

Sister nodded approvingly, "Yes, you look really nice like that."

Carefully we wrapped my long locks in a sack from the school store and popped it into my closet. "Don't say a word to Mother . . . or anyone else," I warned. "I want it to be a surprise to everyone."

Sister giggled and promised to keep my secret. When dinnertime came, I turned the doorknob and hesitated before opening the door. "Well, here goes!" I sighed. Sister nodded and held one thumb up in encouragement.

I stepped out in the hall and we headed toward the stairwell. Two doors down, the girls in the room called out, "Jackie, are you going . . . Oh, I'm sorry. I thought you were Jac. . . . That is you! What have you done?"

I whirled around like a model, patting the hair that lay flat against my neck. The girls ran to me, hugging me and jumping up and down. "You did it! Good for you! It's great!"

Buoyed by their enthusiasm, I continued to the dorm lobby with my head held high.

Auntie Bess and Uncle George were waiting in the lobby for us. As I approached with Sister, the smiles faded from their faces. "What have you done, Alice?" Auntie Bess cried, slapping her hand over her mouth.

With a big grin I slowly turned my head to the right, then to the left. "Do you like it?" I asked coyly.

"Well, yes, I do. You look lovely, but your mother . . . ," she stammered.

"I'll tell her when I'm ready," I replied calmly. "I'm starving. Would you like to go eat now?"

I did not tell Mother about my new look. When she came to visit me for Thanksgiving, she was waiting in my room when I returned from class. As I came through the door, she looked up from her book and let out a scream that could be heard down the hall. "What have you done to yourself?!"

"I cut my hair," I replied calmly. As she continued her tirade, I walked to my closet and drew out the sack containing my locks. Handing it to Mother, I said, "I saved this for you." Curious, she stopped ranting long enough to peek in the sack. "Why, Alice Cornelia? Why?"

"Because I wanted to look like everyone else," I answered honestly.

She snorted bitterly and snapped, "Let's go to dinner."

I never thought about my saved hair again. When I was cleaning out Mother's dresser after she died, I ran across that sack containing my hair. I'll never know for sure what it signified for her. To me, it represented repression, and its absence meant I had at last begun to savor the life Dad had promised me I would enjoy someday.

The other change I did not tell Mother about was my change of major. Evelyn was going to be a piano major, and my mother sent me up to Denton to become a schoolteacher. I knew I had no qualifications for teaching, so I decided I would go the business administration route. This way I could either work in the business world or teach. Not until Mother came to visit in November did I tell her I was not going to be a teacher unless all else failed. She made no comment when she got this news, but her face clouded over and she pursed her lips, and it was clear she disapproved.

My first year at CIA was difficult for, like most freshmen, I did not have good study habits from high school. Also the texts were vastly different from what I had studied in Palestine. I was having a very difficult time, and Mr. Walker King, the registrar who was a good friend of our family, called me in to find out what my problems were and to see if he could help. He soon realized that I was not prepared for college, so he secured a tutor for me who was the blessing of all blessings. After the first semester studying became easier, and by my sophomore year I was beginning to be able to study in an adequate fashion and better comprehend the material I was studying.

However the tutor could not prepare me for the heartache that was brewing.

seven

chapter 7

A FIRST—AT LAST

In early November 1926, my first year in college, the school had a campus holiday. Needing some school supplies, I put on my navy blue serge uniform and my black wool coat and walked downtown to the drugstore which was the hangout for all college students in Denton, from both North Texas State Teachers College, a coed facility, and CIA. While CIA students were not allowed to hang out at Brooks Pharmacy, there was not much the staff could do when we went in to buy supplies and were invited to sit down and have a coke. CIA girls had to sign out when we left our dorm and state when we thought we would be back. An unexpected invitation had to be squeezed into our estimated time of absence, so our stay at the hangout was relatively short, but those were golden moments for any girl who was invited to be part of the group.

This particular day was sunny and crisp. My cheeks were flushed from the brisk walk, and I was smiling at the break in my routine. I relished the lightness of my head as a result of my shorter hairdo and tossed my head dramatically from side to side without even realizing what I was doing. As I walked down the aisle looking for the items on my list, I held my head in a regal manner, thankful not to be loaded down with ropes on my head. A slender young man with a strong, yet kind face and dressed in a stylish navy blue suit and immaculately polished, black shoes approached me. I could not take my eyes off his handsome face. He stopped in front of me and asked pleasantly, "May I help you?"

"Actually you can," I stammered. "I . . . I'm looking for the blue books and can't seem to find them."

"Oh, we have moved them to the other side of the store," he said. "Let me show you where they are."

I followed as he walked right to the pile of little books with lined, blank pages and a blue cover that we used for writing our essays and exams. "Is this what you need?" he asked, handing me one of the thin booklets.

I took it and grinned, "Actually I was hoping for one already filled out. It's too nice a day to be inside writing papers."

He laughed, "Boy, is that right! What's your paper on?"

"Shakespeare, what else?" I sighed. "To be studious or not to be studious: that is the question for a day like this."

"Yes, 'conscience does make cowards of us all; and thus the native hue of resolution is sicklied o'er with the pale cast of thought, and enterprises of great pith and moment with this regard their currents turn awry, and lose the name of action,'" he quoted expertly. "Don't let Shakespeare ruin your day," he grinned. "What would you rather do today?"

Giving in to the game of pretend, I wrinkled my brow and thought a moment. "A picnic and a rope swing from a tree," I decided and waved one hand left to right in imitation of a swing. "How about you? What would you choose to do on a day like today?"

"Do you really want to know?" he asked, his eyes twinkling. "I'd like . . . I mean . . . Here, let me check you out." He abruptly took the blue book and other items I was carrying to the register and efficiently rang them up, chatting all the while. Afraid that I had offended him somehow and ended the delightful banter, I dug in my purse for my coins, and he handed me my package and change. After a slight hesitation he came from behind the counter, held the door open for me, and followed me outside.

As I turned to thank him for his assistance, he interrupted me, "Please do not think I am forward, but I would like to introduce myself. I'm Dick Mason, a pharmacy rep with Brooks. I knew that one of Mr. Brooks' employees had to be out today and so I've just dropped by to help him. I . . . I've enjoyed talking with you."

Now the blush returned to my cheeks, not as a result of the weather. "Well, I have too. . . . I'm Jackie, a student at CIA." We both laughed at the redundancy of that statement. My uniform had already given away my identity.

"I'm from Atlanta, Georgia," Dick went on. "Where are you from?"

"Palestine, a town southeast of Dallas," I replied.

"Oh, I've heard of it."

"How do you know about Palestine?" I queried, amazed that anyone outside East Texas had ever heard of the little village.

"I travel a lot in my work." He dug a hand into his pocket and glanced down at his shoes.

"Would you permit me to drive you to wherever you are going?" he asked, looking up at me suddenly.

My heart skipped a beat and cried out, "Yes! Yes!" while my mouth uttered the awful truth, "Thank you so much . . . Dick . . . but it is against the college rules for a student to ride with someone without written permission. Since I have just met you, obviously I don't have permission, so . . . I'll have to thank you and decline." I couldn't stop my lip from quivering.

In all my seventeen years I had never had a boy show interest in me. If the flutters in my stomach were a typical result of such attention, I was not sure I could endure many more requests for dates.

I made no move to leave. Dick stood rooted to the sidewalk also. He ran one hand through his black, wavy hair and frowned slightly. Then his face lit up and he lowered his voice. "Please let me drive you close to your dorm at least. Maybe there is place I could let you out that would not be too conspicuous for I really want to get to know you."

His eyes penetrated my soul and surely discovered my dilemma. Every cell in me longed for the attention he was showing me, yet I knew the rules—and the consequences for breaking them. Pulling my eyes away from his gaze, I peered into the pharmacy and turned in all directions to see who might be watching. Not seeing anyone I knew, I looked back at his pleading eyes and felt my legs become weak. To dispel the tension, I winked and said, "I know just the place."

He jabbed his fist into the air in triumph and laughed, "My car's this way."

As we drove toward the college, he told me, "You know, it's funny. I stopped by here to help Mr. Brooks, and when I saw you come in the store, I had no intention of letting you out of my sight until I drove you back to your dorm."

My heart was about to jump out of my body for I was into something I had no experience with. I just looked at him, smiled, and shook my head. "No! Not here!" I cried, suddenly aware that he was turning right onto the main campus drive. "I'll be spotted," I laughed as he jerked the steering wheel left and we veered back onto the side street we had been traveling. He slowed the car to a crawl, and we kept up a lively conversation for several more blocks.

"Turn right here," I directed, "and stop in front of the house with green shutters."

Dick followed my instructions and parked the car. Knocking the steering wheel with one fist in frustration, he got out of the car and opened my door for me. Taking my hand, he made no move to help me out of the car. Instead he leaned close to me and whispered, "Can you manage a way for me to come see you tonight if you cannot leave the campus?"

Giddy with excitement and yet filled with apprehension, I answered, "I would more than enjoy seeing you again, but I guess I'll have to forego that pleasure. The dorm mother would never allow me to see you without a permit from my mother."

He nodded soberly and helped me out of the car. He gave my hand a prolonged squeeze and looked straight into my eyes. "I will see you again, if you agree," he said.

"Sure, but how ...," I began.

"I'll think of something," he promised. "Now, you'd best go before someone sees us."

He winked. I laughed, and my laugh cracked as I struggled to hold back tears. How could someone I had just met affect me so much? "Jackie, good-bye ... for now."

I nodded sadly and headed to my dorm at a slow pace. Before I climbed the steps, I turned to see if he had driven off. He had stayed right where I left him and was watching me. Later I realized he was wanting to see which dorm I entered. I smiled wanly and barely nodded my head. I did not dare wave. There were too many windows in the dorm.

That evening Evelyn and I were studying. Well, she was. My mind kept wandering back to my conversation with Dick. So that's what dating was all about? We talked and joked and got to know each other better. The strange feelings in my head and heart would take some getting used to, but I was convinced I would enjoy dating Dick. Then I would tell myself, "He's never going to call again. Why would someone much older than me and sophisticated like him bother with someone as provincial as me? And why did I tell him I liked rope swings? That's for babies. I should have said I liked dancing . . . no matter that I don't know how to dance; I could learn."

At about eight the knock on the door startled me. Languidly, I walked to the door and was surprised to find the dorm assistant, Julia. "Jackie," she said, "your cousin is downstairs. He just happened to be driving through Denton and thought he would stop and say hello to you if you have the time."

"My cousin?" I frowned. I didn't have any cousins who lived near enough to visit Denton.

"Yes. He said his name is Dick Mason," she reported, wrinkling her brow in confusion.

"Oh . . . Dick . . . ," I repeated, hoping the pounding of my heart could not be heard outside my body.

"Sure, I'll take time to see him," I said, composing myself. "He's a traveling salesman and he does travel up this way at times. Let me freshen up and I'll be right down."

I gently closed the door and jumped straight off the floor with a silent whoop. Evelyn, who had heard the exchange, asked, "What's the deal?"

"I'll explain when I get back," I whispered mysteriously, racing to brush my hair and straighten my dress.

Down in the living room, Dick and Julia were politely visiting when I entered. Dick stood and reached out a hand. I shook it, or maybe it was what was shaking me. My legs trembled even as I tried to act composed. After all, a cousin should not have this effect on me. I thought every bone in my body would turn to mush when I walked into the living room and saw Dick so tall, so handsome, and so smug for what he had pulled off.

Julia greeted me and rose from the mahogany, needlepointed chair. "Jackie, you may take Dick into the sitting room to visit. He seems worthy, so he may stay for one hour. Do you understand? I'll just close the door so you won't be disturbed."

I nodded mechanically and forced a cheery voice. "Well, Dick, this is a pleasant surprise. How is the rest of the family?"

Dick followed me into the sitting room, and I was quite aware that Julia did not. It was the dorm staff's prerogative, even duty, to chaperone visits between the sexes. Later I learned that Julia was not as uninformed as I had suspected. She knew the signs of love and did not presume to squelch them.

As soon as Julia closed the door, Dick walked right up to me, gathered me in his arms, and kissed me lightly on the lips. He held me at arms' length and whispered, "I thought you said it was impossible to see you again."

I stretched my arms around his neck and held my head up with my eyes closed. He bent down and kissed me hungrily. Finally I broke away and admitted, "I guess I was not willing to risk the truth of the saying, 'Where there's a will, there's a way.'"

In response he hugged me close. Our lips met again and we lingered until we both had run out of breath. Nervously we sat on the damask sofa and resumed our teasing and chattering from the afternoon. I do not know who watched the time the closest, but a few minutes before the hour Dick said sadly, "I don't want to leave, but I had better go on time. Maybe if I obey the rules, Miss Kemper will say, 'Yes' the next time I come calling."

We stood and crushed each other in a hug. Then Dick tilted up my chin and planted a sweet, soft kiss on my lips. "Till the next time," he smiled. "There will be a next time. Good night, Jackie. I'll write or call real soon if I can't come by."

I walked him to the front door of the dorm, oblivious to others holding their own conversations in corners of the living room. He walked gracefully down the steps, turned, and winked. I nodded and stepped onto the porch so I could watch until his car was out of sight. Even though I did not have a sweater on, I did not feel the slight chill in the autumn air.

Waking from my reverie, I walked to Julia's door and knocked. More forcefully than I intended, I said, "My . . . cousin is gone. Thank you for giving us time to visit."

Julia patted me on the shoulder and smiled knowingly, "He can come back because he minds the rules."

I nodded and slowly climbed the stairs to my room. No sooner had I passed the first room on the hall than the occupants screeched and came running out to hug me and drag me into their room. Within moments nearly every girl on the floor had crowded into the room. "Who was the handsome visitor, Jackie?" "Was that really your cousin?" "How did you get Julia to leave you alone?"

Evelyn bombarded me with more questions than anyone. She knew better than the others how foreign a boy was in my life. I had had enough intrigue for one day, so I told the story honestly as it had happened. Well, I left out the intimate details, but anyone with any life experience could guess from my dreamy look what had taken place.

For days afterwards girls would come by my room and whisper, "Have you had any special mail? Has he called yet?" A phone call would not be a secret since sixteen girls in our wing of the dorm shared one phone. The phone was off limits between eight in the evening and nine in the morning except on Saturdays when we could talk until eleven at night. Every time the phone rang, I jumped and strained my ears, hoping to hear the call, "Jackie? It's for you!"

That never happened, but the following Friday I was walking through the lobby after class when Julia called me into her office. "Jackie, a letter came for you."

Surprised, I thanked her and turned it over to discover the writer. I had not received any mail while at CIA. There was no return address, so I carefully tore open the envelope and glanced at the signature. My whole body flushed, and I stuffed the letter into my purse, fearing that everyone would detect my correspondent. "Thank you, Julia," I called as nonchalantly as I could.

I tried not to run up the stairs, but I did skip halfway down the hall and into my room. I plopped on the bed and pulled a pillow into my lap. Carefully I retrieved the letter from my purse and read each word until I had memorized the short message:

"Jackie,

"I really enjoyed our visit last week and can't wait to see you again. I will be back through Denton Wednesday of next week and surely hope I can make a way to see you. Unfortunately, I'll be in town on a big business deal, and my time will not be my own. Know that I'll do everything in my power to spend some time with you. I've never known a girl whose company I enjoyed more than yours.

"Affectionately, Dick."

The days dragged by until Wednesday. When I woke up Wednesday morning, I was almost sorry that it had come. What if he did not get to see me? Then my hopes would be dashed. As long as it was not yet Wednesday, I had something to look forward to.

After class I raced to my room so I would not miss his call. About four o'clock I had given up any hope of seeing him. Just then a soft knock came at the door. I opened it, expecting one of the girls on the hall to be inquiring about whether he had showed up. Instead it was Julia, wearing a crooked smile. "Dick, your . . . cousin, is downstairs. What shall I tell him?"

I could not hold back a big sigh. "Please tell him I'll be right down. And . . . thank you, Julia."

She merely waved as she turned to deliver the message.

I arrived in the living room just seconds after Julia did even though I had taken two minutes to smooth my hair before I left the room. My steps were quicker than hers since my reasons for getting downstairs were more urgent. "Hello, Dick," I said simply from the doorway. He immediately excused himself from where he and Julia were standing and came towards me. Julia did not budge. She sat down primly on the sofa with her hands folded in her lap. My eyes grew big when I realized that she intended to chaperone this visit.

Dick jumped into the silence. "Jackie! It's so good to see you," he said in a voice that was too loud and he gave me a brotherly hug. "Come sit down with us. Miss Kemper was just telling me about the upcoming homecoming weekend. It sounds like quite a festive occasion."

He motioned for me to sit on the sofa beside Julia, and he perched on a footstool in front of a big stuffed chair.

My disappointment in having a third person in the room closed my mind to participation in the innocuous conversation. Dick, however, bravely kept up a banter with Julia and tried to draw me into the dialogue. Painfully, the precious minutes ticked away as I watched Dick's mouth utter words on ridiculous subjects and I longed to feel his arms around me, holding me close to his chest. Finally the minute hand finished its spin around the clock face, and it was time for Dick to leave. Julia abruptly stood and announced, "I'm so sorry, Dick, but visitation time is over for today. Please do come visit again."

Truly chagrined, Dick stood and apologized to Julia, "Please forgive me. I was so fascinated in hearing about the new language department on campus that I totally lost track of the time."

Julia smiled as she brushed past him. She glided through the door and kept going, not even looking back when Dick hesitated at the door. He stood facing away from me a moment, expecting her to turn around and beckon him to follow. When she did not, he turned around and bumped into me, I was standing so close behind him. "Oh, Jackie!" he moaned, taking me in his arms. "It was torture being in the room with you and not being able to hold you. I hope she'll give us privacy once again."

He kissed me eagerly and ran for the door. I stood rooted to the floor until I heard a car start up and drive away. Then I reported to Julia's room that he had gone. She just shook her head.

Dick's visits became more frequent. Sometimes he would come calling twice a week. The day before Christmas break, he brought me a dozen red roses. Julia just raised her eyebrows and did not say a word.

In the spring Dick and I were allowed to go with other couples on picnics, to attend musical performances on campus, and even to walk downtown to a café by ourselves. The more I knew about Dick, the more I knew I was ready for a new beginning . . . with him.

eight

chapter 8

THE END OF INNOCENCE

By the spring of 1927 Dick and I were visibly in love. Even Julia was resigned to the fact that he was not my cousin and would soon be my husband. One Saturday we were walking hand in hand on campus and stopped to sit on a bench under the spreading branches of a huge oak tree. Another girl from the dorm and her boyfriend were "chaperoning" us and found another bench facing away from us and sat down for their own private time. Dick took my hands and looked at me earnestly. "Jackie, my dearest, I don't know how I am going to survive the summer without you. It's hard enough seeing you only a few times a month." He quickly pulled my hands up to his lips and brushed his lips over them.

He sat up straight and added, "I've been thinking. It's time for my mother and sister to meet you and for me to meet your mother."

I stiffened and tried to pull my hands away. He held on tight. "Don't be afraid. They'll love you. I know they will."

"I'm not afraid to meet your family . . . although it is a little scary. I mean . . . I'm so much younger than you are and all . . . And I'm not sure I'm ready to tell Mother about you."

Dick grinned, "I'll win her over."

His eyes clouded imperceptibly, then he brightened again. "So what do you say? Can I ask them to come over after school is out? I'm not sure how it will work in Palestine, but we'll think of something."

"Dick, I haven't had a chance to tell you yet what Mother dropped on me this week."

"What?" asked Dick with genuine concern. He had heard enough about my mother to be wary.

"I won't be going home to Palestine in May," I began.

"Is it that bad?" Dick frowned.

"Oh, no," I assured him, straightening my skirt nervously. "She is moving to Denton."

"What . . . ? Why?" Dick asked confused.

"She thought it would help our finances," I lied. I couldn't tell him that Mother and Grandmother had continued their animosity towards each other and, without me as a buffer for their dislike, living under one roof had become intolerable the last year.

"Well," Dick shrugged, "that will simplify things. When should I ask Mother and Mary to come?"

"Wait until we get settled, can you? Then we can set a date. I don't want to tell Mother until she is here already." While I dreaded living with Mother and the possibility of her domination, I reasoned that seeing Dick out of a home would be easier than having to contend with the dorm's rules. I hoped the lessons I had learned about making up my own mind would carry me through the difficult transition of having Mother around on a daily basis again.

We found a little cottage in the back of a large, stately mansion across the street from the campus, and she moved down in early June. One evening shortly after we got settled in our new abode, Mother and I sat down to dinner about nine o'clock, our regular mealtime since that was as early as she could get dinner on the table after giving music lessons and doing church work all day.

We had eaten our chicken soup and pineapple salad in silence. Suddenly, I knew it was time. I placed my napkin carefully beside my plate and blurted out, "Mother, I have something to tell you."

She looked up with surprise and did not respond. I took a deep breath and said, "I have been seeing a very nice young man. He intends to marry me when I finish college."

She stared at me as if I had announced that I was going to dye my hair red. I fidgeted under her intense gaze.

"His name is Dick... Dick Mason," I continued, trying to sound confident. Why was this so hard? Why couldn't Mother show some sign of interest, or that she had even heard me? I choked back tears and stopped talking.

"So that's what you have been up to here in Denton?" she asked coldly.

"I haven't been up to anything!" I retorted, insulted at her insinuation. "I've met a very wonderful guy and have fallen in love with him. I want you to meet him." I couldn't bring myself to mention his mother's visit.

"He's from Atlanta, Georgia," I added in a low tone.

"Well, is Texas not good enough for you?" Mother cried out. "It's enough that you sneak behind my back seeing a young man, and now you tell me that you'll be moving to Georgia! Such ingratitude."

Too stunned to reply, I resumed eating my dinner although the soup had no flavor anymore. Fortunately silence had seldom ruined my appetite, and I was not going to let it tonight. Gradually her words took on a new meaning, and my spirit of independence rose to my throat. I realized that she had picked up on his being from out of state and she was afraid my marriage to Dick would derail her long-standing plans for me to take a job in Dallas after graduation so she could live in the city of her dreams.

"I have invited Dick to dinner next week, Mother," I continued as if she had never spoken. "I trust you will be here to chaperone? Is Tuesday or Thursday better for your schedule?"

"Well," Mother snapped, "make it Tuesday. Let's get this over with."

"Fine. What time shall I tell him?"

"Make it eight," she said as she cleared her bowl off the table with half the soup still in it.

Tuesday night I was dressed by six in a navy blue skirt and white blouse. Then at seven I changed into my Sunday dress, a pale yellow linen. I was glad it was summer and I was freed from the monotonous uniforms. I would love to have had a new outfit for the occasion, but knew it was pointless to ask Mother. In fact, it might make her change her mind about having Dick over.

The conversation around the dinner table was strained, but, salesman that Dick was, he masterfully engaged Mother in a conversation about her music. As Mother reluctantly warmed to his interest, she asked him innocently, "And what are your plans for the summer?"

Taking the cue he had been waiting for, Dick replied, "I'm glad you asked and I hope you will be agreeable to what I have in mind."

He shifted in his chair, threw me a glance, and added, "Mrs. Matthews, I am sure you are aware of my feelings for your daughter. After she graduates, it is my fond intention to make her my wife. Since she will eventually be a part of the Mason family, I think it only appropriate that she—and you—meet my mother and sister."

Mother coughed behind her napkin and did not interrupt. I dared not look at her. Dick told me later all color had drained out of her face. He took a deep breath and said, "I have taken the liberty of inviting them to Denton next month to meet both of you. I hope that will not interfere with your plans."

Her silence seemed endless. Finally she nodded slightly and said, "I will welcome them into my home. Please let me know the days they will be here."

I could hardly believe my ears! She had agreed! I could hear wedding bells already.

The visit of Mrs. Mason and Mary lasted four beautiful days. Mother was a gracious hostess and conversed with the visitors as if they were best of friends. She even allowed Dick to tease her a little about her fastidiousness. The Mason ladies were so accepting of me, I was ready to marry Dick just to spend time with these encouraging women. At last I would have a sister, although much younger than I, and a mother figure who knew how to nurture.

The fourth night of their visit, Dick called from work to say that he hoped I would understand that he would like an evening alone with his family. His voice sounded strained. I assumed that was because he was disappointed he would not get to see me that night. "Okay. . . but only if you promise to get off work early tomorrow and come straight here."

"We'll see . . . ," he answered distractedly. "Jackie . . . "

"Yes, Dick," I replied with concern.

"Jackie . . . ," he repeated.

"What's the matter?" I pleaded.

"I . . . can't . . . Oh, Jackie. . . . I've got to go now."

"But, Dick . . . ," I yelled into the phone. The line went dead.

Fortunately Mrs. Mason and Mary were out the rest of the afternoon, and Dick picked them up from their last stop for the day. I paced the floor of my room until I heard the Masons come in and go to their rooms for the night. Sleep had to be coaxed to visit me that night.

At breakfast the next morning I asked our guests how their evening had been. Without answering, Mrs. Mason glanced over at Mary and said, "Retha and Jackie, we need to talk to you both right after breakfast. Do you have a few minutes?"

There was no merriment in her tone, and Mary looked as if she were going to cry. My skin crawled with apprehension, and I could not swallow another bite. Mother must have sensed something ominous because as soon as we all had finished picking at our scrambled eggs and biscuits, she suggested we retire into the living room.

Desperately wanting to postpone the doom I felt was about to descend on my world, I asked if we shouldn't wait for this discussion until Dick could join us.

Mrs. Mason sighed deeply, "No, dear. We can't wait. It's too late as it is."

Mary reached for my hand and pulled me down beside her on the sofa. Mother and Mrs. Mason sat in the straight-back chairs on either side of the coffee table. I had trouble breathing in the tense atmosphere.

"My darling," Mrs. Mason began, leaning forward to look into my pale face, "I don't know how to begin, so I'll just begin at the beginning. When Dicky was twenty-six, you know he graduated from pharmaceutical school."

I nodded, wondering why that was so heavy a topic. Mary squeezed my hand.

"His father and I were so proud that we bought him a blazing red Cadillac convertible." She paused and stared into the past, seeing a grinning Dick grabbing the keys and hopping into the vehicle for a test drive. He roared away and she stood nervously in the yard until he reappeared an hour later.

"He was so excited," she went on, "that he wanted to drive all over the area to show off his new toy to everyone he knew. One night he drove to a party in a neighboring town. When he got out of his car some blocks from the party, he was held up and beaten and his car was stolen. Whoever jumped him threw him into a ditch and left him to die."

Mrs. Mason paused to compose herself. She clinched her teeth unconsciously and continued, "Fortunately, some police came by very shortly afterwards, saw the blood on the street, and stopped to investigate. They found Dicky in the ditch and rushed him to a hospital. By going through his clothes, they found our names and called us to come as quickly as possible." Her voice cracked, and tears formed in her eyes as she recalled the shock of that phone call.

Mary looked at her mother with compassion and added, "For days the doctors did not think he would live. However a greater tragedy occurred. When he finally did regain consciousness, his memory was gone. He did not remember one thing about his past and no one we brought in, even me, his younger sister, or his best friends, helped him recover his memory."

I clapped my free hand to my mouth, and Mary put her arm around my shoulders. Mother's lips became narrower and narrower, although she did not utter a sound.

"It took months," Mrs. Mason picked up the story, "to convince him that he was Dick Mason. He never could accept when we told him that he was a pharmacist. While he went home to live with us, he never really remembered a single instance of his past. There was no choice but to build a new life for him."

I grabbed a pillow from the sofa and unconsciously hugged it to my chest as if to comfort the ache growing inside me.

"His father was a physician and owned a drugstore," Mrs. Mason went on, "so he took Dick into the business and trained him to be a pharmaceutical representative so he could have a trade to make a living. It took a long time before he would make friends. Finally after a year he began visiting with the young men and women in Atlanta."

Mrs. Mason glanced at Mother, then looked directly at me. "Jackie, I'm so sorry. By the time he met you, he had been living in his new world about four years. He had adjusted to being accepted as he was and to living as well as he could."

I interrupted, "That's terrible, Mrs. Mason, but he seems to have made a full adjustment. I mean, he talks with such love about you and Mary. He obviously considers you his family." Hope tried to gain control of my emotions, but it was not given time to succeed.

"My dear, I know how hard this is for you to hear," Mrs. Mason added. "That is not all of the story."

A chill shivered down my spine and my stomach began to churn. "The doctors told us that, at any moment, if there were a shock or stress of any intensity, Dick could snap and his memory could return to where he was at the time of the accident and his current life would be wiped out of that memory. You need to know that this could happen, and if you were married to him, he might not know you or any children you might have."

A cry escaped my lips, and I collapsed to the back of the sofa. Mother jerked forward towards me. Mary grabbed a magazine from the coffee table and began to fan me. I gave in to the tears and sobbed for ten minutes. Once I thought I could speak, I stuttered, "It does not matter! I love him and I will still marry him!"

Mrs. Mason did not say anything. She merely patted my knees and let her tears run unhampered down her cheeks.

Suddenly I sat up and the tears stopped flowing. "Why . . . are you telling me this . . . instead of Dick?" I asked between heaves.

Mary looked down at her hands, and Mrs. Mason just looked at me pitifully. "Was it because he could not do it?"

Mrs. Mason merely nodded. I let out another cry and buried my face in my hands. "So, does he not want to marry me?" I stammered.

"Oh, Jackie, he wants more than anything to marry you, but he feels he has no choice but to break your engagement. He said he could not take a chance on hurting you. He loves you too much."

I could hear no more. I jumped up and ran from the room, yelling, "I will not agree to this! I've got to talk to Dick myself!"

I slammed the door to my room and threw myself on the bed. "Why?" I cried. "Why? We were so happy!"

I wished I could wake up at Aunt Lucy's home in Dallas. Unknown to Mother, Aunt Lucy had been my confidante from the day Dad died. She was everything Mother was not, and Uncle Ernest did his best to fill in for my dad. The Douthitts loved me and understood me, and I treasured them both. Aunt Lucy would know just what to say, but Mother would have thrown a fit if I had suggested going to visit them. I cried myself to sleep every night and wondered if I would ever talk to Dick again.

About two weeks later Dick called. I was alone in the house. "Jackie," his familiar voice rang in my ears.

"Dick!" I cried helplessly. "Where are you? I've been dying to hear from you. When can I see you?"

"I . . . I hope you understand me when I say that I think it is best that we not try to visit at your house," he said. "I wondered if you would drive with me to Fort Worth Saturday. We can visit and make our decisions."

"What decisions are there to make?" I answered hoarsely. "I'm still going to marry you."

"Will you just agree to ride with me?" he pleaded.

I agreed and left a note for Mother to find after she returned home from helping with the church choir practice. I simply wrote that I was out for the day and would be back by ten that evening. I had never gone away without telling her where I was going, but I had had my world fall apart once before and she could offer no emotional support, so I didn't see any reason for catering to her fears and restrictions during this cataclysmic time.

Dick and I never made it all the way to Fort Worth that day. We bought a picnic lunch at a café and stopped at a roadside park to eat and talk. Another family with children was enjoying a meal at the other end of the park. Their laughter and squeals as they chased each other could not penetrate the cloud that followed Dick and me to our concrete table under the shelter. We silently opened the box of food, but neither of us even reached to take a sandwich. We grabbed each other's hands tightly while studying the other's face for a sign of hope.

It didn't matter what Dick said, I would not agree to break off our engagement. I had lost the first man I loved, and I did not plan to lose the second one. Finally, my objections wore Dick out. "Darling," he said, shaking his head sadly, "let's think about this and talk again in a few days." I held on to him as if I were afraid he would evaporate before my eyes. He hugged me back, then gently peeled me away and helped me into the car.

The next Thursday he called, and said that he would be in town Friday and asked me to join him for dinner. Mother surprised me by not objecting to my going out alone with him, especially after my slipping out Saturday without asking her permission.

Dinner was tense, and neither of us had much to say. Afterwards, Dick drove out to the campus and parked along a deserted street. We got out of the car and walked to a bench where we had sat many times the spring before planning our lives together.

"Dick . . . ," I began.

He put his finger gently on my lips and bit his lower lip. "Jackie, this is hard enough. Please don't make it any harder."

I opened my mouth to protest, and he sadly shook his head. "No, darling, this is not going to work. I cannot take the chance on waking up some day and not knowing you. You are the love of my life. The past few weeks I have been haunted by visions of your screaming at me, 'Dick! Don't you know me! I'm Jackie, your wife!' and me staring blankly at you as if you were a lunatic who had invaded my home."

He began to cry. "I can't do that to you! Oh, Jackie, I love you so much. Please help me to do this to protect you."

I fell into his arms, and our bitter tears mingled on our cheeks. A faint summer breeze rustled the leaves on the trees as if in a dirge. Finally, he stretched back and said, "I've thought about this moment so often the last few days and I didn't ever want it to come. I realize that the only way I can go through with this is for me to change territories and never come back. I could not stand being in the town where you are and knowing I could not see you."

Huge sobs escaped from my throat, and I clawed at his back in my anguish. We both cried until we could cry no more. We held hands while we walked slowly to his car and said nothing on the drive home. After he pulled the car into my driveway, he started to get out to open my door. I placed my hand gently on his arm. "Don't get out, Dick," I pleaded. "Just kiss me one more time and then let me go."

He pulled my shoulders forward and firmly kissed my lips as if that kiss needed to last me a lifetime. Finally we parted and looked each other in the eye until mine were so filled with tears that I could not see his face. I scrambled out of the car and ran into my house and into my room, without looking back. Once I was dressed for bed, I scribbled a note for Mother not to disturb me in the morning and left it on the kitchen table. When I finally did get up and went into the kitchen to get something to eat, my mother showed a side of her I had never seen. She walked up to me, put her arms around me in so gentle a way, and said softly, "My darling, I wish I could help. My heart breaks for you both."

The summer days drifted by too slowly. I sat alone many days staring into the empty living room. One morning, no different from the rest that preceded it, something my dad said crept gently into my mind: "This too will pass and God will hold you in the palm of His hand. Life will again open the door to joys for you." And I remembered a psalm that had comforted me at other times in my life, but took on new meaning now: "Weeping may endure for a night, but joy comes in the morning." Gradually I let life begin again.

I continued to correspond with Mrs. Mason and Mary, but I never actually asked about Dick because I could not bear to think of him. The second year I was in Houston, in 1931, I got a letter from Mary, telling me that a girl Dicky was going with wanted to marry him and he had told her that it was not in the cards for him to be married, so, she wrote, at a party the girl gave him a potent drink, got him drunk, and took him to a justice of the peace and they were married. When he awakened, he had a wife, and nine months later he was a father of a little girl who was a beauty for she was his image. I doubled over in pain at the thought of another woman looking deeply into the eyes of the man I loved. Maybe we could have had a happy life. Why did I give up so easily? I threw myself into my work with a renewed vigor, trying to forget him again. How do you forget the love of your life?

When the baby was a few months old, the Masons called to tell me that Dicky had been killed in an auto accident. The news devastated me. As the weeks went by, I realized that I was somewhat relieved for I now could never hope to have him back. I needed a closure, and it had finally come.

Several months later about ten one night our doorbell rang. Mother was asleep, and I walked out on our upstairs porch to see who the visitor was. I was puzzled to see a taxi with the back door open, so I called out, "Who's there?"

A voice called from the dark, "It's Doris Mason, Dicky's wife."

That was not possible! I must be dreaming, but the drone of the taxi motor was real enough. I grabbed a robe, hurried downstairs, and flipped on the front porch light. On the porch stood a pretty young girl with long blonde hair. She was dressed in a simple cotton dress and held a sleeping baby in her arms.

Still not believing what was happening, I cracked open the door. She jumped at the sound of the door opening and peered into the dark house. "Jackie?" she asked timidly.

"Yes," I answered hesitantly.

She abruptly pushed open the door and shoved the baby out towards me. "Dicky never loved me," she cried out. "He always loved you and so this is rightfully your baby and I am bringing her to you."

I staggered back as if I had been hit. Doris just stood holding the sleeping child out to me. I shook my head violently back and forth. "There is no way I will take this baby!" I declared, afraid that I was caught in some nightmare. "Look, you pay the driver and come on in and let's talk."

One look at Doris's wild eyes told me that if I had any chance of influencing this girl, I had better pay the driver and keep Doris with me until the matter was settled. I took Doris gently by the elbow and guided her into the living room and seated her on the sofa. "Here. Lay the baby down and I'll take care of the taxi." I raced up to my room, fearing that Doris would disappear in my absence. I grabbed some money out of my purse and ran out to the taxi. Fortunately Doris was sitting placidly in the room when I returned. By this time Mother had heard the racket and had joined us.

While I made the bed in the guest room, Mother brewed a cup of tea and sliced a cold biscuit and topped it with homemade apricot jam. Doris ate it with relish. The baby woke up and was comforted with a cup of warm milk. I rocked her to sleep while Doris accepted our offer of a bath and a place to sleep for the night. We talked until two in the morning when I insisted I had to go to bed. Since going to work the next morning was out of the question anyway, I decided to sleep on the couch outside the guest room in case Doris decided to take her leave during the night.

Fortunately she slept through the night, and I was awakened by the happy coos of a ten-month-old. At breakfast I suggested we call the Masons and tell them what had happened and then we would make flight arrangements for her to return to Orlando, where she and Dicky had lived.

Doris vigorously objected. "But, Doris, what else are you going to do?" I reasoned with her. "I cannot take your baby, and you need to be near the Masons so they can help you raise her."

She looked at me a long time, then sighed, "They'll never forgive me."

"Of course, they will," I encouraged her. "Here. Let me hold the baby and you go call them. Tell them you realize your mistake and are coming home on the next plane."

I did not hear the conversation although it seemed there was more silence on Doris's end than words.

At last she reappeared and said, "They said to let them know when the plane is to arrive." She looked out the window and added as if to herself, "How stupid of me. How stupid."

I handed her the baby and went to look up the number to the Houston airport. Fortunately there was a plane leaving that afternoon for Atlanta. We hurriedly made some sandwiches and put some applesauce into a few jars for the baby and drove to the airport. I stayed with Doris until she disappeared down the runway. When I drove into my driveway, I was so exhausted emotionally and physically that I hardly knew my name. To my delight, Mother was teaching at her studio across town so I had the house to myself most of the day. I took a long, hot shower and called and told Mrs. Mason that Doris was on an Eastern flight and would be arriving within about four hours. Then I flopped into my bed and slept until nearly three in the afternoon.

When Mother came home that evening, I was preparing dinner. The Mason family was never mentioned that night or ever again. Some fifteen years later I was at a meeting in Amarillo, Texas, and I went out at noon to a nearby restaurant with some colleagues. I shook my head in disbelief when I spotted a girl who looked just like Doris, who was seated with an older woman and man. So sure was I that it was a strange coincidence, I decided not to acknowledge their presence. Out of the corner of my eye, however, I saw the older woman turn her head in my direction and stare. Slowly she got out of her seat and approached my table.

"Excuse me," she said hesitantly. "You aren't by any chance Jackie Matthews, are you?"

I shrugged and said, "Yes, Doris, I thought I was seeing you again, and I see now that that must be your daughter. How are you?"

"I'm okay," she smiled. "I'm . . . I'm sorry . . . ."

"Hey," I interrupted, "no need for that." I waved my hand in dismissal.

"Will you come meet my husband and my daughter, Mary?" she asked in relief.

"Of course," I agreed and excused myself from my confused companions.

It was like playing a trump card to see her daughter. Her husband seemed pleasant enough. I was glad to have seen them and equally as glad when we left the restaurant. Another heartache, another reminder, and for what?

Maybe I needed to be a stronger and more understanding Christian, I thought, and maybe I needed to face reality and let God direct my future. I certainly seemed to have complicated it on my own. Some years later Mary wrote me that her mom had died and that she was being married and would be moving to New Hampshire. I thanked God again for a love I was privileged to have enjoyed and for guidance to deal with it in a way that made me realize that God would always be my strength, no matter what came my way. I made a pledge to repay the care He gave me by doing my best to serve Him wherever I was needed. I have kept that pledge through many subsequent new beginnings.

nine

chapter 9
THE END OF THE BEGINNING

When Mother moved to Denton at the beginning of my second year at CIA, we found an adorable little bungalow in what was known as Taliaferro Court. It was owned by the family in the big house in front of us. Next door was another little house occupied by a good friend of mine, Myrle Justin, who was then a senior, and her mother. The Justins had a car, so we four shared lots of good times together. Often we would pool our dinners and have a feast. Mother was surprisingly agreeable to almost any activity that Mrs. Justin suggested. As a result, we went to concerts in the city and on campus and occasionally even tagged along on a shopping trip to Dallas. Following her pattern, Mother was a delightful companion—while in the company of the Justins or anyone else besides me. Her students and friends thought she was a well-bred, gracious Southern lady. Few saw behind her facade.

With Mother's arrival, I was heartsick at falling back into the repression of my earlier years. Fortunately I had tasted freedom and did not readily relinquish it. Mother rented a studio across town to teach first through fifth grade students, and the last three months we were in Denton, she took over as organist at First Methodist Church. Since I was in class most mornings and she was gone most afternoons and into the early evening teaching, we managed to coexist without many explosions. She still expected me to obey her without question and to stay hidden in the house except when I went out to class. The first week of my sophomore year, she spoke harshly to me as I left for class one morning. "Alice Cornelia, I was not happy that you took an hour to return home yesterday after class. I expect you to come straight home today. Is that clear?"

"Yes, it is," I retorted. "However, I have a club meeting, so I won't be home until about five."

She blinked and looked at me as if I were a stranger who had walked into our house by mistake. I had never crossed her this bluntly before. Feeling chagrined at my defiance, I added as I walked out of the room, "It's the Chaparral Club. We are raising money for library books, and I am in charge of the community support committee."

I had been so pleased at the end of my freshman year to be asked to join this exclusive literary and social club. Members were selected on grades and character. Each year the club organized a project to raise funds for some charitable purpose. This year the CIA library was to be the benefactor, and I was to solicit donations from businesses in the community. It was my introduction to finance, and the exposure to businesses' outreach efforts proved to be useful experience as I worked my way through the banking hierarchy in later years.

Another benefit I derived from the Chaparral Club was friendships, or actually my membership was the result of friendships, which made it even more precious to me. When I went off to college, I wondered if I would know how to make friends although I felt I would know how to be a friend. One day early in my first semester I was sitting under one of the wonderful oak trees on campus when one of my classmates walked up, sat down, and said, "I've just come from the drugstore. On the way home I noticed that the Methodist Church was having a bake sale and I bought some cookies." She reached into a brown paper bag in her hand and pulled out a thick oatmeal cookie and extended it to me. "Would you like to share these with me?" This was my first invitation to friendship since Chicago, outside of people I went to school with in Palestine. That day a long-time friendship was born with Ila Joe "Jean" Leslie. A beautiful friendship it was too, one that lasted until she slipped away to her just reward in 2000.

It was such fun to have another friend besides Evelyn, who had been a friend for many years. The girls in our dorm were also were becoming special friends. These were friends I had choices with—they invited me to go downtown or to sit with them at lunch and I could decide yes or no. Mother could not orchestrate my interaction with them. What fun it was to have someone to talk to, to go study with, and to ride the bus with to downtown Denton. Sometimes we shopped and on occasions when we were allowed to do so, we enjoyed lunch together at one of the restaurants on the courthouse square.

It was so special to have one of these wonderful friends come to me and say, "I have to have someone to talk to" or "Do you have time to talk to me?" I soon realized that having someone's confidence is the greatest compliment anyone could ever be paid. I cherished every moment of sharing with these new friends, for I had never before had a "best friend."

One day I was at the library doing research for an English paper when I realized that in the same room with me were girls I felt very close to. In surprise I began looking around to see how many were in the library whom I could actually call by name and knew a little about. It was amazing that out of twenty girls there, I knew the names of fifteen and frequently walked down the halls with them or maybe over to the dining room or sat by them on the bus. This was a real thrill, more so than the "A" I hoped to receive on my paper.

Suddenly I made a resolution. We had approximately 980 students at CIA my freshman year. I decided I would make an effort to know the freshmen, sophomores, and juniors by name by the end of the semester. I decided not to concentrate on the seniors because many of them lived across campus and had their own houses, dining rooms, and activity centers. I made an effort and, by the time school was out, I could call the names of well over half our campus population. It was a great feeling to belong and be asked to share friendships.

Possibly my deprivation in this area during my growing-up years made me want to reach out and mother anyone who was in trouble or seemed unhappy. It was not long before I gained the reputation as the mother confessor on campus, and how thrilled I was to have this identity. The girls who confided in me gave me far more than I ever gave them.

For financial as well as personal reasons, I elected to finish school in three years. I knew my earning a paycheck would ease Mother's burden, and I was ready to break away from her domination for good. I started going to summer school the summer after my sophomore year, taking nine hours. Because of my good grades, the dean allowed me to take six extra hours the beginning of what would have been my junior year. Because of summer school I already had senior hours. The extra hours were a real burden, but with the banking difficulties of the Great Depression shaping up, I felt I had to finish and get a job as quickly as possible. By taking extra courses, I did graduate in the summer of 1929 and if ever there was a tired college girl, I was it.

The last month Mother and I were in Denton, Nell King, the registrar's wife, came to see us one afternoon and asked if we would like to give up our house for the two weeks before graduation and stay with them until we left Denton. This let us release the house early enough for the Taliaferros to rent it to another couple who would be on campus for at least four years. So Mother and I packed up our things, shipped back to Palestine what we didn't need for those two weeks, and moved in with the Kings.

It was a special two weeks. Several times when I would get home and Mother would be at church or teaching piano at the studio, Mrs. King would suggest that we go play tennis or maybe take in a movie. She was precious, and it is a shame they never had children for they would have been great parents. One evening Mr. King asked me to go for a hike in the woods with him.

I donned my jodhpurs and joined him on the front porch. For a fleeting moment the creak of the porch swing as he waited for me reminded me of Dad. I sadly brushed aside the memories of our frequent talks as we swung back and forth on our porch on pleasant evenings. Mr. King led the way to a path behind their house and covered the pine needle carpet with long, rapid strides. When we were out of earshot of the houses, he slowed down and waited for me to catch up. "So you are almost finished with school," he began softly, reaching up to snap a low branch that protruded into the path at face level.

"Yes," I said with a grin. "Just two more weeks and Dallas, here I come!"

"So the position with Magnolia Oil worked out?" he asked.

"Yes. I'll be making seventy-five dollars a month," I reported happily.

I did not bother to tell him that the dream of my mother's life was to live in Dallas, and so she orchestrated my getting this position through some friends of hers. It wasn't my first choice, but I needed a job, so I gratefully accepted the offer.

Mr. King stopped walking and reached for my hands. "Jackie, I'm so happy for you. You will do well. I'm so glad you chose to come to CIA and join us for dinner as often as you did. If only . . . I mean . . . I just wish Mrs. King and I had asked you to live with us throughout your school career. Then we would have felt like we had a daughter."

His voice cracked, and he stopped talking. Sensing Dad's presence in this conversation, I gently squeezed his hand, leaned up to kiss his cheek, and said, "Let me be that one now."

I stepped back and looked up at him. He bent over to give me a hug, and tears shimmered in his eyes. He merely nodded and smiled. As he started abruptly back down the path toward the house, I saw him reach in his back pocket, pull out a brown plaid cotton handkerchief, and hastily wipe his nose. When we reached the house, he opened the door for me and winked without a word.

A week before graduation Mrs. King asked me at dinner one night, "Jackie, what would you like for a graduation gift?"

That day I was exhausted because school had been very demanding that summer. I sat down my glass of iced tea and replied, "Do you really want to know what I want? Mrs. King, the day of graduation I want to come home to one of your fried chicken dinners with crispy biscuits and homemade ice cream, and then I want to go into your guest room, get in the bed, and be left alone until I wake up—no matter when it is. And I don't want Mother coming in checking on me saying I have to drink water or eat or whatever she feels I need to do either."

Both Mr. and Mrs. King could hardly suppress a giggle. Without a moment of hesitation Mrs. King clapped her hands together and promised, "Darling, you will have your wish." She turned to my mother, who had flushed at my pronouncement, and said, "Retha, this is my house. True she is your daughter, but when the day of graduation comes, I will call all the shots. Is that clear?"

Mother nodded defensively and averted her eyes from mine.

Mrs. King made good her promise. The morning after my last final exam I stumbled into the house at noon, hugged Mrs. King, and allowed the fragrance of fried chicken and biscuits draw me into the dining room. I fought back tears when I saw the table set with her finest white linen tablecloth, sterling silver flatware, and the Sunday china. Heaping plates of fried chicken, fresh garden beans, mashed potatoes, and homemade biscuits were waiting for our consumption. A bowl of fresh roses in the center of the table flanked by white candles in silver candlesticks applauded my efforts of the last three years. While I was tired beyond description, I just stood and shook my head in astonishment. The elegance of the celebration compensated for the many birthday parties I had not been allowed to have. I threw my arms around Mrs. King's neck and wept. Shortly, Mother returned from her piano lesson and we indulged in my chosen menu, followed by creamy, homemade vanilla ice cream with fresh strawberries on top.

I thanked Mrs. King profusely and headed straight for the guest bedroom. Closing the door, I sighed, dropped my books on the desk in the corner, and started to fall into the bed. I stopped long enough to notice that the corner of the rose-colored comforter had been turned down already, inviting me to crawl in. At the foot of the bed lay a demure cotton nightgown with lace appliqué along the hem of the long skirt. I ran my hand admiringly over it, kicked off my shoes, and climbed into bed fully clothed in my uniform. I was simply too tired to change into my gift gown.

I did not know until later that about eleven that night, after I had slept for ten hours, Mrs. King saw Mother approaching the guestroom and reaching for the doorknob. "Retha!" she called out. Mother snapped her head around and looked sheepishly at her friend. "I . . . I was just going to check to see if she is alright," she began lamely. "It's been a long time since she got home and if she's going to eat . . . ."

"Now, Retha," Mrs. King admonished gently, moving her back to my door and crossing her arms across her chest. "Remember what I promised Jackie? No interruptions. None. She knows where to find a bite to eat if she wakes up in the night. She has been working very hard for three years, and it's high time she got caught up on her rest."

"Well, . . . ," Mother started as her face flushed, "I just . . . ."

"I know what you 'just' wanted with her," Mrs. King answered without a smile. "You run on to bed now."

Mother stammered, frowned, then turned and disappeared into her room. Mrs. King waited a few minutes and when Mother did not reappear, she cautiously walked away.

I finally awoke at six the following morning. For a moment I tried to remember what final I had that day and worried that I had fallen asleep in the middle of studying. Then I remembered that I was finished with college and the day was mine. I stretched and snuggled back down into the comforter. Feeling rested for the first time in months, I plumped the pillow and turned my head toward the window. The summer sun was already balancing over the horizon and the birds were chirping a salutatory song. I closed my eyes and savored the moment of rest. With a contented sigh, I jumped out of bed and pulled on a jumper Auntie Bess had made me for graduation. It felt so freeing to dress in something other than a uniform, just as it had felt so freeing to don the uniform three years earlier. I felt ready for the next new beginning.

Sauntering into the kitchen, I found Mrs. King waiting for me. Mother was teaching a piano lesson. Mrs. King jumped out of her chair and gave me a long hug. "Congratulations! You did it! I'm so proud of you."

She hustled me to a seat at the kitchen table and brought me a glass of orange juice. "I'll fix you an egg if you like, and I do have your favorite pimento cheese if you'd like a sandwich instead," she offered.

"Oh, that sounds good!" I exclaimed, taking advantage of the pampering.

"I sort of thought you'd like that," she smiled, "and here is some bread fresh out of the oven."

I gulped down the sandwich and smiled contentedly.

"Would you like a bite of homemade ice cream?" Mrs. King asked, obviously pleased to meet my every request. "I made some chocolate this morning." She removed the wet towels from the top of the ice cream freezer and scooped the cold, brown mounds into a dish for me. "You can have as much as you want—even if there is none left for lunch," she laughed as I dug into the dessert with relish.

The next day as Mother and I loaded our bags into our car to return to Palestine, Mr. and Mrs. King hovered around us. "Did you remember your hanging clothes?" Mrs. King asked.

"Here, let me help you with that box," Mr. King offered.

Mother impatiently sat in the car while I hugged the Kings one more time. "Thank you," I started. "I can't thank you enough . . . ."

"Now, Jackie, it has been our pleasure," they assured me. "You write us when you get to Dallas, okay?"

"Of course," I promised. "I'll have a car before long and will come visit often. I promise."

Mother stuck her head out the window and snapped, "Alice Cornelia, we have to get to Palestine by five for my lesson. You have said everything already. Please get in the car so we can go."

I hugged both the Kings once more and slid into my seat. I waved until we disappeared around the corner.

Sadly I did not go to work in Dallas as planned. While we kept in contact, I never saw the Kings in person again. Mr. King died the following fall semester. Mrs. King sold their house and moved to Kerrville to live near her sister and died two years later before I could get out to that far end of Texas.

After graduation Mother and I returned to Palestine to live once again with my Grandmother Wagner. It was good to see my high-school friends and this time to plan a big picnic with other class members without parental dictation. My attention was also directed to my future life in Dallas. As a graduation present Mother had given me a trip to Houston to visit Auntie Bess, Uncle George, and Sister Saunders. These special friends had recently moved to Houston. Little did Mother know that this visit would change our lives completely and it would derail her plans to make her future home in her beloved Dallas.

If ever I experienced change, I did during college and I learned full well what it meant when someone would say, "So life always begins," for indeed it did for me. When I would ask the inevitable "Why?!" I was comforted by God's promise to Jeremiah, "'For I know the plans that I have for you,' declares the Lord, 'plans to prosper you and not to harm you, plans to give you hope and a future.'" Clinging tightly to that hope, I bravely stepped into my future.

ten

chapter 10

A TASTE OF INDEPENDENCE

Shortly after Mother and I returned to Palestine after my graduation from CIA, I left for my graduation trip to Houston to visit Auntie Bess, Uncle George, and Sister Saunders. Of course I was delighted, for not only would I be traveling alone, but I would be visiting without parental domination. Even though I was now a college graduate and nearly twenty, I was still a minor. I looked forward to a taste of personal freedom and the opportunity to test my decision-making abilities. Mother called and made the arrangements for me to go, and within three days I was on the Missouri Pacific Railroad headed for Houston. Neither Mother nor I knew that a surprise of great proportions awaited me there.

The Saunders met me at the train. I was so excited to see Houston for it had been quite a number of years since I had been there when Mother was having eye surgery. We rode a streetcar back to the Saunders' house, and I enjoyed the new experience as much as if it had been an amusement park ride instead of the common mode of transportation.

After we got home and were all settled in, Auntie Bess came into my room and announced with a twinkle in her eye, "Alice, I want you to plan dinner for tonight. You can have anything and everything you want. There are no limits."

I could hardly believe my ears. After Mrs. King's kind offer earlier in the summer, I could get spoiled by this kind of attention. Without hesitating, I ran to Auntie Bess and flung my arms around her waist. "Oh, you doll!" I cried. "That's an easy assignment. You make the best fried chicken on earth and biscuits that melt in my mouth. Will you make those for me please?"

"Flatter me like that, and I'll make you anything you want," Auntie Bess laughed. "I want to see you eat two or three biscuits slathered with all the gravy you want, and then there will even be leftovers to be toasted for breakfast. What else?"

"I'll leave the rest up to you," I replied, knowing that whatever she made would be delicious.

That evening she served a large white ceramic platter of crisp fried chicken, bowls of creamed potatoes and fresh black-eyed peas, flaky biscuits, and a lemon pie topped with a tall meringue. I don't know who had more fun at that meal, me or Auntie Bess. She beamed as I asked for more of every dish, knowing how seconds were discouraged at Mother's table. "Sweetheart, if you want a third glass of milk tonight, you may have it," she coaxed. Not wanting to be greedy, I declined, but I felt so grateful that the extra had been offered. If this was freedom, I welcomed it with my whole being.

After dinner we moved out onto the front porch to catch some evening breeze and I told them about graduation. "You know, Mother almost missed the ceremony because she had gone to Dallas and the bus was late on her return trip," I reported.

"What was she doing in Dallas?" Uncle George asked, settling back in his white wicker chair and placing a fresh glass of iced tea on the table next to him.

"Well, she was making plans for our next move," I answered, thinking that should have been clear without an explanation.

"Your next move?" Uncle George questioned, leaning forward in his chair to see me better in the waning light.

"Yes," I said, trying to sound upbeat. "You know Mother has always wanted to live in Dallas. She went to visit with Miss May Grigsby, a longtime friend whom you know and who is executive secretary to the president of Magnolia Oil." This company eventually became Mobil Oil Company. I fingered the folds in my yellow cotton dress and pictured my mother saying nice things to her friend about me that she would never say in my presence. Bitterly, I thought that she would allow the compliments to exit her mouth because they would benefit her.

Realizing that that sort of thought was totally counterproductive, I resumed my story. "Mother told Miss Grigsby she wanted to live in Dallas and she was making inquiries about a job for me. She told me that Miss Grigsby said, 'Tell your daughter to look no further. Magnolia will gladly hire her as a secretary September 1. We will pay her seventy-five dollars a month.' I understand that's the going rate for girls just out of college. Anyway Mother accepted the offer for me and spent some time looking for apartments. She hasn't found one yet, but we still have a few weeks. She says I am to pay for rent and she'll furnish the food."

"No!" Uncle George bellowed, pounding his hands on the arms of his chair for emphasis. I jumped as he rose and paced the length of the porch. I just watched him, knowing he would verbalize his thoughts as soon as he filtered them for my hearing. He knew too well the repression with which I had been raised, and Auntie Bess had stopped him more than once when he had started to protest my mother's rules in my hearing.

I smiled, realizing that he must consider me an adult now to be speaking against my mother in my presence. He whirled around and shook his forefinger at me for emphasis, "You are not going to live in Dallas. Houston will be one of the largest cities in America in a short time, and Houston will give women a chance to advance whereas Dallas never will." His words had the strength of truth, and even today I believe this to be true.

Without warning I began to cry. Auntie Bess came to sit beside me and put her arm around my shoulders. She reproved her husband gently, "Now, George, see what you have done."

"No, Auntie Bess," I whimpered, "he's not done anything wrong. He is right. I see the signs myself with all the oil companies settling in Houston. Its economy is diversifying faster than Dallas' and its attitude is not as old-guard as Dallas'. And if I lived here, I could see y'all whenever I wanted!"

I sighed deeply and wiped my eyes with the handkerchief Sister had retrieved from the house. "I know Mother would pitch a fit if we did not move to Dallas, and I just don't think I can take that," I shrugged.

Uncle George opened his mouth to reply and Auntie Bess jumped in, "Darling, he doesn't mean . . . ."

"Bess," Uncle George interrupted her, "I will take care of Retha. Alice, be ready tomorrow morning at eight and we will take the streetcar to some of the major oil companies here to apply for a position. Unfortunately Humble is out of the question since I work there. They have a nepotism policy, you know. However, we'll go to Shell first because I have lots of friends among the officials." Uncle George had worked for years as claims agent for the Missouri Pacific Railroad. When the company wanted to transfer him to St. Louis years before, he declined. Immediately, friends got him an interview with Humble, and he was hired because of his excellent reputation in claims. He had worked in Humble's claims department for several years, eventually becoming manager.

I put my hand to my chest and took a deep breath of fresh air. A smile spread across my entire face, and I clapped my hands together like a child at a birthday party. Maybe the walls were not closing in after all.

At the Shell Building the next morning we were directed to the personnel office on the third floor. Uncle George spoke to the receptionist, who led me into a room with eleven other applicants. We each filled out an application and waited for the next step. Shortly an employee came in, and starting at the opposite end of the room from where I sat, she picked up each application and said to each applicant, "We appreciate your time and if we have an opening, we will gladly call you."

Her attitude miffed me. I thought, if I have worked three years to graduate just to get this kind of response, I am going to Dallas, Uncle George or not. Finally she arrived beside the table where I was seated. Everyone else had been dismissed, and I was reaching for my purse, knowing what she was about to say. However, she picked up my application and said as if in surprise, "Please wait here. I'll be back shortly." Puzzled, I watched her disappear and close the door after her. An hour passed and I was miserable. I needed to find the ladies' room, I needed a drink of water, and I needed some air as the room had no windows and air conditioning was not an option in the humid coastal city in 1929.

At last a tall, commanding lady in a black tailored suit opened the door, introduced herself as Florence Dunn, personnel director for the Southwestern Region of Shell, and invited me into her office. I followed timidly down a long corridor of offices. She turned into one, strode over to a large mahogany desk and pulled out a padded, swivel chair. She motioned for me to take a seat in the black overstuffed chair on the other side of the desk. While she arranged some papers on her desk, I glanced around at the large office. I was stunned to realize that this was her office; she was not the secretary to a man in that position but an executive in her own right. Uncle George's prophetic words took on more meaning.

Miss Dunn looked up from her papers and spoke, "I apologize for keeping you waiting so long. We did not realize at first that you had graduated from the College of Industrial Arts in Denton. We almost always hire everyone who comes to Shell from there because their students are the best prepared students from any university or college anywhere."

My mouth felt even drier than a few minutes ago as I dared hope the direction this conversation was taking. I smiled and continued to sit up straight as Mother had always taught me. I kept my legs crossed at the ankles and did not fidget with my hands.

Miss Dunn stood up and walked around to my side of the desk. She stopped in front of me and smiled, "While you were waiting so patiently, we were creating a position for you as supervisor of the filing section for four key divisions in the company—leasing, land, paleo, and the geophysical departments. Would you be interested in that position, Jackie?"

Before I could answer, she laughed, "Well, I'm sure you are interested in knowing the salary before you give an answer." She reached across the desk, picked up a piece of paper, and glanced down at it briefly. "Your beginning salary will be one hundred ten dollars a month," she reported, "with a promise of a twenty-five dollar increase in ninety days if all works out well and a fifty-dollar raise at the end of your first calendar year. What do you think?"

"I think . . . ," I started and leaned forward to shake her hand. Suddenly the breath was knocked out of me as my mother's face appeared before me—ashen and angry. "I think that is a very interesting offer," I said as I composed myself and rose. "Will you please give me a day or two to consider it and let me get back with you?"

"Well, of course," she smiled, shaking my hand. "Take whatever time you need."

I waited until I was out the front door of the building before I broke into a trot. I needed to talk to Uncle George, and I was to meet him and a Shell executive for lunch at the exclusive Rice Hotel a few blocks away. I dashed to the hotel and found them already sitting at a table with a white tablecloth and a lone red rose in a silver vase. I apologized for being late and gave my order to a waiter in a black tuxedo with tails and white gloves.

Mr. Miller, Uncle George's friend, smiled at me and asked, "Well, did the folks at Shell treat you well?"

I laughed, "Oh, they treated me so well I think I'm dreaming."

Uncle George winked and said, "So they offered you more money than Magnolia did?"

I nodded slightly and blushed. Personal finances were never discussed in polite company.

Mr. Miller sensed my discomfort and laughed, "Jackie, Houston is always going to pay higher salaries because of our oil position, and there will always be more opportunities for women in Houston than in Dallas."

I agreed totally, but there was still one flaw in this perfect picture. How was I going to break this news to my mother who in her mind was already living in Dallas? We finished our meal with talk of the oil business, and nothing more was said about my job offer.

When Uncle George came home that night, he was one jump ahead of me. "Alice," he said as his lips twitched, "I have spoken to your mother."

My eyes widened and I unconsciously shrank back into my chair. "I told her you would be staying in Houston with us and she could go on with her plans to move to Dallas."

I coughed and shook my head to be sure my ears were clearly hearing what he was saying. "And I also suggested that since she had made all the arrangements for your employment at Magnolia that she call Miss Grigsby and tell her in detail what has transpired. I told her I felt sure her friend would understand."

I jumped up and hugged Uncle George so tight that he almost lost his balance. "Thank you, Uncle George!" I cried. "I never thought something like this could happen!"

The next day I called Miss Dunn and accepted the Shell position. My new adventure had begun. I loved living with the Saunders, having Sister to confide in, and Auntie Bess and Uncle George to encourage and spoil me. I felt God was smiling graciously on me, and I was thankful.

My first paycheck was like a ticket to heaven. I had so much money to spend any way I wanted! I had thought all month about what I would do with it and had spent it several times over in my mind. After my gift to the church and a bit stuck away into a savings account, I still had plenty left. The Saturday after payday I rode the streetcar downtown and disembarked at a shoe store a block away from the Shell Building. I had often walked by it on my lunch hour. The windows were filled with high heels of every color and numerous styles very different from the clunkers I still had from college. I was at the door of the store when it opened at ten. "May I help you, miss?" asked a salesman.

"Yes, I'd like some shoes," I answered with a quivering voice.

"What style would you like to try on?" he pressed.

“How about this one? ” I said, pointing to a purple heel with a gold buckle on the toe.

“Fine. That is very popular with the working ladies,” he agreed. “Would you like to try the red one next to it? It’s a little wider in the toe and has a slightly different feel.”

“Well, yes,” I decided.

Within half an hour I had tried on fourteen pairs of shoes. I had not had on that many pairs in all my life put together. The weary salesman asked, “And have you decided which you want?”

Rashly, I answered, “Yes, I want them all.”

He looked up from his stool where he had sat to place each shoe on my foot and shrugged, “Okay. All it is!”

I importantly wrote a check on my new bank account, and then my jaw dropped. How in the world was I going to get all those boxes home on the streetcar! And what would Auntie Bess and Uncle George say if they saw me carry in all those shoes! “Sir,” I stammered, “there is one small problem.” I explained my predicament to him. He offered helpfully, “We can hold them for you and you can come get them as you want over the next week or so.”

I sighed with relief. “Yes, that’s a good plan. Thank you!”

Every day the next week I retrieved two more pairs and stuffed them into my closet when I got home. Fortunately no one at home commented on my many purchases.

Every day I wore a new pair of shoes and loved the feeling of being in style, if only from my ankles down. The next paycheck would go toward a new wardrobe. Auntie Bess had graciously made me two suits and Sister had given me a few of her blouses so I would look like a corporate employee. However I wanted the luxury of wearing a different outfit every day of the week.

A few days after I brought home the last of the shoes, I opened my closet to choose which ones to wear. I was surprised to realize that I was not as pleased with my purchases as I had been the day I made them. I had worn only five of the pairs; many were the same style shoe but in different colors. My wardrobe was not large enough yet that I needed all the colors I had picked out. The boxes cluttered the closet and made it awkward to get to my clothes. What was I going to do? I didn’t need all these shoes.

The next day at lunch I walked to the shoe store and saw my salesman through the window. He waved. I smiled and bravely reached for the door handle and pushed the door open.

“Hello,” he greeted me. “What would you like to try on?”

“Oh, nothing . . . ,” I stammered. “I don’t know how to say this, but I’ve decided I don’t really need . . . I mean . . . .”

"You want to bring some shoes back?" he interrupted with a smile.

"Yes," I sighed heavily. "How did you know?"

He smiled. "Was it your first paycheck you spent on those shoes?" he asked, walking to the cash register.

"Well, as a matter of fact, it was," I answered shyly.

"It happens all the time," he went on. "Girls get giddy with their first money, and shoes are a good place to start spending. Lots of them didn't have many shoes growing up and want to change that."

"Yes, well, . . . what do I . . . . I mean, can I . . . ?"

"Just bring back what you don't want and haven't worn," he helped me out. "It's not a problem."

Over the next few days I returned seven pairs of unworn shoes. Freedom still felt good—the freedom to set my own limits.

The next months were such fun for I was developing into a thinker and a decision maker and learning how to be a business leader. Even better than my raise was the day my boss came into my department and asked, "Jackie, the lease department needs to be able to retrieve their old reports in a more efficient fashion. Do you have a suggestion?"

I had noticed that a change of procedures would serve that department better but was too unsure of myself to offer my suggestions. Now that I had been asked, I told him my ideas without hesitation. He readily agreed, "Why, that's a marvelous idea. I think that will solve their problem. Thank you for being so observant. I'm really glad you are on our team."

I didn't need high heels to feel tall that day.

As my confidence grew, so did my social schedule. I had been attending church regularly with the Saunders and after a few months joined St. Paul's Methodist Church and began teaching in the Children's Department as well as singing in the choir. I was also privileged to take voice lessons from Helen Flake, a neighbor and foremost voice teacher in Houston.

After a few weeks I looked up Father Lee, my good friend from Palestine. Shortly after I moved to Houston in 1929, he was sent to Villa de Matel in Houston as the resident priest. The Villa was a nunnery, which included a school for girls who wanted to be nuns, a small retirement facility, and a small hospital for retired nuns. One Sunday a month I had dinner with him at the Villa and visited for a couple of hours.

About a year after I arrived in Houston, I held his hand the day he died. It broke my heart when he said weakly, "Colleen, it is not too late to tell me you will join the church." Before I could answer him, I squeezed his hand, leaned over to kiss him, and felt his hand let go of mine—a blessed moment for me, who did not have to say more, and for him, who did not have to hear me again say, "No." He knew I was happy and active at St. Paul's yet he still wanted me in the official fold of the Catholic church.

I also began participating in the Houston chapter of the alumnae group for the College of Industrial Arts. By the third year I agreed to serve as president. Then fourteen alums who had graduated with me decided to sponsor a project to benefit the Louis H. Hubbard Literary Club at CIA, named after the current president of the school. Each year we raised funds to give three books to the school library. The friendships I enjoyed through this group were worth much more to me than the time I gave to the organization.

My life in Houston was taking root and I was beginning to feel at home. Being loved and having friends and a family who made room for me was like a dream come true. I wondered if this was what Dad had in mind when he told me that he felt sure I would have an extended family one day. I came to love Saturday mornings when I could arise when I wanted and spend the day as I wanted. Even during the week no one told me to eat this or avoid doing that. The Saunders placed no restrictions on either Sister or me. They trusted us enough to make good decisions on our own. Sister continued to live at home until she married in 1936 and moved with her husband back to Palestine.

Mother visited only a few times in the three years I lived with the Saunders. While she was unhappy that Uncle George had found me a job in Houston, she was glad I was living with people she knew and approved of. About once a year she came to Houston to check with her eye doctor. She would arrive on the train in the afternoon, spend a night with us, have her appointment the next morning, and catch the return train directly from the doctor's office. That was acceptable to me since we really did not have much to say to each other.

For Christmas in 1930 the Saunders gave me a present of a train ticket—roundtrip—to Palestine. It was fun seeing some of my friends who were home and comparing notes on how our lives had changed. Most of the girls in my class, as well as most of the boys, were now married. My time had not been designated, but I trusted that the Lord would make a way for me in His good time. In the meantime I loved my extended family, my job where I was appreciated, and my freedom.

This was the real beginning of my understanding that life always has its beginnings and its endings. The beginnings challenged me. For instance, I was developing capabilities through my position with Shell and those who took such a marked interest in me and my work. I thanked God many times for this wonderful knowledge of how things always begin. I experienced that He never left me, that He had a plan for my benefit, and I was willing to trust Him in both the beginnings and the endings.

eleven

chapter 11

NOTHING EVER STAYS THE SAME

My experience at Shell was absolutely delightful, and my progress seemed assured from the first day. I loved the people I worked with, and I loved the work I did for them. One day I was terrified, however, when the vice-president, George Luhn, called me into his office. My legs were shaking—and not from the exercise—as I walked up the three flights to his executive suite. I reviewed every detail of my last few days, trying to discover what I might have done to displease this man whom I admired and with whom I thought I enjoyed a friendly relationship.

His secretary showed me into his office. The large window with a view of downtown and the walls lined with oak bookcases merely reinforced my fear. I felt like a novice piano student again, waiting for the scolding of my mother.

"Oh, hello, Miss Matthews," he began pleasantly enough, but with no mirth on his face. "Please have a seat." He pointed to a burgundy, tufted-leather chair with padded arms. I sat nervously on the edge of the seat and managed to force a smile.

"Miss Matthews, I wanted to talk to you about some suspicious expenses that are showing up on expense accounts," he continued without returning my smile.

My heart began to pound and my throat went dry. "Sir," I replied weakly, "you must have me confused with someone else. I don't have an expense account."

He looked at me with a quizzical expression, then burst out laughing. "Of course, you don't, Miss Matthews," he guffawed and slapped his knee with one hand. Then he regained control of himself and said, "No, no. I was not accusing you. I need your help."

My breathing became more normal, and I nodded for him to continue.

"Your supervisors have told me of the . . . the integrity with which you conduct yourself at your work," he smiled at last, "and that is the quality I am looking for in the person who will accept a very important assignment—the one I want to explain to you. I am hoping you will be agreeable to taking on this challenge."

I felt my back relax, and I sat forward in anticipation.

"What I am about to tell you must remain in strict confidence, do you understand?"

"Yes, sir," I replied, wondering what a vice-president could possibly want to confide in me, a clerk with less than a year's tenure at Shell.

"Well, to be blunt, we have noticed a number of questionable items showing up on expense accounts, and we need someone to look into this for us. I would like to put you in charge of auditing all our expense accounts and automobile reports each month and questioning the men about anything suspicious. Will you do that for us?"

I swallowed hard and frowned slightly. I hated the thought of confronting men who had been with the company for years. I was a girl of just twenty and a newcomer. Besides, I had begun to establish friendly relations with many of the executives for whom I worked and knew how confrontation could tarnish relationships.

"Are you sure?" I questioned.

Mr. Luhn laid back his head and howled. "I knew that's how you would respond," he chuckled. I just sat waiting for an explanation.

"Yes, I'm very sure, Miss Matthews," he assured me, putting his forearms on his desk and leaning in my direction. "You are an unusually bright girl with a strong sense of right and wrong. Those are the qualities we need in this position. Will you accept it?"

Knowing that God opens doors and expects us to walk through them without question, I replied, "If you have that much confidence in me, I won't let you down. I'll give it a try."

"Excellent!" he exclaimed, slapping his hands on the desktop. "I'll get Margie to show you how the system works and move you up next to her office right away."

As I waited for him to make arrangements for my move, my heart suddenly stopped as I remembered one particularly handsome, redheaded young man whose reports I would have to review. My heart beat quicker whenever Makaja McGehee, whom we called Mac, passed my door, and I felt myself blush each time he spoke to me. How in the world was I going to deal with men like this one and some much older if there were a problem? Well, I had given my word and I would have to trust that God knew what He was doing.

Most of the men who had expense accounts were either executives or fieldmen who worked in the oil fields or the territories where Shell hoped to purchase leases. When their expense account reports were due, the men came into town to turn them in and meet with their department head or division manager. It usually took the entire week they were in town for their reports to be checked and processed. I asked Mr. Luhn if I might meet each presenter the first time he turned in an expense report that I was to review. We could talk about the report before I scrutinized it. He thought that was a wonderful idea and set up appointments with each man.

To my dismay, the first presenter I met with was the handsome Mac. He swaggered in wearing an expensive double-breasted suit, probably from Hart Schaffner and Marx, a new overcoat, and a pair of shoes that shone like polished glass. I had to take a few deep breaths to get my heart to stop racing at his image. I knew these thoughts were futile because he treated me as one would a clerical employee. He never spoke to me unless I addressed him first. Then his reply was brief. I was obviously the new "little girl" in the office, in his view.

Mac walked into my office without even knocking at the door. In four big strides he covered the distance to my desk and handed me his report. Taken aback at his brashness, I thanked him with a stilted smile and quickly glanced over his report. I had trouble concentrating on the task at hand, knowing such a handsome man was just feet away from me. Finally, I turned to the last page and saw his signature. Then I glanced at the front to see where his territory was. He worked out of Plaquemine,

Louisiana, a town of maybe a thousand at that time. I tried not to react visibly when I saw his meal tabs—breakfast, five dollars plus tip; lunch, seven dollars plus tip; dinner, nine dollars plus tip. Those prices were unheard of in those days, even in fancy Houston restaurants. I did not want to start off on the wrong foot, so I merely stated, "Mac, I understand that these figures represent your expenses for the previous month."

He nodded.

"Is there anything you want to explain to me that might not be obvious in the report?" I continued.

"No," he replied brusquely, shifting impatiently from one foot to another.

"Well, thank you very much. I'll call you if I have any questions," I said as pleasantly as I could.

Without a word he scowled and turned toward the door. As he walked out, I thought I understood now why he wore such fine clothes, but I had to be sure. This was no time for assumptions. The consequences could be very severe, so I had to be certain of my facts. In those days receipts were not required to be turned in with expense reports, so I had to scour the report to find the name of this high-powered café in this out-of-the-way town. Finally I located the name of the place and called information to find a telephone number. I dialed the number.

"Cajun Kitchen," the voice answered with a distinctive French accent.

"Hello," I replied. "I am in Houston and I would like to get a copy of your menu. Can you send me one?"

"Hello?" came the reply. "Are you sure you have the right place?"

"Is this the Cajun Kitchen in Plaquemine, Louisiana?" I repeated.

"Yes, ma'am."

"Then I have the right place," I went on. "Will you please send me one of your menus?" The lady on the other end of the line laughed, "That's the first time anyone out of town has wanted one of our menus."

"I just need it for my files here at Shell Oil," I explained.

When the menu arrived in a few days, I took it straight to the vice-president's office.

"Mr. Luhn, I'm sorry to disturb you, but I think you need to see what I have discovered," I said, handing him the report and the menu. "Please note the prices on the report for the meals and notice that no meal on the menu costs that much." The most expensive breakfast on the menu was $1.95, lunches cost between $3 and $4.50, and no dinner was more than $7, including steaks.

Mr. Luhn looked up at me and commented without batting an eye, "I did not realize how damn smart I really am!"

I shifted my weight from foot to foot, not knowing what he meant. "I knew you would catch on pretty quick and you have not disappointed me," he continued, extending his hand to shake mine. "I realized that Mac was wearing a lot of new expensive clothes. I was curious to see what you would come up with the first time, and you have met my expectations. These new clothes will come to an end, you'll see," he said, lifting his eyebrows and nodding his head vigorously. "Please come back tomorrow at one and we'll talk to Mac."

I dreaded that meeting. To prepare, I dressed in my most professional suit and high heels and spent an extra few minutes putting on my makeup and combing my hair. The morning dragged by, and finally the hour arrived. I had no choice but to face the handsome Mac. With my heart beating fast, I arrived in Mr. Luhn's office just seconds before Mac. I noticed that he did not walk right in to Mr. Luhn's office as he did into mine, but he waited for the secretary to show him in.

He strode in wearing yet another expensive suit and shook Mr. Luhn's hand confidently. He did not look at me. Mr. Luhn began, "Well, Mac, it is so good of you to come visit with us."

Mac nodded cursorily in my direction, and I thought I detected a slight frown on his forehead.

When he turned back to Mr. Luhn, the vice-president did not say anything. He merely held out the printed menu from the Cajun Kitchen. As soon as Mac saw it, he paled. He knew his game was up. There was no need for words. Mr. Luhn merely nodded towards Mac, who swallowed hard.

Wanting to diffuse the tension, I spoke up, "Mac, I'm sure that you want your expense account figures to be correct, so I am asking that you furnish receipts with your report from now on—for every expense. That way no one will have any questions. Will you agree?"

"Why, yes... of course ...," he stammered. I noticed a bead of sweat had formed on his brow.

"Fine," Mr. Luhn replied, looking intently into Mac's eyes. "Thank you, Mac. That will be all for today."

I sighed heavily when Mac left. Mr. Luhn thanked me for my thorough research and said, "I doubt we'll have to repeat that scenario."

Sure enough, word got out that Mac had been caught red-handed. Two fieldmen even came to me and awkwardly asked for their reports back so they "could correct a mistake" they had noticed. This padding of expense accounts had gone on for years, so naturally I was not the most popular employee according to some. I ordered menus or price lists from all the businesses that showed up on expense reports, and soon all the reports were turned in with reasonable and accurate amounts—and with receipts.

I even received a letter of commendation from our division manager for the orderly way I was addressing the expense account checks and the automotive reports. Verifying the automotive reports was a little harder than working with the expense account reports since there were no receipts to get except for car repairs and gasoline. However, those figures were usually reasonable. To cheat on the mileage on an automotive report was silly since I had all the distances for every fieldman, including the size of the town near which he was stationed.

Honesty paid off for when I got my first three-month evaluation I received a fifty-dollar raise instead of twenty-five. Finally the executives and fieldmen became friends with me, and checking reports and accounts was fun and, above all else, honest.

Just when I could predict a bright future at Shell, the economic crash of the thirties hit like a bolt of lightning out of a blue sky. Houston and Texas did not feel the crunch of the Great Depression as heavily as other parts of the world did because we were in the heart of a booming oil business. However when I had been with Shell two years and seven months, the operations officer called me to his office. This was not unusual, but for some reason I had the jitters about going this day. When I entered his office, he seemed to sense my nervousness. "Jackie," he began, without even offering me a seat, "I will get right to the point—although this is very hard for me. Our New Orleans office is being moved to Dallas, as you know. We have just received word that the Houston office will also be moved and anyone with less than three years service will not be transferred."

I staggered and sat down heavily in a chair. "I'm really sorry," he went on with sincere concern in his voice. "I did everything I could, but the higher-ups will not break that rule for anyone—even for a valuable employee like you. If there is anything, anything I can do, please don't hesitate to call on me."

I nodded numbly and rose. "We will move the first of next month," he added softly. "If I hear of anything, I'll let you know. And I'll be happy to give you a glowing recommendation."

"Thank you," I mumbled. "It's not your fault."

Walking home that evening in March 1932, I tried to shake off the news as if it were a bad dream. I had to keep my wits about me and could not give in to despair; that I was sure of. Besides supporting myself, I contributed towards the expenses of my mother and grandmother back in Palestine. Mother still taught piano students and worked as the church organist, but she did not make enough to support herself and her mother, who was not able to work any longer. I had no experience in job hunting, and I did not know where to turn in this dismal economy. I could not afford to make a mistake in securing income since I had no backup funds.

This time Uncle George could not be of much help to me because his world had been the railroad and the oil company, and both were in trouble because of the downturn. That night as I said my prayers, I added earnestly, "God, you have never given me something I cannot handle, so please hold me tight and help me see a way out of this dilemma." Before I drifted off to sleep, it dawned on me that my mother had a cousin who was secretary to the president of a well-known bank in Houston. I decided to call her and see if she had any ideas.

God did use Gertrude Chambers to solve my crisis. Gertrude did have some ideas, and I went over the next day to meet her and talk about how she could help me. She was delighted to hear of my experiences at Shell and offered me a good job as an administrative assistant to the attorney for the bank, Guardian Trust, with no cut in pay.

So once again life began anew with marked uncertainties but also with marked certainties. This was my introduction to a future in finance whereas until that day I had thought oil would provide my future. We never know how a day will begin or end, but as long as we are following God's lead, we know the day will turn out alright.

twelve

chapter 12

STAKING OUT NEW TERRITORY

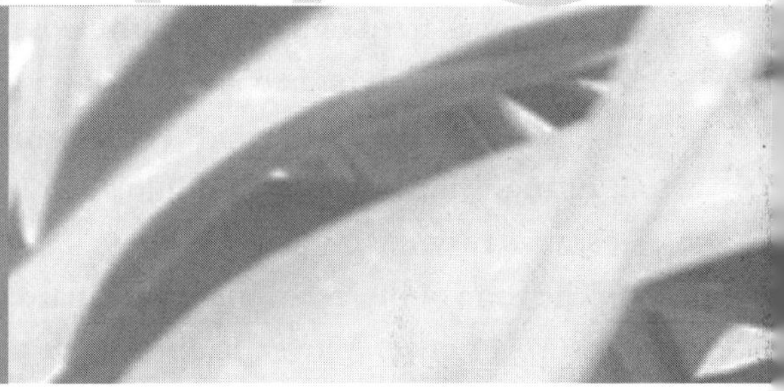

My assignment at Guardian Trust Company was administrative assistant to Clyde Odeneal, the chief counsel for the bank, a treasure of a man. In keeping with his goal of helping women get ahead in the professional world, he tutored me in all sorts of legal matters and gave me projects to oversee. Small though the bank was, it was the lender for subdivisions such as Riverside Terrace, the area around North and South MacGregor, and also to some extent River Oaks, an expensive area where well-to-do families built mansions on tree-lined boulevards. He told me later that he recognized my leadership skills and determined that I would not be a secretary the rest of my life.

In an unusual move for a man of that era, Mr. Odeneal delegated some of his responsibilities to me. He taught me how to find the documentation for each parcel of land; go to the courthouse to check titles, deeds, and abstracts; and build a file for each lot. Then he reviewed my work from a legal standpoint. His point was to help me develop managerial skills. The confidence he showed in me also boosted my morale immensely.

Working in the Legal Department threw me in contact with all the departments of the bank. On our same floor were the Trust Department and the Real Estate Department. I enjoyed the interaction among these divisions.

Also I was frequently in the office of the president, Clarence Malone. I came to learn that although he had a reputation as a crusty banker and seemed to delight in being gruff, he had a soft heart. Perhaps my being the cousin of his secretary helped our relationship; however I do think he respected the way I stood up to him and did not shy away when he snapped at me.

The tone of our relationship at Guardian was set the day I went to work for the bank. Every new employee had to have a session with our president before he or she actually began work. When I walked in his office that first day, I was so glad that Gertrude had accompanied me. Again I felt inadequate walking into such a large, airy office with gilded plaques adorning the walls and important leather-bound volumes lining massive bookcases. Mr. Malone had hardly introduced himself when he blurted out, "We surely are paying you a lot of money for someone who has had no banking experience."

Gertrude had told me when I applied that Guardian could not pay me what I was making at Shell, and I told her I could work for no less because I had a family I was responsible for. She finally said they would pay what I asked but warned I would likely not get a raise for a year. I could live with that and readily agreed to the position she offered.

Although I was unprepared for Mr. Malone's statement, I answered humbly but with confidence, "True, I do not have banking experience, but my three years at Shell were not wasted. I learned a lot about communications, melding into a working environment with integrity, and how to take responsibility. That is worth something."

He stood up, reached his hand across the desk to shake my hand, and smiled, "I accept your explanation." From then on we got along just fine, both speaking our mind freely. Many were the times I would knock on his open door and walk in without waiting for him to give permission. One day I did that, not knowing that a co-worker was watching the episode. As soon as I put one foot in his office, Mr. Malone barked, "I'm busy!"

I continued up to his desk and asked my question, which he answered.

Later the co-worker asked me amazed, "How did you have the nerve to go on in when he hollered like that?"

I shrugged. "I told him what I had was the bank's business too and I needed an immediate answer."

"Aren't you afraid of him?" my friend pressed.

"Why should I be?" I responded, honestly stunned. "He wakes up and dresses just like you and I do."

When his birthday came around my first year at the bank, my cousin told me about the event and suggested I buy him a card because no one else at the bank would. On the morning of his birthday I handed him the card and smiled, "Happy birthday!"

He frowned and said gruffly, "Why are you giving me a card?"

"Because when I get to be your age, I hope to look just as good as you do," I teased.

He threw his head back in a roar of laughter. "Some people are just crazy," he grinned at me.

"Yes, you are a little crazy, aren't you?"

He laughed again. I noticed that my card stayed on his bookcase for days.

While I already knew about standing my ground from other experiences in my life, during my two years at Guardian Trust I also learned about holding my tongue and being very sure before I spoke my mind in some situations. As during my college years I seemed drawn into mentoring relationships, and I learned what a heavy responsibility that role carries and how sound my advice needed to be because it would often be taken without much evaluation on the part of the person I was mentoring.

One of my first relationships of this ilk at Guardian involved an adorable young lady in the Trust Department named Emma Vestal. With her bobbed hair and large brown eyes, she looked fourteen but was actually about nineteen. Emma was the secretary to the head of her department, Mr. Whitmire. Mr. and Mrs. Whitmire never had the daughter they longed for, and so they "adopted" Emma. She was easy to like because of her ready laugh and encouraging spirit.

We quickly became friends. Soon I noticed that more and more frequently Emma would bring a problem to me and we would try to solve it together. After I had been at the bank about a year, Guardian hired a young man, Pat Emmott, to be a messenger and perform some clerical duties. He was tall and utterly handsome, and I soon was aware that the inevitable had happened. Pat had spotted Emma.

My office was on a mezzanine that was connected to the balcony of the Esperson Drug Store located on the first floor of our building. Esperson's provided a coffee bar for those of us on that floor. It was a great place to take customers for a little relaxation and food and also a nice place for the staff to take our breaks. I had begun to notice that Pat and Emma were visiting with each other quite frequently on the mezzanine. Eventually I begin to worry, as all mothers—acting or actual—do, because I knew that Guardian heavily enforced its nepotism policy. After much thought I decided to exercise my motherly responsibility and bring Pat and Emma individually into my office when the boss was gone and have a talk about this policy.

So one morning I saw Emma coming down the mezzanine headed for the president's office. I stepped to my door and said, "Emma, on your way back, will you come see me please?" When she returned, I closed the door and point-blank asked, "Emma, are you and Pat going together?"

She blushed and looked confused. "Don't worry," I assured her quickly. "No one has said anything. I just wanted to be sure you knew about the bank's nepotism policy."

She paled and shook her head. "I don't know what you mean," she confessed.

"Here," I replied, opening the policy manual and pointing to the paragraph that prevented more than one member of a family from working at the bank.

"Oh!" she exclaimed. "I didn't know about that." She quickly gave me a hug and said, "I'll be sure Pat knows about this. When . . . I mean, if . . . things work out, that could make a big difference in our plans."

I nodded. "Just let me know if there is anything I can do for you two."

"Thanks, Jackie. I will. Pat is really nice," Emma sighed.

"Yes, I know, dear," I answered with a knowing smile.

Nothing more was said for about three months, although I continued to see the two together frequently, and their body language inferred more than a casual friendship. I had seen budding romances before and recognized the signs. One day I was startled to see Emma running towards me along the mezzanine, crying as if her heart would break. I motioned her into my office and closed the door. At first all I did was hold her and kiss her softly on the top of her head. As the sobbing subsided, I whispered, "Do you want to tell me about it?"

I walked her to a chair and guided her gently into it. Then I reached for a box of tissues and handed it to her. She patted her eyes and managed to say between sobs, "Mr. Whitmire could not see me, so I've come to you. Pat has broken up with me!"

While lovers' quarrels are nothing new, that fact did nothing to ease Emma's pain. Mostly I listened to her hurt and tried to comfort her from my limited experience with love. I felt a pang of sorrow as I remembered Dick and our ill-fated love of five years back. Finally Emma and I agreed that she would come talk to me every day to see how she was progressing in dealing with the ruptured romance.

The meetings seemed to be helpful. One day after a few weeks I was expecting Emma for our little visit and was surprised to look up from my desk to find Pat. He made no effort to hide his tears. He told me that the break-up a few weeks ago was actually their second one. "And I can't live without her, Jackie! What can I do? Will you help me get her back?"

Knowing this was exactly the way Emma felt also, I wanted to help this confused young couple. However, I knew that any reconciliation would have to come from them, not from a third party. If they were to have a healthy marriage, they would have to learn how to solve their problems by themselves, for problems surely come to every couple, no matter how devoted they are to each other. "Pat," I said, hugging him like a mother, "let me do some groundwork and I'll see if a plan emerges."

"Okay, okay," he agreed. "Just think of something! I'm really desperate."

I was afraid to do anything because I realized how much both of them were counting on me to mend their relationship. Any false move on my part could shatter this tenuous rapport beyond repair, so I took three days, much to Pat's dismay, to think the matter through. Finally when I felt I could act with maturity and reason, I called Emma and asked her to go to lunch with me.

We picked a place a few blocks away from the bank, where it was unlikely that co-workers would spot us. As we settled into a green plastic booth in the corner and placed our orders, I sighed, "Well, Emma. Tell me what is happening between you and Pat today."

She shrugged, "Nothing. He's quit."

"Quit?" I echoed. "What do you mean?"

"Well, he doesn't speak to me any more," she said bitterly. "When we pass in the hall, he just nods his head towards me and keeps walking. You'd never know we had ever talked about getting married."

"That must hurt a lot to see him so indifferent," I sympathized.

She just nodded and stared out into the crowded café.

"Do you think he might be acting like that because he isn't sure what you are thinking and he can't bear the thought of having you confirm the rift as permanent? As long as you don't exchange words, there is not a chance you might patch things up," I said, trying not to give away my plan too soon.

Emma brought her eyes to focus on my face and replied, "I wish I could believe that, but I don't. He doesn't love me anymore or he'd try to make up." The waitress placed our blue-plate specials in front of us, and we hungrily tasted the hot mashed potatoes and chicken fried steak smothered in white gravy.

"Emma," I began again in a few minutes, "what would you say if I told you that I think you are mistaken about Pat's feelings?"

"What do you mean?" she frowned, buttering a hot yeast roll.

"Do you trust me enough to come to my office after work today to meet with Pat—the three of us?"

Emma shivered and stared at me. Slowly the words formed on her lips, "Sure, what can it hurt?"

By the end of our evening visit, Pat had invited Emma out to dinner that very night. She eagerly accepted. That night as I lay in bed, I prayed, "God, I don't know what your will is for Pat and Emma. I just know it's hard to see them both hurting so much. If it is your will that they marry each other, please show them both your direction. Thank you, Lord."

My prayers did not always receive such rapid answers. By the end of that working week, Emma called me. "Jackie, can you stay after work today so Pat and I can come talk to you?"

"Well, sure, darling," I answered. "Be here about five."

I fully expected to hear that they were going to be engaged and I rejoiced at the thought. When they arrived, they were holding hands. They both hugged me and began talking at the same time. "Whoa!" I laughed. "I can't hear either of you. Pat, what's going on?"

He glanced at Emma and grinned, "We're engaged. I'm so glad you pointed out the nepotism policy so we knew to plan around it. I'll be leaving the bank because I have more diversified skills, and Emma will stay on because she has worked here longer than I have."

Emma broke in, "And we want to be married at your home and have our reception there. That is all right, isn't it?" Her big eyes focused such hope on me that I could only stand up and hug her tenderly.

Sometimes mothering requires instant solutions. My home life had changed drastically just a few weeks before this conversation, and my new circumstances did not complement their request. However, as any good mother would do, I exclaimed, "You bet! When shall we get together to plan?"

thirteen

chapter 13

A STEP BACKWARDS

By the time I began playing matchmaker to Pat and Emma in 1932, I had gained confidence in my future at Guardian Trust Company, even though it was a small bank. I felt as if my world was gliding along smoothly in its orbit, and I was enjoying the ride.

Wanting to learn as much as I could about banking, I joined the American Institute of Banking's educational program and began their arduous series of courses and certificates which was the equivalent of a two-year college degree in finance. My first courses were in business letter writing and public speaking. It took me seven years to complete all the courses and earn their three certifications in general banking, commercial banking, and trust work, but I did finish and with honors.

One day in early January 1933 my phone rang at work. I was surprised to hear Auntie Bess's voice. It sounded strained. "Is everything alright?" I asked with concern.

"I just thought you should know right away about a letter I just received," she answered. "It's from your mother. She says she has decided to come to Houston . . . and live with you."

A cry escaped my lips, and tears blinded my eyes. The phone slipped from my hand and banged on the desk. My breathing became shallow, and I felt like I were choking. Sobs wracked my body. Finally I became aware of a scratchy noise coming from the phone receiver. It was Auntie Bess frantically trying to make contact with me.

"I'm here," I said weakly into the receiver.

"Oh, thank goodness!" she exclaimed. "Darling, you gave me a scare. Now you listen to me, Alice. I know how devastating this news is to you. I share your fears, but I don't know what either of us can do about it."

"Hmm," I acknowledged her concern. I pulled several tissues from a box on my desk and patted my nose.

"You and Retha can stay with us a couple of months. In the meantime, I'll help you look for an apartment, and I'll be here to help you through your adjustment. Uncle George and I will see you through this, you hear?"

"Oh, Auntie Bess, I love you!" I cried as more tears blinded my eyes.

"We'll talk about it more this evening when you get home," she said. "I love you too."

I carefully placed the receiver back in the cradle and buried my head in my hands. I loved my life, and I didn't want Mother to sail back in and try to take control again. Suddenly a thought hit me forcefully. I would have to support us both, plus Grandmother. Also, I would have to take time from my activities to find a place to live. The sobs returned, and I didn't even bother to close my door.

Gertrude happened to walk down the hall and waved cheerily as she passed my office. She had taken two steps beyond my door when she reappeared in the doorway. After one look at me, she gently closed my door and came around to hug me. "What in the world is the matter, Alice?" she inquired.

Briefly, I told her my dreadful news. She tsk-tsked and then startled me with a question, "Have you been to lunch?"

I shook my head.

"Well, let's go," she ordered.

Although I just wanted to be left alone, I followed her like a lost child. We walked to the café where Emma and I had eaten and discussed her relationship with Pat. The fresh air revived me. Over a bowl of comforting vegetable soup, Gertrude sympathized with my plight. She too had had a bitter childhood and resented never being able to marry and have a family because she had to take care of her mother. She had truly walked my same path, but for a longer time than I.

She told me, "Alice, I hate that this is happening to you, but it is and you may as well just try to make the best of it."

She shook her fork at me for emphasis. "The main thing you must do—as soon as your mother arrives—is to set boundaries. Tell her that you have established your life with friends and organizations and you intend to continue those relationships. If she protests or tries to rein you in, remind her—gently but firmly—that you are no longer a minor in the eyes of the law and that you, after all, will be the sole support of your family unit. She may not like your talking to her like that, but she will see the logic of what you say."

I nodded as if in a stupor. The thought of the confrontations to come made me wince in painful anticipation. I did not wish Mother any harm. I just did not want her restricting the freedom I had come to enjoy—and was handling responsibly, I had to admit. If I were making bad or foolish choices or if she had financial difficulties, I would not be surprised at her moving in. As it was, she was escaping an intolerable situation in Palestine, and she either did not see the parallel in her situation with her mother and mine with her or she did not care how her decision affected me. Both explanations irritated me and reminded me of other self-centered choices she had made without regard for my needs and feelings.

As Gertrude and I were finishing lunch, I reached for the ticket. Gertrude snatched it before I could touch it and said as if she were a teacher instructing a student, "Now I want you to take your money and go across the street to the Majestic Theater, where there are a great vaudeville show and a super movie playing. Go see them both and when they are over, go home."

"But . . . ," I protested. Even though the president was out of town, I could not imagine not going back to work after lunch. How would I explain my absence?

She laughed, "You are still a novice in the ways of the working world. Remember whom I work for. I will tell him I sent you home as you were not feeling well, and that will be it." I agreed since I knew I would not be productive the rest of the day anyway.

The news about my mother arrived on Thursday, and on Saturday Auntie Bess and I hopped into her car to hunt for an apartment. The newspaper was our only guide for apartment locators were yet to appear on the business scene. We made a list of the conveniences we had to consider since Mother and I would have no car. We had to be close to such places as a grocery store, drugstore, bus stop, church, and doctors.

Auntie Bess knew of a rather new development called Temple Terrace just off Taft Street, and we decided to start there. Fortunately it met all our needs, including my ability to pay for it. The four-unit facility was broken into one-bedroom apartments with a kitchen, small dining room and living room, bath, and front and back stairways. The most convincing feature was that the units were furnished and rather nicely. We of course owned not a stick of furniture since we had always lived with Grandmother in her house and had no need for furniture. I signed the lease for 301 West Clay #4 and asked the landlady if she would put more pieces of furniture in our apartment, even if she increased the rent a little.

She thought for a moment and replied, "The apartment below is going to be vacated in a few days, and it will become our office. If you can use any of that furniture, you are welcome to—and I won't raise the rent."

When I saw the furniture in the lower unit, I was pleased and asked if we could have the nightstands, coffee table, two needlepoint chairs, twin beds, and a pie stand for the kitchen. "And," I asked timidly, "do you think we could switch out the sofas? I really prefer this blue one over the green one in my apartment." The blue sofa had a nicer fabric and carved mahogany arms showing whereas the green one had no wood showing.

The landlady said, "Sure, why not? We'll want to paint and clean before you move in. That will take about two weeks. Is that satisfactory?"

When we got back to the house, I called Mother and told her about the apartment. "I will come home next weekend and select a couple of things out of the house that we'll need."

When no reply came for a few minutes, I asked, "Mother, are you there?"

"Yes," she answered crisply. "There is no need for that. Grandmother has said that none of the furnishings are to leave her house under any circumstance."

I sputtered and decided to save my anger for Grandmother.

That Friday night as I sat down at Grandmother's dining room table to a sparse meal of chicken noodle soup and homemade bread, I confronted my grandmother. "I was surprised to hear Mother say that you would not let us have any of your furniture for our apartment in Houston. Surely she misunderstood you?"

Grandmother straightened her back and looked at me over the rim of her glasses. "She did not misunderstand. Everything in this house is mine, and it will stay where it is."

"Well," I shrugged to dissipate my anger and looked at Mother. "I tried."

Mother's face wore a smirk and Grandmother frowned.

The next morning I saw Grandmother out in her flower garden, pulling the few weeds that dared grow in that well-tended bed. She did not look up as I approached. "Grandmother, would you permit me to pick a few of your flowers to take to Miss Margsue tomorrow? I'm going to a luncheon at her house and thought it would be nice to take her something for the centerpiece."

Grandmother straightened up and placed her hands on her hips. "Sure," she answered, "take whatever you like."

Surprised, I retorted without thinking, "Thanks. I wish you had been as generous yesterday with the furniture you really don't need."

She did not answer. Just then I caught a movement out of the corner of my eye and recognized a neighbor walking down the street. "Mrs. Doyle!" I cried out, turning from Grandmother to visit with an old friend. "How are you? It's been ages since I've seen you."

Sunday after church, I was packing my things to catch the train back to Houston. Just as I closed my suitcase, Grandmother appeared in the doorway to my bedroom with a bundle in her arms. "What is that?" I asked curious.

"These are some sheets and pillowcases you might need in Houston," she said and handed them to me.

"Why, these are lovely, Grandmother!" I exclaimed, taking the pile of linens to the bed and sifting through them. "These are the ones you hem-stitched and monogrammed. Thank you so much!"

I hugged her awkwardly since neither of us had shown affection to the other very often in all our years together.

She stiffened and turned to leave. She threw back over her shoulder, "Before you go, select whatever furniture you want for you were right. I don't need all of this stuff anymore."

Back in Houston, Auntie Bess and Uncle George met me at the station and I told them about the furniture. Uncle George was going to Palestine the next week on business and said he would arrange to have it crated and shipped down to me. Then he asked, "When is your mother coming down?"

"I don't know," I admitted. "We didn't discuss her arrival. It wouldn't matter anyway. When she's ready, she'll tell me and come on."

At breakfast the next week I told the Saunders that I would move into the apartment over the weekend. That way when Mother did arrive, I would have some idea of what our new lifestyle would be like. Actually I enjoyed decorating my very first apartment. I picked out white crocheted doilies to go under the new painted, ceramic lamps I found at a sale downtown. Sister helped me pick out some pictures for the walls and an inexpensive, floral tablecloth with matching blue napkins. I even splurged and bought wicker wastebaskets for each room and asked Auntie Bess to make colorful yellow daisy curtains for the kitchen window. All in all, the apartment had a friendly feel to it.

I was eager to move into my newly decorated apartment, but I dreaded having Mother in the same abode. I had had three lovely years with the Saunders, so I could not really complain. Family obligations, after all, carry more weight than an individual's preferences. I did try to enjoy my freedom each day because I knew her arrival would mean a return of my former world of criticism and control. I would see whether the thinking skills I was learning at work would suffice in my private world.

Debates raged within me as the time drew nearer for Mother's arrival. Uncle George noticed my increasing reticence as the day approached and finally commented one evening when I was eating dinner with them, "Alice, is there something you would like to talk about? You have been very quiet of late."

I looked at his sincere eyes and slightly wrinkled brow and sighed, "Oh, Uncle George. I'm being so selfish. I don't want Mother to come."

"I know, child," he reassured me lovingly and patted my arm. "You've had a real taste of independence and it will be hard to revert to living with your mother."

"Am I just awful . . . ?" I stammered. "That is, I know the Bible says I am supposed to honor my mother, and yet I don't know if I can obey her every whim. Then I tell myself that I will be our full support, and therefore I can do what I please—and that sounds so rebellious, which I know isn't right. What shall I do?"

"First of all, you can stop flogging yourself," Uncle George smiled. "Of course, it's hard to think of living with a parent again. I think the fact that you will be supporting the two of you carries some weight. I do think you would be wise to set some boundaries from the very beginning. You have begun to establish your own identity, and I do not see continuing that as rebellious. Use as much grace and tact as you can muster in explaining your limits to your mother, but by all means set limits. You have proven to be a very capable, responsible adult, and there is no need to revert to a subservient role. Remember Paul's advice to Timothy: Let no one despise your youth, but set an example in speech and conduct, in love, faith, and purity."

He paused while I let his words sink in. Then he reached out and patted me on the shoulder, "Do you think you can do that?"

"I don't know, but I'll try," I promised bravely.

"Honey, you know that you are welcome to come visit with Bessie and me any time things get rough. Even your mama would not want to squelch the lovely woman you are becoming. She'll come around—and to be sure, Auntie Bess and I will be praying for you every day, just as we do now."

I sighed and nodded—not convinced I could pull it off.

The day of Mother's arrival came much sooner than I had thought—or hoped—it might, but I was ready to welcome her to our new home that I had fixed up quite attractively. The night of her arrival Auntie Bess invited us to dinner, so I went straight from work to the Saunders' home. Sister had picked Mother up at the train station, and she had not yet seen the apartment. After dinner we told Mother about the places nearby to shop and also about the church we would be attending. I really wanted to continue attending St. Paul's Methodist Church. The problem was transportation. On Sunday the bus schedules were quite different from during the week, and it would take us over an hour to get to church and the same time back home. Sister shouted out suddenly, "Hey! I don't know why I didn't think of this before. Florence Conway lives near you. I'll call her this evening and see if she would be willing to drive you on Sundays."

"Oh, that's a wonderful idea," I agreed. "Tell her I'll be happy to pay her."

So it worked out that we had a ride every Sunday and to most of the church activities since Florence was an active member.

While Auntie Bess served a rich chocolate pudding for dessert, Mother began to talk about the things she would be doing and the things she would expect me to do. The queen was already on her throne, but this time she had no ally. No sooner had all the rules been spelled out that Uncle George interrupted with a face as red as if he had taken a bite of hot pepper jelly. "Retha, you are no longer the queen," he scolded. "Alice is the queen for she is the breadwinner, the new provider, and she is old enough to make decisions and wise ones too."

Mother had prepared for such a contest and had her weapons ready. "George, Alice Cornelia is the child and I am the parent, no matter who earns the living, so I most certainly will run the house. In fact until she marries, I will always run the household."

Auntie Bess coughed and threw her napkin onto the table. She spoke in a tightly controlled voice, "It's time we took these folks home." Mother laid her spoon down on her dessert plate and pushed back her chair without a word. I managed to swallow two bites of the delicious pudding before Auntie Bess added, "Retha, grow up and recognize that this young lady right here is the one who will keep you alive—and I mean that literally."

Not a word was spoken as Uncle George and Auntie Bess drove us to our apartment. When we pulled up to the building, Uncle George carried Mother's luggage upstairs, and I went around the car and kissed Auntie Bess and Sister. I said bravely, "God bless you and thanks so much—for everything."

I went straight to the bathroom to get ready for bed. I had to get up at five because I walked to work and it took me almost an hour. The bus I could ride that would take me directly to the bank was quite far from us, and the one closer to the apartment would require me to transfer buses, so I walked. I was surprised when Mother came into the room after I had crawled under the sheets of my bed and said, "Alice Cornelia, the apartment looks very pretty and I look forward to meeting the other residents."

Afraid to risk more conversation, I grunted and turned toward the wall. The next morning while I was showering, Mother opened the bathroom door and called, "What do you want for breakfast?"

Irritated at the invasion of my privacy and leery of boundaries already crossed, I answered from behind the shower curtain, "Don't worry about it. Go back to bed. I'm used to fixing my own breakfast."

Stepping back into the bedroom, I immediately detected the aroma of bacon and I knew full well the queen mother had taken the throne and it would be wise for me to accept the inevitable. Sure enough, when I got to the dining room table, my place was set with eggs, bacon, toast, and a glass of milk—just like I had every morning in Palestine.

Trying to remember Uncle George's advice, I said, "Thank you for fixing breakfast. I already have chicken and vegetables in the ice box for our dinner tonight, and you'll find tuna fish and canned soup in the pantry for your lunch."

After breakfast I started downstairs and I realized I had not given Mother my phone number at the bank, so I dashed back up the stairs and scribbled my number on a piece of paper on the drain board. Mother watched my frantic actions and commented imperially as I reached for the doorknob once more, "Now, I want you home early tonight so I can get out of the kitchen at a reasonable hour."

I looked at her, did not trust myself to say a word, so slammed the door and flew down the stairs. Just as I came running out the back door, our neighbor across the hall was backing out of the driveway. She stopped and inquired, "Can I take you somewhere, Jackie? You seem in a hurry."

"Well, I'm on my way to the bus. I'm going to Guardian Trust downtown," I explained.

"Really! That's just where I am going. Hop in and I'll give you a ride." From then on whenever she had business downtown, she went early in the morning so I could ride with her.

Walking home that evening, I dreaded reaching the apartment. I walked in and did not greet Mother, who was standing in the kitchen spooning sweet potatoes onto our plates. I threw my purse onto my bed and sat down at the dining room table.

"Where did the sweet potatoes come from?" I asked confused. "I didn't buy any."

Mother made another trip to the kitchen to retrieve our glasses of iced tea and a slip of paper and sat down. She bowed her head and I dutifully followed her example. "For this food we are about to receive, we give thanks," she prayed. We lifted our heads and placed our blue cloth napkins in our laps. "I met the owner of the apartment today," she explained. "She took me to the grocery store and I bought some things we need."

She handed me the piece of paper. I looked at it and let out a squawk. It was the bill from the grocery store. So our roles had been defined so soon. I managed to withhold my anger at her lack of gratitude and avoided making eye contact with her. We ate in silence. Eventually, I shifted my eyes to the attached living room and choked on the bite in my mouth. "What have you done!" I cried, standing up suddenly. I realized that every piece of furniture had been moved to different places from where I had placed them.

"What do you mean sashaying in here and rearranging everything? Isn't it enough that you are rearranging my comfortable life!" I erupted. Mother said something, but I had already stomped into the kitchen and did not stop to listen. I was too tired for a confrontation, so I carried my dishes to the sink and washed them along with the pots and pans. Mother stayed in the dining room until I finished and went straight to bed.

Just as I was turning off the overhead light, Mother stuck her head in the bedroom and announced, "I called several of my friends today. I will be going to lunch with them Saturday and also to dinner."

I smiled to myself. At least I could sit on the throne that day. I thought bitterly that life always begins again—but we never know if it will bring sunshine or showers. Tears wet my pillow as I silently cried myself to sleep wishing for Dad. I remembered his saying that eventually the apron strings would be cut, but when? The Bible said there was a season for everything under the sun. I seemed always to be learning "how to be a big girl" without the chance to prove my growth. I would welcome the season that allowed me to display my abilities.

I felt so crowded in that bedroom with Mother tiptoeing as she got ready for bed, but the most confining boundaries were the ones I allowed Mother to place around me again regarding my activities. She lived to be eighty-two, and it was only then that my real identity had a chance to blossom. She constantly reminded me that I was never to grow up, that she was the mother in charge—and I allowed her to rule.

That is, except for one time. When Emma and Pat said they wanted to be married at my apartment and have their reception there as well, I agreed without consulting Mother. "Of course, you can," I had consented. "It will be as you wish." The logistics escaped me at the time, but I knew we would work something out. Emma came from a very large family out of town, so her mother was not available to plan the details of the wedding. Pat's mother did live in Houston, but the wedding and reception were not supposed to be the groom's family's responsibility.

"Now you realize, I hope," I warned the happy couple, "that my apartment is small and you will have to choose carefully whom to invite."

They nodded, probably without even hearing me, so engrossed were they in each other. "You'll have to limit the festivities to twenty people," I added. That was about half the number of people in their families, not even counting friends. They were agreeable; they just wanted to be married.

The day of the wedding, in late January 1933, I moved all the furniture except the dining room table and the sofa and chairs into the bedroom, pushed the remaining furniture against the walls to make as much room as possible in the center of the room, and helped a florist arrange an attractive altar area in the living room with palms and white lilies. A friend of Mother's furnished a decorated white cake and a centerpiece.

The weather cooperated and dawned clear and just a bit chilly. The parents of the bride and groom arrived first; then gradually a few relatives and a couple of friends came. As soon as the preacher arrived, we gathered everyone into a circle for the ceremony. Before he could say, "Dearly beloved . . . ," the doorbell rang. To my amazement about ten people stood on the front porch, and more were arriving behind them. There was nothing to do but crowd into the apartment. The ceremony was lovely. Emma of course was radiant and Pat awed at her beauty. The table looked quite pretty with a white damask table cloth, two-tiered cake, and punch bowl flanked by more white lilies in a cut-glass vase. It did not take long for me to see that there was not enough cake, punch, or even nuts, and guests were still arriving. We made the most of a situation over which we had no control, cutting the pieces of cake smaller until only crumbs were left. To this day we are all still family and love each other and laugh over the miscalculations of that day.

Pat became a very prominent banker in Houston and at one time was elected mayor of Bellaire, a small community adjacent to Houston. They have three beautiful daughters and one very handsome son and wonderful grandchildren. Pat slipped away from us in 1999 and how we do miss him. Emma, Pat Jr., the girls and I are still a loving family, and we visit and talk often. I shall ever be grateful for the privilege of being chosen to be a confidante to these two special people and learn through their situation to be a mentor. I applied the lessons I learned through their plight many other times in my life, and hundreds of people benefited from the confidence Pat and Emma placed in me.

On March 5, 1933, a few months after the wedding, I arrived at work that Friday and approached the outside door of the building with my key. I jumped when I noticed an imposing-looking man in a military-type uniform with epaulettes on the shoulders blocking the doorway. He said, "Excuse me, miss, but I need to ask for your identification."

"What's the problem, officer?" I asked as I dug into my purse for my bank ID card.

"I'm Officer Rodney," he explained officiously, "with the U. S. Treasury Department. President Roosevelt has declared a bank holiday. All banks in the country are closed indefinitely."

While I tried to take in the amazing news, the federal officer flipped through some papers he had on a table beside him. "Ah, yes, Miss Matthews," he continued. "I see your name on my list, so please go ahead into the building." He opened the door for me, and I started to step into the foyer. I stopped long enough to read the sign I just noticed taped to the glass door: "By Order of the President of the United States all Banks of America are closed indefinitely." I knew the Great Depression had extended its devastating tentacles all through the country and into most industries, but I could not fathom what this drastic step meant—for the country or for me. When would the banks open again? Would I even have a job when they did?

Staying at work that day was pointless, but we all stayed anyway and together pondered our fate. The president's order included a temporary moratorium on all banking transactions. Storekeepers would not allow customers to buy unless they had cash to pay. Fortunately the banks were allowed to open again on Tuesday, but it was not business as usual. Federal officers were stationed in every bank for a week to ensure there was not a run on the bank. The government put a limit on how much cash each investor could withdraw from his account in one day and limited the frequency of withdrawals. Since banks were not required to hold one hundred percent of their deposits in ready cash, officials were afraid skittish customers would close their accounts and leave the banks without sufficient funds to pay all their depositors. That scenario could have been the beginning of the end of the American economy. The bank holiday had been a bold step to bolster our economy—and it worked.

Even countries, it seemed, experienced new beginnings. I hoped and prayed this was not a precursor to another new beginning for me. My world had been rocked rudely enough lately, and I was not sure I could weather any more rumblings.

fourteen

chapter 14

INVOLUNTARY MOVES

One day in 1934, after I had been at Guardian Trust Company approximately two years, the president of the bank called a meeting of all the bank employees after the bank closed at two o'clock. As I was coming down the steps to go to the lobby for the meeting, I heard one of the officers say to his secretary, "I heard at lunch today that our bank was going to merge with another bank and so I wonder if that is what this meeting is all about."

Merge? I had never heard of a bank merger. Even a bank failure was a new phenomenon of the last troubled economic year in America. However a few minutes later I heard our president announce we would be merging with the Second National Bank of Houston within six months. "As far as I know," he assured us after the ripple of exclamations died down, "you will all likely be moved to the new bank, but if you feel more secure about getting out and finding another position, I will give you time to do that if you will let my secretary know. I cannot thank you enough for your good services. I will sincerely miss our little closely knit family." He took out his monogrammed handkerchief and blew his nose loudly.

Returning to my office in a state of amazement and some trepidation, I saw that I had a call from my immediate boss, Clyde Odeneal, asking if the announcement had been made. I called him to report on the meeting. "Now, Jackie," he said, "I do not want you to worry about employment. Unfortunately, you will not be going to the new bank. They have no legal department as such since they do no developmental work on large properties."

I could feel my hands growing clammy, and I gripped the side of my chair for support. This was no economy in which to be looking for work.

"However," he continued quickly, "I have called San Jacinto National Bank about you. They have a place for you, so I am willing to release you at any time."

On his advice I called one of the bank's executive vice presidents, Leslie Coleman, and had a successful interview the next morning. I was relieved and grateful to accept a position with San Jacinto doing work similar to what I was doing at Guardian—and at an advanced salary. Returning to the Guardian building, I immediately went to report to Mr. Odeneal. He did not seem surprised at my being hired. "And what will they be paying you?" he asked dryly.

Embarrassed to be discussing my salary with someone other than the boss who would be paying it, I blushed and mumbled, "A hundred eighty-five a month."

Mr. Odeneal broke into a wide grin. "Good!" he laughed, slapping his hand on his thigh. "When I called Leslie, I told him we were paying you a hundred fifty and were planning to give you a raise to one eighty-five. I said that I sure hated to see you miss out on that raise."

Suddenly all my tension dissolved and I laughed with Mr. Odeneal. The Lord was taking care of me as He always had and using this dear man to accomplish that.

My work was finished within a month at Guardian, and so in March of 1934 I moved from the Esperson Building at Travis and Rusk, once the tallest building in Houston, to the San Jacinto National Bank on Main and Lamar, where a Foley's store now stands. I was the only employee in San Jacinto's legal department besides the lawyer on staff. Because of my experience at Guardian, I was capable of making decisions, answering questions, and handling mail and phone calls. Since the bank did not have any big projects underway, most matters were routine. My boss spent an inordinate amount of time at the courthouse, which left me virtually in charge in his absence. I made deposits and took a great deal of responsibility off him. I enjoyed the confidence placed in me.

I continued singing in the St. Paul's choir, teaching a Sunday school class of fifteen to sixteen year-old boys and girls, and serving as president of the Houston chapter of the CIA Alumnae Association. In 1937 Mother and I moved to another apartment in Temple Terrace and could not easily get to St. Paul's on the streetcar, so we moved our membership to Bering Memorial Methodist Church. There I enjoyed being the soprano soloist in the choir and teaching a class of twelve active eight and nine year-old boys. Two brothers in the class were constantly creating trouble. The class met in a basement room with windows that looked out onto the ground. Once I left the room for just a few minutes to retrieve some supplies and came back to find that the brothers had stacked chairs to the windows, climbed out, and were outside playing. After a number of similar episodes I complained to the parents. They replied indignantly, "They just have surplus energy. You are not to discipline them in any way."

After a few more months of tiring struggles with the boys, I spoke again to the parents. "Since you don't have children of your own, you obviously do not know what you are doing," they retorted.

I could take no more and called the superintendent of the Sunday school. "It's either them or me," I stated. In all my previous experience with children, these were the only two I could not manage—and in all my future contacts with children, I never encountered another whom I could not control. The superintendent supported me and moved the boys to another class with a male teacher. He also tired of their disobedience. Eventually the superintendent had to call the parents and have them remove the boys from Sunday school. They refused to rein in their children in any way, and the boys were completely unruly. Unfortunately both boys had difficulties as adults.

Everywhere I was given roles commiserate with my growing maturity, integrity, and responsibility. Everywhere except at home. Mother was as rigid as ever, the queen mother who ruled over her child. Even though I was the main support for both of us, she expected me to do exactly what she wanted—when, where, and how. Once when she refused to allow me to have a friend over for dinner, I protested. She responded icily, "You will do as I say. I will restrict your activities whether you like it or not."

She apparently did like placing restrictions on my life. I could not date or drive or invite friends over. Mother continued burying herself in her career. Since 1935 she had run three piano studios in Houston in the East End and the Heights. She taught children from the first to the fifth grades. A private school she worked with allowed children to leave the campus for piano lessons in the morning. Then she taught children after school on weekdays. On Saturdays she rotated lessons among the three studios. At one time she even substituted as organist for Congregation Beth Yeshurun and St. John's Methodist Church downtown while the regular musicians were out on maternity leave. St. John's then allowed her to use their organ to give lessons to adults. I recognized her immense musical talent, but that did nothing to make meal conversations more pleasant or to encourage my social life.

As my relationship with my mother had not improved with my expanding role in Houston, neither had my relationship with my grandmother. After I moved to Houston in 1929, I went back to Palestine only for the Christmas holidays. Most of my days in Palestine were spent visiting friends. Even when Grandmother and I were in the same room, we had little to talk about because the work to which I devoted my days was foreign to her experience. In October of 1936 Grandmother had returned home from taking ten friends to the hotel for lunch, then to a movie and the ice cream parlor. She suddenly complained of a sharp pain in her chest and died of a heart attack. The last few years she had not tried to dictate my activities because I had been gone from home so long. While she did not treat me as much like a child or a foreigner as she had while I was living at home, she did not correspond with me except with a card on my birthday. Her death was sad more for what I did not feel than for what I did.

The following spring of 1937 I had been at San Jacinto three years when I found a letter on my desk telling me the bank would be merging with the Second National Bank, which later became Bank of Southwest and is now Bank One. My boss suggested I look for other employment since the new bank did not have a legal department. History was repeating itself. With two mergers and a temporary moratorium in such a short time, I decided banking was no longer for me, and I looked outside the banking world for a new connection and career.

Fortunately I had friends all over the city because of my banking experience, and soon these paid off. I accepted a position as an assistant vice-president at T. J. Bettes Company, the largest mortgagor in the state and one of the largest in the nation. I would be assisting one of the vice presidents who was responsible for mortgage lending.

What I learned about lending at T. J. Bettes had little to do with money and much to do with priorities and sharing myself. At the mortgage company I quickly made new friends, one of which was Marie Word, the switchboard operator. She was tall with big brown eyes, curly brown hair, flawless skin, and the face of a child. Although she was shy, she came alive on the dance floor. At our company dances she was a very sought-after dance partner.

Marie came to me one day with boyfriend trouble, and apparently something I said was helpful. After that she regarded me as her mother confessor. One day I was eating lunch in our break room when Marie entered. She glanced around and seemed to sigh with relief when she noticed that I was alone. "Jackie," she began in a low voice, "do you mind if I join you?"

"Be my guest," I smiled, wondering why she asked since we had often shared meals together.

She opened her lunch sack and removed a ham sandwich and apple. Before even taking the sandwich from its wrapper, she leaned forward toward me and pleaded, "Jackie, what am I going to do?"

I stopped eating and gave her my full attention. Thoughts of Emma at Guardian Trust flashed through my mind.

"You know I like working here," she began almost defensively, "but I don't want to stay at this job the rest of my life. I want to be a stenographer for an oil company." She stated her dream with the fervency of a child saying she wanted to be a movie star.

"And what is stopping you?" I asked gently.

Tears came to her eyes and she bit her lower lip. "I don't have the money for the training," she answered simply.

"Can anyone in your family help you?" I asked, peeling my banana.

"No," she sighed. "They are all in the same boat."

"Can you cut any of your expenses—like move to a cheaper place to live?"

Each suggestion was met with a discouraging answer. She was living on the edge as it was. Finally another employee walked into the lunchroom and our discussion was over. "Let me think about this," I told Marie, "and I'll get back to you." She nodded without much enthusiasm.

The following Saturday I called Droughan Business School to ask about tuition costs and how long it took to complete a stenographic course. Then I began to put some ideas together. I did not know what Marie was paying for rent, but in the 1930s after the economic crash, I figured it was probably fifty to seventy-five dollars a month for a furnished apartment. If Marie came to live with Mother and me and did not have to pay rent, she could use that money for her tuition. She would not eat enough or use enough utilities to make a large difference in my bills. If she could live with us for those two years, she could afford to complete her course and find the position she so desperately wanted. I figured I could pay her hundred and twenty-five dollar tuition for two of the four semesters and allow her to save up for the remainder of the cost.

Sunday night at supper I told Mother what I was planning to do. "You can't do that!" she glared at me.

"Yes, I can and I plan to," I answered quietly, steadily meeting her gaze.

"But you are still a minor, so that's not your decision to make," Mother retorted, scooping up another bite of green beans.

"You forget that I was born in 1909 and this is 1937, so in the eyes of the law I am old enough to make decisions for myself, even if you try to stop me," I responded. "A young girl needs help and deserves that help. I'm in a position to help her and will not allow you or anyone to thwart me in this."

Mother sputtered and protested, but I would not allow her to win the argument. Finally, she just left the table.

On Monday I asked Marie to go to lunch with me and I posed my offer. She reached over, grabbed my hand, and burst into tears. I patted her hand while she cried. Finally she sniffed, "Oh, Jackie, you don't know what this means to me. I thought my dream was beyond my reach, and now it is going to happen—all because of you!"

Several weeks later one evening after work Marie had a friend deliver the two of us and a few suitcases of her things to our one-bedroom apartment. I had spent the past few evenings rearranging furniture in the living room where Marie was to sleep so she would have some private space for her things. As I opened the door, I caught my breath. Everything was back in its original place! Mother did not come to the door when I called, "Mother, Marie and I are here! Where are you?" I motioned to Marie and her friend where to put down the luggage they were carrying and went to find Mother.

She was standing at the kitchen sink peeling potatoes for a vegetable soup. I stomped up beside her and hissed, "What do you think you are doing?!"

She reached around me to pick up another potato and attacked it with the peeler. She did not say a word.

"Mother," I continued under my breath, "Marie is living here whether you like it or not. This will be the last antic you pull while she is our guest. Do you understand?"

She cut her eyes up at me and returned them to her task.

Marie appeared at the kitchen door asking, "Are you sure this is not going to be too much trouble?"

A faint smile flittered on Mother's face and quickly disappeared.

"Don't be absurd!" I exclaimed. "Marie, I want you to meet my mother, Retha Matthews. We are delighted you will be living with us."

Mother turned slightly to acknowledge Marie and nodded her head silently before swiping the peeler over another potato.

"How do you, Mrs. Matthews?" Marie said politely. "You are so kind to allow me to stay with you and Jackie." She hesitated. "I promise not to be a burden."

Getting no response, she looked inquiringly at me. "How many more suitcases do you have?" I asked with more enthusiasm than I felt. "Let's go see how we can move the furniture to make more room for you. I meant to do that last night and just got busy with other things. Come see if you agree with my plan."

When we had successfully moved furniture back into the new arrangement, Mother announced that dinner was ready. Marie complimented the soup and the homemade biscuits as if they were the first she had ever eaten. I kept the conversation focused on work and current events. When the meal was finally over, Mother stood and reached for her dishes to take them to the kitchen. "Oh, no, Mrs. Matthews!" Marie cried, scampering to Mother's side and picking up her dishes. "That's my chore from now on. You were so nice to cook for me. The least I can do is take over washing the dishes. Just show me where you keep your soap and towels, and I'll be happy to wash up for you."

Mother raised her eyebrows and shrugged. "If you insist . . . ," she responded.

While Marie continued to pile sincere compliments on Mother and located the essentials for cleaning the kitchen, I heard her naïve chatter and laughed to myself. "Mrs. Matthews, I hope I will have the opportunity often to hear you play the piano," she said as she turned on the water. "Jackie has told me so often what a wonderful musician you are. I'll be glad to help with the cleaning around here too. . . where do you keep the broom? . . . . oh, OK . . . but please don't ever ask me to sing. I admire people who have the gift of music. I'm just not one of them. How did you get so interested in music?"

Twenty minutes later Mother emerged from the kitchen and walked straight to the piano with Marie at her heels. She sat primly on the piano bench and began swaying to the melody she drew from the keys. Marie sat on the couch, listening intently. After a few minutes, I whispered to Marie, "Please feel free to unpack and do whatever you need to do to get your things arranged."

"Oh, I'll get to that," Marie smiled. "I'm enjoying listening to your mother play."

I saw Mother's shoulders rise with a big breath, and she increased the tempo and force of her hands on the keys. Her head bobbed and the little curls on the back of her neck danced as she banged out the music.

One piece followed another until it was late into the evening. Finally Mother lifted her hands from the keys and turned to face Marie. "You must be tired after all your packing. I'll leave now so you can go to bed."

Marie stood and held out her hands to Mother, "Thank you so much, Mrs. Matthews. That was so beautiful."

The corner of Mother's lips raised slightly, and she put her hands into the pockets of her light blue cotton dress. "Well, good night, Marie."

"Good night, Mrs. Matthews," Marie replied, dropping her hands awkwardly to her side. "I'll see you in the morning."

I peeked around the corner of the room and asked, "Is there anything I forgot to show you? The linens are in the bathroom cabinets. If you can't find anything, just pretend that you are at home and open cabinets until you find what you need." I walked over to Marie and hugged her. "I'm so glad you are here."

"Thanks, Jackie," she said. She didn't let go of me right away and whispered, "Is it . . . ? I mean, are you sure it's OK with your mother for me to be here?"

I forced a smile. "You bet it is!" I exclaimed. "She wouldn't have it any other way."

Marie was a dedicated student, taking four classes the first semester: business English, arithmetic, law, and rhetoric. She attended class for three hours after work and most of the day on Saturday and studied after we got home from church each Sunday. She still made time to assist us with grocery shopping, housecleaning, and other chores. After about a year we moved to a two-bedroom apartment nearby. Marie and I shared one bedroom while Mother had her own.

Shortly before Marie completed her two-year course, I received a call from the registrar at her school telling me that Humble Oil Company wanted to employ one of their better students to train in a position that would open within six months. The job entailed working for one of their junior executives. The registrar said, "From what I observe, Marie is more than ready academically for this challenge. However she is young; you know she is just twenty. I would like your candid opinion on whether you think she has the maturity to deal with executives."

I beamed like a parent and responded, "You cannot go wrong with Marie. She is a hard worker and a gracious young lady. She has the poise as well as the work skills to be an asset to Humble."

After Marie took her exams and got her ending grades, she was told that this position was available, pending an interview at Humble and their testing of her skills. Subsequently she was offered the position and accepted it.

As she relayed the good news to me, Marie sparkled with enthusiasm. "I'll give

Bettes a month's notice that I am leaving for a better position." She reached out and hugged me tight. Then she stepped back and looked me square in the eye. "Jackie, but for you, my dream would never have come true. How can I ever thank you?"

I swallowed hard and squeezed her hands. Placing a kiss on her cheek, I smiled, "Work smart to be successful. I am very proud of you."

After her ninety-day probationary period was over and she was approved as a permanent employee, she felt she should move to her own quarters. "And, Jackie, I am in a position now to repay you for all you invested in me during my school years."

I shook my head decisively.

"Please, Jackie. I couldn't have. . . ."

"Marie," I told her, "what I want you to do is save your money, buy some Humble Oil stock, and start a methodical program of savings."

She did move out and started her savings account. The first Saturday after she moved, Mother told me, "Jackie, call Marie to come eat with us tomorrow. She'll be tired from working all week and might not have time to cook a nutritious meal."

I turned so Mother would not see my grin. Marie was happy to accept, and this became our routine for several months. One day a few months later Marie called me at the bank. "Jackie, is there any way you can go out to dinner with me tonight? I have something I have to talk to you about."

"Of course, darling," I promised. "Where and when?"

The moment I saw the gleam in her beautiful eyes, I knew what the news had to be, but I was careful not to spoil her telling of it. As soon as we had ordered dinner, she reached over and took my hand. "Jackie, were you aware that I have been dating my boss?"

Genuinely surprised, I confessed ignorance. "You never bring him around and never mention him. Why should I suspect that?"

"We tried to be as inconspicuous as we could," she laughed. "I guess it worked!"

I nodded with a big smile on my face, trying to ignore my concerns that he was much older than she. I quickly asked God to give them the wisdom to make the right decision about their relationship.

"He's giving me a ring for my birthday in a few weeks. Then we'll announce our plans to marry before the end of the year. He is being moved to New York the first of the year and says he won't go without me," she beamed. Her confidence was well placed as they enjoyed more than fifty years of a loving marriage and home life.

After this second successful mentoring experience, I managed the rest of my days to find someone to reach out to and offer to be a mom, an aunt, a big sister, or whatever role was needed to bring comfort, encouragement, or guidance. In this way I have built a remarkable extended family of "children" and "grandchildren" who love me and are pampered by me with as much affection as natural offsprings. It is certainly more blessed to give than to receive because I have ended up receiving so much more than I could have asked from these special people. It has always been a pleasure to be a small part of someone else's experiencing pleasant new beginnings.

One surprisingly fertile soil for my extended family was classes in the American Institute of Banking's educational program. After I received the last of three certificates through the program, I began teaching classes in 1940 in personnel administration and public speaking. I lost only two students, and that because their families moved away from Houston. I was the only teacher who had ever had such a record. I don't credit that success to my great teaching ability although I did try to make the classes challenging and fun. What I offered my students was useful information and my desire to see them learn. They responded with enthusiasm and friendship. I had to give up this enjoyable activity in 1957 when my new employer refused to let anyone have time off to participate in such organizational responsibilities. I still keep up with some of those early students and have experienced with them life beginning again and again as they progressed in their careers with what they learned.

fifteen

chapter 15
WELCOMING A NEW LIFE

One day in January of 1939 my phone in the Legal Department of T. J. Bettes Company rang. "Alice Cornelia," Mother's shrill voice came loudly through the receiver. "Novella has taken quite ill." Novella Chambers was the mother of my cousin Gertrude, who had gotten me the job at Guardian Trust Company. "Gertrude is concerned about having someone with Novella day and night," Mother went on without even asking if I had time to talk. "I want the two of us to take the night and early morning duty. We'll start tonight."

There was silence while I tried to process what I was hearing.

"Go to her house after work today instead of coming home," Mother added as if I had readily agreed.

"No, wait . . . ," I cried, getting up out of my chair in panic. "I can't sit somewhere all night! You forget I have to be at work at eight in the morning." I glanced wildly at the stacks of paper on my desk vying for my attention.

"But Gertrude needs some relief," Mother protested. "She can't stay there twenty-four hours a day."

"Well, I know she needs help, but I can't help in this way. Maybe I can cook meals for her, do some shopping, something else . . . anything else but stay there all night. I have to have some sleep to function at my job."

This time the pause was on Mother's end. "I've already told Gertrude we would do this," Mother finally answered.

"How could you!" I exclaimed, making a fist as if to choke my frustrations.

Mother did not answer. Finally I sighed with resignation, "What time did you tell her we would be there?"

"From six at night till eight in the morning," she responded crisply.

"OK, I'll leave here in time to be home by 5:30. I'll need the car to drive to Novella's by 6. Then I'll come pick you up at 1 in the morning and take you to Novella's while I get a few hours of sleep. I'll pick you up again at 7:30 so you can drive me to work by 8."

"Good," said Mother and she hung up.

After three weeks of this schedule I was totally exhausted. One night as I checked on Novella, I was frightened by her labored breathing and restlessness. I immediately called the doctor and woke Gertrude, who was asleep in an adjoining bedroom.

The doctor arrived in about twenty minutes and examined Novella while we waited outside her door. He looked tired as he came out of the bedroom with his finger to his lips and led us to the living room. "I'm sorry, ladies," he began awkwardly. "I don't think your mother will last through the night. She is very weak. I gave her a shot to make her more comfortable. Just check on her occasionally. She should sleep peacefully now."

Gertrude and I cried and talked for hours until we were both emotionally wrung out. "Go on to bed," I told my cousin. "I'll be here and will call you if there is any change."

Gratefully Gertrude went to bed. The room was stuffy and oppressive with musty medicinal smells. I felt slightly nauseated and my head ached. Around eleven o'clock I decided that Novella would be fine without me in the room for a few minutes.

I wandered out to the front porch and sat heavily in the swing at the far end of the porch. I remembered nostalgically the many sweet conversations I had had with Dad in a similar swing and drew comfort from the memories.

Just then I froze as I realized that a car had driven up in the driveway and a male was exiting the driver's side. If I tried to run for the door, he could easily beat me there. I decided to hold still and hope he would not spot me.

As he reached the bottom of the steps, I let out a sigh as I realized it was Kenneth Greer, a young man who rented a room from Novella. I thought as I did almost every time I saw him what a handsome person he was with his sandy blonde hair, clear blue eyes, and ruddy complexion. Apparently, I was not alone in my assessment because his phone was constantly ringing with women pursuing him. He did not know he was handsome, and his sweet, unassuming manner was irresistible to some females. When we had first met five years ago when he moved into the house, I sensed that he was interested in getting to know me better, but my heart was still too raw to risk joining competition for the man's affections. I enjoyed his company at frequent meals at Novella's, and that was as far as our friendship had developed.

I must have moved as he stepped onto the porch because he swung his head around and saw me. "What in the world are you doing out here at this time of night?" he asked, quickly coming over to the swing.

"Novella is dying," I told him. "She is sleeping peacefully for now, and I just had to have some fresh air."

"Well, you just rest here," he said decisively. "I'll be right back."

I lazily pushed myself back and forth in the swing and thought fondly of family gatherings with Novella and Gertrude. Soon the front door squeaked open. I could smell Ken's light cologne as he approached and sat beside me. "Now, what can I do for you?" he asked with genuine concern.

I smiled inwardly when I realized that Ken had showered, shaved, and changed clothes. A chemical engineer by training, Ken worked for the Martin-Senour Paint Company, the fine paint portion of the Sherwin Williams Company. In the mid 1930s someone had developed a climatized paint and tried to sell it to Martin-Senour. The company officials doubted the claims. However they did agree to test it, so they hired Ken and other engineers to go around the country planting chips of the new paint and studying them on a regular basis as they were exposed to the elements. Ken's Texas territory included the Rio Grande Valley, Houston, Beaumont, and north to Huntsville and Navasota. He had approached farmers asking for a tiny spot on their barn to place the paint. Every five weeks he made the rounds, collecting the chips, placing more, and analyzing those he collected. The project was to last five years. I thought it nice that he had changed his dirty clothes for me.

"I can't think of anything I need, thank you," I answered. A yawn escaped my lips involuntarily.

"How long have you been here?" Ken asked, sitting in a wooden rocker beside the swing.

"Since six," I answered sleepily. "I'll be leaving soon to get Mother to take my place."

"You sound like you have a routine," he observed.

"I guess we do. We've been doing this for three weeks," I explained. "I'll be fine. I appreciate your concern."

"You may have forgotten," he said as he stood and held out his hands to me, "that I attended medical school for a few years. I want you to go lie down on the couch and I'll watch Novella until one. You need the sleep." Ken had mentioned that he had dropped out of medical school in Lincoln, Nebraska, where he was training to be a surgeon, when his father died and he had to go home to provide for his mother and three siblings.

"Oh, I can't do that," I protested, covering another yawn with my hand.

"And why not?" he asked.

Before I could answer, I heard a strange noise. "Do you hear that?" I asked, jumping up.

"Yes!" he answered, following me to Novella's room.

Her breath was raspy and uneven. The air rattled as it exited her throat. I headed for Gertrude's room as Ken said, "I think the time is near."

Gertrude came into the room in time to kiss her mother gently on the cheek. Then there was no sound. Novella had left us. I called Mother and told her that I would not be picking her up at one.

The next hour was a blur of hushed activity and tears. After the undertaker left, Ken said, "Jackie, let me take you home. There is no point in waking up your mother just to come pick you up."

I readily accepted the offer. As we drove, Ken asked about my work schedule. "How do you get to work?"

"I walk," I laughed, leaning my head wearily on the back of the car seat.

"Isn't that pretty far?"

"Yes, it's 35 blocks," I said.

"And what time do you have to leave home to make it downtown by eight?"

"I'm fine if I leave by 7:10," I assured him.

"It's already two!" he pointed out. "You'll have to sleep fast."

"I know," I sighed. "Thankfully I have a light day tomorrow at the office. Thank you so much for your assistance tonight. I really appreciate it."

"My pleasure," he grinned as we pulled into my driveway. He hopped out of the car to open my door and escorted me to my front door.

I fell gratefully into bed. When the alarm went off later that morning, I felt as if I had slept only ten minutes. I longed for Mother to offer to take me to work. She owned the car and would not allow me to drive it, except for the last three weeks to exchange places at Novella's side.

No offer came, so I wearily opened the door at 7:10 to begin my hike. My heart raced as I saw a familiar car in the driveway. It was Ken!

He jumped out of the car and ran up to me.

"Good morning!" I laughed in surprise. "What are you doing here?" Then I collected my thoughts. "Is anything wrong at Gertrude's?"

"Oh, no," he assured me. "I just thought how tired you looked last night, so I decided to come drive you to your office."

I had to restrain myself from hugging him. Once in the car I was almost lulled to sleep by the motion and the sun streaming in on my side. I must have dozed because Ken's voice startled me, "Well, here's your office."

"Oh, I'm sorry I was such a dull conversationalist," I apologized. "You were so thoughtful to help me out like this."

He reached out and took my hand between his. "My pleasure," he repeated with a penetrating gaze.

At his touch the tiredness dissipated and my body felt light and tingly all over. I smiled and walked to the door of the building. Without thinking, I looked back to where his car had been. He was leaning against the side of the car with his arms folded against his chest, watching me. When I turned, he grinned and waved. I waved back. As I entered the building, I felt something special in the air, but I was too tired to figure out what it was.

I dragged my tired body through the routine of the morning. As lunchtime approached, I stopped by the switchboard operator and told her I would be taking a long lunch hour, then I headed out the door. As my eyes adjusted to the sunlight, I broke into a wide smile and picked up my pace. There where Ken had left me that morning was the handsome Ken. While he was just five feet, ten inches tall, he had a solid build and classic facial features.

"What ever are you doing here?" I laughed.

He took my arm to guide me to the car. "I've come to take you to lunch—if you will permit me," he answered with a gallant sweep of his other arm.

"I'd be delighted," I replied, feeling my heart flutter and my face flush.

The next few hours I forgot how tired I was—and all about my shopping. We ate a leisurely lunch and never had a pause in the conversation.

As he opened my car door back at the office, I tilted my head and began, "Ken, I don't know how to thank you for being so thoughtful . . . ."

"That's not hard with you," he interrupted.

Our eyes met and lingered. After a few seconds I became aware of an unfamiliar sensation in my heart. Not even with Dick had I felt so weak in the legs and so . . . special.

All afternoon I found myself daydreaming about Ken and recalling how he tossed his head back when he laughed and how his eyes sparkled when he looked at me. As I pushed open the door of the bank to leave that evening, I wished that he would be in the same parking space waiting for me. And he was!

He scampered up to me, leaned over, and brushed my cheek with his lips. He took my hand and said, "I hope you are not surprised to see me this afternoon."

I managed to say feebly, "I really hoped you would be here."

As he pulled into the traffic, he looked over at me with a quizzical look. "Do I remember correctly that your mother is out of town for a few days?"

"You remember correctly," I responded, smiling at him. "She went to Palestine to see friends and take care of some long-standing business."

"Then will you let me take you out to dinner?"

"I'd love to go!" I replied, clasping my hands like a school girl.

"Where do you want to go?" He laughed at my enthusiasm.

"How about . . . oh, no!" I gasped.

"What's wrong?" he asked, braking suddenly.

"Oh, no emergency!" I assured him. Frowning, I added, "I just remembered that I have an alumnae club meeting tonight. As president, I really have to be there."

Before I could ask for a rain check, Ken suggested, "Well, how about if I take you home to freshen up, we grab a quick bite, and I'll take you to the meeting? Then I'll pick you up at whatever time you say. Is that a deal?"

"Oh, yes!" I cried. "Thank you so much!"

I quickly changed out of my business suit and into a more casual dress, and we ate a hurried dinner at the cafeteria. When Ken dropped me off at the home where the meeting was held, several other members were walking up to the door at the same time. After I was inside the house, they converged on me, "Who was that handsome man? Why have we never heard of him before? Are you dating?"

Not knowing myself what was happening with Ken, I shrugged off their inquiries. "He's a new friend," I said mysteriously. Later I learned that no one who saw us together that night doubted for a moment that Ken was someone very special to me. I hurried the club members through the old and new business and dismissed the meeting a little earlier than usual. When I peeked out the window, I blushed to see Ken's car already there as if he could not wait for the appointed time either.

We drove to a nearby House of Pies for dessert and coffee. As we talked, I realized that Ken was the dearest man I had ever met and I did not want to wake up and find this only a dream.

"Jackie?"

"Oh . . . yes?"

"You didn't answer me. Are you OK?" Ken said with concern on his face.

"I'm sorry. . . . I'm . . . I'm just still tired from the other night. What did you ask me?"

"It was nothing important. Let's go. You need your rest," Ken said, motioning to the waitress for the check.

Ken slid the car into my driveway and turned off the motor. He took the keys from the ignition and reached his arm around me, pulling me close to him. He kissed me with a fervor I had never experienced—or had never wanted from anyone I had ever known. I did not want the moment to end.

Finally he held me at arm's length and whispered, "Darling, I want to marry you. You are the first and only woman I have known I ever wanted, so please say yes."

To buy time while I caught my breath, I teased, "What about all those other women who keep calling you?"

"Who said I wanted to hear from them?" He gently kissed the tip of my nose.

"Oh, Ken, I love you too. Yes, I will marry you!"

His lips hungrily sought mine, and I relaxed in his arms. Soon we realized it was after midnight. Since the next day was Saturday, we went upstairs and sat on the porch. Wrapped in jackets against the chilly air, we talked and talked about our families and dreamed about our life together. Ken kissed me tenderly again and suddenly I stiffened. Ken looked at me and frowned, "What's wrong? Are you cold?"

"I just remembered that I have to tell Mother about our plans," I admitted, "and I don't relish that."

"Look, Gertrude has told me about your restricted life," he said holding both my hands firmly in his. "Don't you worry about your mother. You are mine now and we will do what we want to do. If it pleases us, that is all that counts. There had best not be any interference for I will not tolerate it . . . ever. Do you trust me in this?"

Tears formed in my eyes as I nodded, remembering how much I had missed having Dad play the role of my protector. To think of having that support again was too wonderful to imagine.

“Oh, Ken,” I whispered, “I love you.”

We called Ken’s mother, Alta Greer, in Illinois the next day. She was so happy and instantly became the mother I had never had. She periodically sent me little presents and often told me how happy she was that I was to be in her family. She made several trips to Houston before the wedding and stayed in my room. She insisted that I call her Mom. It was easy to do. We remained best of friends until her death at 91 in 1979.

Even with Ken’s pledge of support I waited several weeks before telling Mother of our engagement. One evening when Ken was visiting our house, I nodded to him and mouthed, “It’s time.”

He nodded and said to Mother, “Mrs. Matthews, I’m sure you have guessed by now that I love your daughter very much, and I want you to know that we are planning to get married next year.”

Mother looked from him to me and back. “Well, I wish you well,” she said. “I guess I’ll move back to Palestine and leave the apartment and furniture for you two.”

“Thank you, Mother,” I stammered, in shock at the ease of the announcement. “That is very generous of you.”

“And we’ll have your announcement party in February,” she stated.

“Oh, Mother,” I protested, “you don’t have to do that. That’s a lot of work, and I know you can’t afford it. We can just tell people . . . .”

“Now what kind of mother would I be if I did not give you an engagement party? Decide on the weekend and let me know.”

So the next February dozens of people attended a trousseau showing to celebrate our engagement. Friends made sandwiches and cakes. Guests brought gifts, and the apartment overflowed with well-wishers for three hours one Sunday afternoon.

For the next six months Ken and I planned our wedding and enjoyed merging our lives together. He introduced me to his business associates and his golfing buddies at the River Oaks Country Club. Several years later one of the builders of the Texas Medical Center in Houston told me that he had always admired Ken’s stance on the golf course. One day he told him, “Ken, you have the perfect hands for a golf club—and for being a surgeon.” He did not know of Ken’s thwarted plan to be a doctor. Ken shot two holes-in-one at the country club, a record that was not broken for many years. One of the shots was on a hole that had not been conquered by one of the professional golfers at the club, and being beaten by an amateur really irritated the man. Ken played golf on Sunday mornings while I went to church. I knew that eventually he would come around and join me at church.

As the wedding approached, I became paralyzed. To me marriage meant more than being with the man I loved every day. It also meant being free to be a human being, being around someone who really loved me, making decisions together, and going about life without confrontations. I was afraid something would prevent my enjoying this happiness.

However I did not let my fears spoil the fun we were having. For the first time in my life I had a social life. Many friends hosted parties for us, which we gladly reciprocated after our marriage.

The week before the wedding Mom came down from Seaton, Illinois, a few days early. While Mother was busy teaching piano and getting ready for the reception, she allowed me to borrow her car during the day. Mom rode downtown with me in the mornings, joined me for lunch, and sometimes met me as I got off work and stayed downtown for dinner or a movie. She became a welcome companion.

Shortly after Mom arrived, Mother moved into an apartment with a Houston friend while she waited for the house she had rented in Palestine to be vacated. I anticipated her moving away with great relief.

Amid a gardenlike atmosphere Ken and I were married on August 3, 1940, in Bering Memorial Methodist Church. Three-tiered candelabras holding long white tapers flanked the altar. Each was draped with fresh garlands of greenery. The altar was punctuated with white roses and white carnations. Small palm trees beside the altar and on the level below the altar completed the garden effect. Ken beamed as Hugh Huffmaaster, Mother's organ teacher, pounded out the "Wedding March," and I appeared at the door of the church in a traditional Chantilly lace and tulle dress with long sleeves and a long lace train. Will Lacey, a dear friend from Palestine, escorted me down the center aisle that had been covered in the traditional white satin. Each pew was decorated with a garland of greenery, white chrysanthemums, and white ribbons. Under the veil Ken could see my wide smile. My seven attendants were attired in light green Chantilly lace dresses. The seven groomsmen wore white tuxes. To round out the wedding party, we had a flower girl, a ring bearer, and a junior maid of honor.

Helen Flake, my voice teacher, sang "I Love You Truly," and Ken and I recited our vows. The day was so steamy that the pedestal fans in the sanctuary merely stirred up hot air. The 500 guests crowded into the sanctuary did not help the temperature. Some guests had to stand because there were not enough seats. However I was not aware of anything except the handsome man waiting for me at the altar who was to be my husband.

As the minister was saying, "These rings are an outward and visible sign of an inward and invisible love . . . ," there was a commotion beside us. The minister gasped, and Ken and I turned to see one of the ushers running up the aisle, slipping his arms out of his jacket as he ran. One of the candles had melted, tilted, and caught the carpet under it on fire. Before any damage was done, the fire was out and the ceremony resumed. After Helen sang "The Lord's Prayer," the minister announced, "By the authority of the state of Texas and as a minister of God, I now pronounce you man and wife. You may kiss the bride."

Ken planted a slow, tender kiss on my lips while the congregation laughed and began to applaud. Then we swept down the aisle to the chords of Mendelsohn's "Wedding March."

We retired to a reception at the Woman's Club, a lovely two-story house that was a popular spot for parties. Because of the cost, we had invited to the reception only fifty of the guests—the seventeen in the wedding party and the out-of-town friends.

Ken and I were enjoying a piece of wedding cake and fruit punch with our guests when Mother came flying over to me. "Who are all these people?" she demanded.

Confused, I looked where she was pointing. It seemed as if everyone from the wedding had come to the reception even though they had not been invited! "We don't have enough refreshments!" Mother growled. "Where are they coming from?"

"They are friends from church and business acquaintances, Mama Jack," Ken informed her. He called her Mama Jack when he was unhappy with her. At other times he called her Gretchen because she reminded him of a German gretchen, or blonde girl.

"Why have they come when they weren't invited?" Mother repeated. "We are completely out of refreshments." She jabbed her hands on her hips and waited for his explanation.

"I don't know," Ken told her, winking at me, "but I'm not going to let their presence interfere with my enjoyment of my wedding day. They are not due anything and they don't get anything." He turned his back to her as he greeted another guest. Fortunately the invited guests knew that we had taken photographs before the wedding, so they had come straight to the reception and had been served. The uninvited guests had lingered at the church, assuming we were taking pictures, and finally drifted towards the reception when they realized we had all gone.

After being congratulated by hundreds of friends, Ken and I drove to our apartment, where I changed into a suit. Meyer and Violet Rednick Lipton picked us up and took us to dinner before dropping us off at the Ben Milam Hotel, where Ken had parked his car and where we spent the night. Violet had been a friend in college, and she had lived with Mother and me for about eight years after Mother moved in with me in Houston in 1932. She and Meyer later adopted a boy whom they named after Ken.

The next day Ken and I drove to Austin for our honeymoon. Aunt Zetta Cockin Pearson, Mother's best friend in Palestine, stayed to visit with Mother after the wedding and offered us her lovely house in Austin. When Mother had started a kindergarten in Palestine right after she had graduated from college, Zetta, also a recent graduate, was one of her teachers. She married Clarence Pearson, who started a printing company in Palestine. They had four children, including one they named Retha after Mother. Uncle Clarence had gotten the printing contract for the state government, and his family lived in a large house near the Capitol.

One day Ken and I drove from Austin to San Antonio. He had not been exposed to the mariachi bands and Hispanic atmosphere of this part of the state and fell in love with the city. Another night we drove up to Mount Bonnell, a high hill overlooking the city of Austin. As we stood with our arms around each other's waist, Ken predicted, "Some day this mountain will be full of houses. One of them will be our retirement home." I nodded dreamily, not believing his prediction. The mountain was then owned by the government and was lined with trees. Sure enough, though, within two years building began on the exact side of the mountain he had predicted.

It was hard returning to Houston after a lovely few days alone. However we both had to go back to work. Actually starting our married life together was just as much fun as the honeymoon trip. We planned everything together. On Monday nights we made the grocery list for the week. On Friday nights we shopped for groceries. Many Saturday nights we hosted card parties or went out to dinner with friends. This was how life was meant to be lived—enjoying being together, no matter what the task at hand.

But Mother had not gotten the message. About a month after we married, Ken forgot some papers and returned to the house in the middle of the day to retrieve them. He was puzzled to see Mother's car at the curb. He ran into the apartment, worried that something had happened to me. What he saw stopped him in his tracks.

Mother was busy moving furniture in our living room. When she saw him, she stiffened and froze with a lamp in her hands. "And just what do you think you are doing, Mama Jack?" he boomed, walking up to within inches of her face.

"Alice Cornelia loves furniture change," she replied lamely, "and I'm doing it for her."

"No!" Ken yelled. "Jackie does not like furniture change—that you initiate. Everything is going to stay as it is, do you hear me?"

He took the lamp out of her hand and set it on the end table. Then he took her by the arm and pulled her toward the front door. "Come with me, Mama Jack," he hissed between clenched teeth. He marched her downstairs and out the door. He let go of her arm and narrowed his eyes. "Hear me clearly, Mama Jack," he began. "You will come back to this house when I invite you and not before. Jackie is not to speak to you until I give her permission. She is no longer your daughter to push around. She is my wife now, and we make the decisions about our life."

Mother spun around and stomped to her car. Ken watched until she had pulled away from the curb. When he told me about the incident that evening, he said, "Jackie, I'm sorry it had to come to that, but she has to understand that she no longer manages your life. We had to break that habit."

I jumped up from the sofa and flung my arms around his neck. At last I had someone to stand up for me. I didn't hear from Mother or speak to her for three weeks. She never confronted me about Ken's ultimatum, so I guess she figured she had been dethroned and she would abide by Ken's rules. A week later Mother's apartment in Palestine was ready, and she moved as planned.

Now there were no obstacles to my happiness. Ken and I loved getting together with friends and being spontaneous. Everywhere we went, however, a shadow trailed us. Hitler was moving against Romania the way he had conquered France, Belgium, Luxembourg, and the Netherlands earlier in the year. Reports of bombings in England and talk of war filled our lives like smoke from an incinerator. The U.S. government had even approved a draft by a narrow vote. We already knew some who had been drafted, and others had enlisted. I dreaded receiving each day's mail, afraid a draft notice would end the life I cherished and had waited so long to enjoy.

However the days became weeks and the weeks turned into months, months of absolute bliss. In between work and an active social life, Ken and I often talked about the possibility of war. Like most American men at that time, Ken felt it was his duty to join the armed forces and fight for his country if necessary. At first I protested, "Ken, I've just found the first happiness in my life. I don't want it to end!"

"I know, darling," he would answer, "but the threat to our freedom changes ordinary life. A lot of people are having to give up or at least postpone whatever plans they have made. Why should we be any different? If Hitler has his way and draws us into the war, it will take lots of people—in uniform and out—to defeat him. I feel I should do my part."

"I know how you feel, but can't you just wait to see if you are drafted?" I would beg.

"But others have gone and are giving up careers and families. I feel I should volunteer too," he would argue.

Finally in about January 1941 I stopped my protests. "I understand how you feel, Ken, and I'm proud of you for it. I won't stand in your way any longer."

For the next few days I felt lethargic and slightly nauseated. I was surprised because heartache had never affected me physically before. Ken noticed. "Darling, are you feeling alright?" he asked one morning before I got out of bed. He placed his palm on my forehead to check for a fever.

"Not really," I answered honestly. "I feel like I have a stomach bug or something, but I can't imagine why I'd be sick."

"Are you nauseated?" Ken asked, looking intently at me for any clue as to the problem.

"Yeah," I sighed. "I have been most of the day for a couple of days."

"Do you think eating a piece of toast before you get up would help?"

"Now that sounds good," I replied, not moving a muscle to get out of bed and dressed for work.

Ken sprinted to the kitchen and made toast and hot tea. He brought them on a tray and found me asleep. "Darling, here is your breakfast," he said, gently rousing me with a touch on my shoulder.

"Oh . . . thanks," I said sleepily, rising to a sitting position. "Ohhhh," I groaned and quickly lay back down.

"What's wrong?" Ken frowned.

"My stomach is upset," I complained. "Give me a few minutes and I'll try again."

Suddenly Ken grinned. "Jackie, have you gained a few pounds in the last few weeks?"

It was my turn to frown. "How did you know?!" I cried. "I didn't think it showed that much!"

"Well," he said, "I think I detect some extra weight right here." He placed his hand on my abdomen and let out a whoop!

"Jackie, darling!" he yelled. "Do you think you might be pregnant?"

"Well, I . . . I . . . ." I grabbed his hand and held it tightly against my lips. "Oh, Ken, I was afraid even to consider that I might be. Do you really think so? Oh, that would be too wonderful!"

He hugged me as best he could while I was still lying down and kissed me on the forehead. "A baby!" he shouted. "We're going to have a baby!" He did a little tap dance and clapped his hands.

I laughed and reached for the toast. He held my head up so I could swallow a few sips of the tea. In a few minutes I tried again to sit up and managed to stay vertical long enough to finish breakfast and settle my stomach.

For two weeks we made a routine of his bringing a light breakfast to me before I tried to get out of bed. I kept crackers at my desk at work and nibbled on them throughout the day when the nausea began. I didn't tell anyone about our fabulous news, but I glowed inside just thinking about the new little life that would share our home. I wished it would be a boy so Ken could teach him about fixing things. I wished it would be a girl so I could break the cycle of heartbreak in my family and dote on her every action. Whichever, this was an answer to a prayer we both had prayed—for different reasons. Of course we both wanted a child to grace our lives. I also was aware that a child would buy Ken a year's deferment from the Army.

At night we would talk about the little one who was to invade our home and discuss our ideas on parenting.

"Will you be sad to end your career?" Ken asked.

"I like what I do," I admitted, "but I can't imagine anything more special than guiding a child into being a responsible person."

One morning in late February I was drinking my tea before getting up and I suddenly bent over in pain and cried out, "Ken!"

He came running in from the kitchen. "What's wrong?" he asked as he grabbed the tea cup and set it on the bedside table.

"My stomach . . . ," I moaned. "The cramps are so bad . . . ."

"Can I help you lie down?" he asked helplessly.

"No, don't move me," I whispered, clutching my abdomen and wincing.

In a few minutes the pain had passed and I lay down. When I woke up, it was 10 a.m. Ken had left me a note saying he had called the bank to inform them that I would not be in—again—and asked me to call him as soon as I could.

I stumbled to the phone, weak but no longer in pain, and dialed Ken's number. "Hi, darling," I said. "I'm sorry for the scare. I'm fine now."

"Well, I'm glad to hear that," he responded with relief. "Just to make sure everything is OK, I've made an appointment this afternoon at 3 with Dr. Frank Iiams, a leading obstetrician. I'll pick you up about 2:30 and go with you."

Wanting to do the best for the baby, I agreed. Dr. Iiams examined me and grinned, "You most certainly are pregnant. I'll give you something for the nausea and it should be gone in a few days. Call me if it's not and we'll try something else."

His diagnosis buoyed my spirits, but it did nothing for the nausea. In fact that increased and the scales showed that now I was losing weight. By March Dr. Iiams was concerned at the weight loss and sent me to Dr. Martha Woods, a respected diagnostician. She performed the "rabbit test," the common pregnancy test of the day, and reported with compassion, "I'm sorry, Mrs. Greer, but you are not pregnant. I would see Dr. Iiams again and try to determine what your problem is. It is not pregnancy."

"But . . . ," I stammered, fighting back tears, "how can that be when I had all the symptoms?"

"False pregnancy is not unheard of," Dr. Woods explained. "A woman exhibits all the symptoms—enlarged abdomen, increased weight, morning sickness, etc. Sometimes there is an emotional basis for the condition. With these uncertain times, it is not surprising. I'm terribly sorry because I know how excited you were."

That evening Ken asked about the doctor's appointment before he had even hung up his coat. "Oh, honey," I began and buried my head on his shoulder. "We're not . . . I mean I'm not . . . there is no baby!"

I could feel his body stiffen, and I looked up after I heard a choking sound. Ken broke into sobs and we held each other and cried more tears than we knew were possible. Every time Ken tried to voice his pain, the sobs began again. He cried off and on most of the night as if he had just buried the child he had wanted so much. Realistically we had suffered a harsh loss. There would be no child, no extension of our love, no deferment.

After another day at home with nausea, I staggered back to work. I had already missed several weeks and did not want to impose upon my coworkers any more than necessary. About a week later I was preparing breakfast and suddenly realized that I had not been sick that morning or the morning before. Just as quickly as the symptoms had begun, they were gone. They had left a void, a grave, inside us, and we would never be the same.

A few days later, in March 1941, Ken came home and put his arms around me. He held me longer than usual, and his kiss seemed more tender. Finally he caressed my face with his hands and said, "Jackie, I tried to enlist today . . . ." A lump sprang into my throat, but before I could utter any sound, he went on, "and they rejected me. My feet are too flat!"

With that he picked me up and twirled me around and around.

"Oh, Ken! That's wonderful . . . I mean, I know you are disappointed . . . that you felt it was your duty to join the military, but . . . I'm so happy!"

I hugged him as if I were afraid that he would evaporate before my eyes if I let him go. The next few days I found it hard to concentrate. The worst I had feared was not to be. Ken was safe. There would be no new beginning this time—and I was so thankful.

sixteen

chapter 16
THREE STARS

On Monday two weeks after Ken's attempt to enlist, he picked me up at work as usual. It had been so handy to have his company car. I could not drive it, of course, but we had the use of it when he was in town. I was so glad not to have to walk to work except when he was out of town, checking his inventory of paint chips. Driving through the tree-lined streets to our house, Ken suggested, "Jackie, let's go eat at the Mexico City Restaurant."

"On a Monday?" I giggled, still marveling at the fun of breaking the routine of everyday life.

"I figured it was a safe invitation," Ken answered, "since I could not imagine you ever turning down a Mexican food dinner."

The restaurant was not crowded, so our meal was served quickly. The chili con queso arrived, and I hungrily dipped a tortilla chip into the creamy sauce. "Guess what Mr. Painter assigned me to do this week?"

Ken did not answer. I noticed he had not even sampled the appetizer.

"Are you OK?" I asked, reaching across the table to touch his hand.

"Jackie," he said, his voice cracking. "Jackie, I've already been home . . . and . . . there was a telegram from the government. They want me after all."

My skin tingled and I dropped my chip. I felt the blood drain from my face.

"What!" I cried.

"I'm to report to the enlistment center tomorrow," Ken continued in a flat voice.

"Oh, Ken!" Tears spilled down my cheeks, and I covered my face with my hands. Ken jumped out of his chair and came around to my side of the table. He put his arms around my shoulders and held me tight. "I was not expecting this either," he said trying to console me. Other patrons stared in our direction.

He stood up and motioned to the waiter to box up our food. My legs were weak when I stood up, and my heart ached as if someone were squeezing it and preventing it from beating.

I hardly knew where I was the next day at the office. My mind was on Ken, and I wondered what he was learning about his tour of duty. That evening felt like a funeral. "I've been accepted into the Army," he reported. Then he frowned, "And I am to report to base camp in two days."

"Two days?!" I cried. "Oh, Ken, I know you have to go, but that doesn't make it any easier. I love you, and I don't want to be away from you." I buried my head in his chest and cried.

Ken stroked my hair until the sobs subsided. Then he put his finger under my chin and tilted my head up so he could see my eyes. "You know I'll come back," he smiled. "Nothing will separate us, you hear?"

I could not stop the tears from falling again. The man I loved, the life I loved, was about to disappear for who knew how long? How could I go on alone? I knew I would survive, but two days! That was not enough time to say all I wanted to say to Ken, to make plans, to enjoy some last celebration. I had to work both of the next two days. Wartime did not take breaking hearts into account since everyone's was breaking in some way. Because of men who had been drafted or had enlisted, we were short-staffed at the office. Every day someone was saying goodbye to a loved one, and it was not possible to allow everyone a few days off, even to say goodbye.

The second morning after the telegram's arrival, Mother drove Ken and me to the Union Station, the train station in downtown Houston that is now the site of the Minute Maid Park, a baseball stadium. She said goodbye to Ken and stayed in the car while I walked with him to the train that would take him to boot camp in Wichita Falls, Texas. Dozens of men with small duffle bags were lingering around the station with their arms around wives or mothers or sisters. We did not recognize anyone but felt a kinship with all of them. They were all shelving plans and dreams, some forever. They all looked hesitant to leave those they loved and yet they were eager to get on with the grim task assigned to them—to protect from a mad man the freedoms we cherish.

Ken and I talked of silly things and of serious things, although we had said them all before in the previous months and in the last two short days. Really, there was nothing left to say except "I love you." We could never say or hear that too much. Finally the moment came that he hugged me hard one last time, kissed me passionately, and broke away. At the door of the train car he glanced back and blew me a kiss, then disappeared. I could not see through the car's windows, so I just stood with my arms crossed, kneading my upper arms with my hands until the train's shrill whistle pierced my heart and the huge machine lunged forward and chugged out of sight.

Even after I could no longer see the train, I stood where he had left me, unaware of the sobbing of other family members who had just seen their loved one depart. My world was breaking apart and I thought if I could avoid breathing, the moment and the smell of Ken's cologne would never end. I don't know how long I stood there, seeing my handsome Ken in my mind's eye and resisting stepping into my future without him.

Eventually I returned to Mother in the car. Neither of us said a word as she drove me back to the apartment. She had voiced her anger over his trying to enlist to the point that I had forbidden her to mention Ken to me. Being apart from him was painful enough without Mother blaming him for our separation.

Mother dropped me off at the apartment. I stood at the door several minutes before I turned the knob. The emptiness lunged at me and dragged me into its den. I stumbled to the sofa and sat heavily on the cushion, just staring into the air. In my mind I could hear Ken walking through the rooms and expected him to appear at any moment and encircle me in his arms. But only the silence encircled me.

I dreaded entering the apartment each night as I came home from work because the silence only reminded me that Ken was missing from my life. At the end of the month Mother announced that she had given up her apartment and would be moving in with me to save money. She had moved from Palestine to Houston about a month before and had rented an apartment near us. I was still so numb from Ken's departure that her pronouncement did not register until she appeared at my door one Saturday morning. "What are these?" I asked as I opened the door and found her balancing two cardboard boxes on my front porch.

"My linens," she answered curtly. I just stood looking at her without comprehension.

"May I come in?" she asked impatiently.

"Well, sure, but . . . ," I stammered. Then it registered that she was actually moving in.

It did not take her more than a few days to rearrange the furniture to her liking and to lay down the rules for the household. Sometimes I would have to study the ring on my left hand to convince myself that I was really married.

I did not hear from Ken for two weeks after he left. I forced myself to go through the motions of working and teaching Sunday school and leading the alumnae group, but my mind was always on Ken. What was he doing? How was he holding up to the physical strain of training? When would he be able to contact me? Where would he go next? When could I see him?

Finally I got a call. "Hi, darling," his cheery voice said.

"Ken!" I screamed into the receiver. "Where are you? How are you getting along? How long do we have to talk?" My whole body was grinning, and I jumped up and down like a schoolgirl.

"Whoa," he laughed. "One question at a time. Goodness, it's good to hear your voice. I've really missed you."

"Oh, Ken, I've missed you terribly," I said, swallowing hard to push the lump out of my throat. I did not want to waste this time of connection by crying. There would be plenty of time later to shed tears—of joy for hearing from him and of sadness for being so far away from him.

"Actually I have just three minutes for this call," he apologized. "Training's not so bad. I've been promoted to staff sergeant. I'm getting on a train for Pierre, South Dakota, in a few minutes. I'll write or call when I know how you can reach me. Oh, oh, the drill sergeant is calling us to fall in. I love you, darling. Know that I think of you every day—and especially every night. I gotta run! Bye!"

"Ken!" I called, but the dial tone answered me. I held the receiver for several minutes, feeling it somehow was a lifeline to my husband. Eventually the beeping of the phone line broke through my reverie, and I gently placed the receiver in the cradle. Then I let the tears come, and they fell for half an hour.

The next time I heard from Ken, he reported that he had been assigned to the Army Air Corps and was training to be a ball turret gunner on a B17 plane. "What's that?" I asked.

"The ball turret is a little cage that hangs down under the belly of the plane, " Ken explained.

"That sounds awfully vulnerable," I said, hugging myself involuntarily with my free hand. "And pretty scary."

"You can see a lot from that vantage point," Ken said, ignoring my fears. "Actually if it weren't for the reason I'll be up there, it would be a great carnival ride."

"But isn't it dangerous?" I pressed.

"Darling, war is dangerous," Ken reminded me. "Anyway I'll have a big gun and can see people on the ground better than they can see me. I'll be fine. I've gotta go. There is a long line to use the phone. I'll try to call again soon. I love you!"

I was supposed to be able to call Ken on one particular day a week within a two-hour period, but it was nearly impossible to get a line through. Obviously lots of other family members were trying to reach their soldiers at the same time. The whole nine months he was stationed at Pierre, we spoke only six times.

One of the early conversations revealed one of the paradoxes of wartime. People went out of their way to reach out to strangers—in uniform. Ken relayed an extraordinary tale. The female governor of South Dakota drove an entourage of cars to his base every Sunday and took ten soldiers to her home for dinner. Ken was lucky enough to be selected early in his stay at the base. As the only Texan in the group that day, he drew the attention of the governor. "You don't sound like a Texan," she teased him.

"Actually I'm a native of Illinois," Ken explained. "I've lived in Texas only a few years."

"Well, I like Illinois a lot," she admitted.

And so they developed a rapport. Later in the afternoon an employee came to the governor while she was visiting with Ken and whispered something in her ear.

"Are you sure?" she asked peeved.

"Yes, ma'am," the man answered. "I'm sorry." He walked away and the governor frowned as he left.

Ken asked, "Is something wrong?"

"Well, yes. I was going to serve our evening meal on the lawn and Frank can't get the outdoor lights to come on, so I guess we'll have to eat in here again."

Ken stood up and replied, "Would you like me to take a look? I've done some electrical work. I can't promise anything, but I don't mind looking into the problem."

"Well, that's awfully nice," she said. "Frank! Frank! Please come back."

Frank returned with a puzzled look on his face. "Please show Sgt. Greer here where the breaker box is and let him check it out. Thank you."

Frank shrugged and led Ken to the utility room of the governor's mansion, then he brought a ladder so Ken could climb up and inspect the light fixtures themselves. After a few minutes Ken located a loose wire. When he tightened it, he told Frank, "Maybe that had something to do with it. Go try the switch again."

Light flooded the dark yard. The governor was ecstatic when Ken returned. "You are quite a handyman! Thank you so much."

The next Sunday she specifically asked for him to be her guest. This time she mentioned that a number of her staff had been drafted. "I understand the need for men, of course," she confided to Ken, "but maintenance has really slipped around here. I hate for this house to be in disrepair when it represents the state to visitors."

"What needs doing?" Ken asked.

"Oh, just things like painting and cleaning the high light fixtures," she said with a shrug.

"I'll be glad to help," Ken offered, pausing with his fork in his hand.

"Oh, my, no," she laughed. "I could not let a guest work around here. You soldiers are out here to relax." She picked up a bowl of rice pilaf and passed it to the soldier at her right.

"It's not work to me," Ken explained, "if it's someone else's house. Really it would be a nice break from what I do all week."

"Are you sure?" she asked incredulously.

"I am. Of course I don't dare get paint on my uniform," Ken laughed as he cut into his ham. Meat was a rare commodity during the war, so this meal was a special treat.

"Well, we can find some work clothes if you really want to do this," she suggested.

"I'd like to," Ken assured her. "Let me see if anyone else wants to help."

He rounded up four other soldiers who thought painting would be a welcome diversion. Frank brought the paint supplies and work clothes to the men and led them to the dining room.

Ken opened one of the cans of paint and asked the governor, "Uh, excuse me, but are you sure this is the color for this room?"

"I believe so. Why?" She walked over to the open can and peered inside.

"Well, this has a yellow cast to it and the paint on the woodwork has a reddish tint. I just thought they might clash."

"Well, let me look. I never thought of that." The governor had him paint a swipe on a scrap of wood, and she held it up to the door jam. "You're right!" she exclaimed. "This won't look right at all. Do you think it will work in the entrance?"

Ken took the swatch to the foyer of the mansion and decided the color would look fine. The soldiers completed the paint job before they returned to the base that evening. For weeks after that, the governor asked for Ken to join her for lunch every Sunday, and he helped with whatever chores her staff had not been able to finish.

One day as he showed his handiwork to the governor, she turned to him and smiled sadly, "Ken, you know I never married, so don't have children, but if I did, I would want a son just like you."

Ken nodded, treasuring having a "family" of sorts while he was so far away from his own.

My first thought when I heard the news of the attack on Pearl Harbor on December 7, 1941, was, "How will this affect Ken?" I'm sure most wives and mothers had the same reaction. I had learned that it was futile to ask Ken about future plans and destinations because the purpose of the Army was preparedness—to be ready to go wherever you were needed on a moment's notice—and secrecy. I ached to hear from Ken and knew he would let me know of any moves. About two months after the attack Ken called.

"Hi, honey!" I gushed when I heard his voice. Even from thousands of miles away he could produce goose bumps on my skin. "What's up?"

I didn't expect his answer. "Darling, can you come to Kansas next week? Our unit is going to Salina, Kansas, and we'll debark from there to Europe. I've got to see you again before I go. It's been way too long, and who knows how much longer this war will go on." He sounded sad and lonely.

"Well, I don't know," I hesitated, running work obligations through my mind and twisting the phone cord in my hand. "It's pretty short notice to give. You know I'll do what I can." I dropped into a chair by the phone since I was feeling a little faint—whether from dread or from the excitement of seeing him, I didn't know. "Oh, Ken, I miss you! Tell me where I need to go if I can get permission."

"I'll arrive Friday evening. Can you be there Friday sometime?"

"Somehow I'll be there, honey! I can't wait to see you!"

As in most companies during wartime, the mortgage company officials understood the sacrifices families were called upon to make, and they accommodated their employees as best they could. Permission was granted for my trip, and I was on a train to Kansas Wednesday morning. I arrived in Salina Friday morning and took a bus to a hotel in town where I was to stay. The day drug on and I was impatient, knowing I was so close to Ken and yet could not be with him. Finally a knock on my door startled me out of the magazine article I was trying to concentrate on.

I jumped up and opened the door. My heart leaped when I saw Ken in his uniform. He had never seemed so handsome. His eyes sparkled as he enveloped me in his strong arms. Suddenly the world disappeared, and only Ken and I existed.

I wanted it to stay like that forever.

That evening we ate a simple supper at the hotel. There was so much to talk about, and yet the words seemed so inadequate to express our thoughts and feelings. We were both trying to sound cheerful and upbeat although we were both a breath away from tears.

Saturday we relaxed around the hotel, strolled around the little town, and talked incessantly. There was so much to catch up on and so much emotion to try to form into words. For reasons I never understood, there were no other military families staying at our hotel. The servicemen had been asked to stay close to their assigned hotel, so we did not see anyone Ken knew. We had breakfast delivered to the room, ate lunch at a cozy little place nearby, and enjoyed the hotel fare for dinner.

We talked about care for both our mothers and made plans for how we would resume our lives when Ken returned. Although I was aware that I had as much chance to see Ken again as not to, I refused to let that thought rob me of the delight of being with him. Sunday morning arrived like a thief. We woodenly nibbled at breakfast, hungrily feasting our eyes on each other and packing our mental suitcases of precious memories.

Finally the time for parting arrived, and we clung to each other desperately. Then Ken let go and turned to pick up my suitcase. He lifted it up and sighed heavily, "Let's go." I nodded and bit my lip to keep back the tears. They would only interfere with our last few moments together.

As we walked out of the hotel, Ken's pilot happened to be approaching. Ken introduced us and we smiled awkwardly. "You watch after him really good, will you?" I pleaded.

He merely nodded and tipped his cap and walked on.

Ken walked me three blocks to a bus that would take me to the train station, from where I would catch my train home. He was not allowed to accompany me to the train. Again he did not see anyone he knew and I did not meet any other wives. Actually I was grateful for not having to make pleasant conversation when my heart was being crushed. When the bus driver said, "All aboard!" Ken and I hugged briefly. We had already spent our passion and our words, and there was nothing left to do but leave. I scooted into a seat and locked my eyes with his until the bus pulled slowly away. I hurt like when I peeled a band aid slowly off my skin, aching as it resisted turning loose of every cell it was attached to.

The next day, Monday, Ken's squadron left for Europe. I did not know where he was being sent. I received my first letter from him about ten days later—from London. I knew there was an Air Corps base there, so I assumed that was where he was stationed. Weeks later I heard from the mother of one of the officers in Ken's squadron that a friend had seen some men from Ken's squadron in a pub in London. That just confirmed my guess. He, of course, could not tell me exactly where he was at any given time.

The way I was introduced to the officer's mother is one of the ironies of wartime. While some people are fighting us, others are being drawn to us whom we would never have met otherwise. One day I received a letter addressed to Mrs. Ken Greer. After reading the first few lines, I realized that it was written to a different Mrs. Ken Greer. I wrote Ken to tell him of the mistake. Eventually he wrote back that two other men in his squadron had his same name, Kenneth S. Greer. While my Ken's middle name was Sidney, the other two were Samuel and Schuller. He gave me the address to forward the letter to. The mother lived in Galesburg, Illinois, not far from Ken's family. I looked up her phone number and called her frequently. Once when I visited Mom, I went to meet her in person. In a mystical way talking or visiting with her made me feel closer to my Ken because her heart was in the exact same unknown place with her Ken.

Back in Houston, as in cities all over America, my sacrifice was no different from that of many families. I went to work every day and wrote Ken every night. Occasionally I would hear from him. His letters, of course, were censored. Often they took two weeks to reach me. I read and reread those I did receive and caressed the paper, knowing that Ken had touched it.

I missed his companionship, and I missed his protection. I was too emotionally drained to care what Mother did or said. When she would make her royal decrees, I would just shrug and go into my bedroom. I didn't have enough excess energy to argue.

She began teaching piano again in Houston although she had fewer students than when she had had her studios. To encourage families to spend some of their limited funds on a nonessential like music lessons, she reduced her fees. She loved children and really did want them to have a musical background, so she sacrificed her livelihood to make her services affordable. Whereas she had charged ten dollars a month before the war, she now gave four lessons a month for seven dollars.

Besides the ache for Ken and worry about his safety, I was reminded of the war at least three times a day—at meals. We could buy sugar, cooking fats, eggs, and meats only on certain days and even then they were not always available. Since I was not a big sweet eater, the limitations were easier on me than on others. Once I was able to get a ten-pound bag of sugar and it lasted us for months. For meat we often ate canned tuna or salmon or that horrible substitute, Spam™. I hated the taste, but it did add a meaty flavor to a soup or stew. Sometimes a friend would luck into a ham and would call special friends and offer them a few slices. Fresh vegetables were so expensive we didn't eat too many. Lots of families cultivated their own Victory

Gardens to grow their own fresh produce. I talked the owners of our apartment into converting their rose bed into a garden. I grew lettuce, mustard greens, and radishes and had enough to share with the owners for several weeks.

I was indecisive about listening to the war news on the radio. I wanted to know what the prospects for the end of the war were, and at the same time I was afraid I would hear Ken's Squadron 84 mentioned. I knew he was based in London, where the medical units were housed and wounded soldiers were brought for treatment.

After he had been in Europe about two months, I was awakened about two o'clock one morning by the ringing of the phone. I stared at the instrument while it shrieked for me to pick it up. Finally my sleepy brain reminded me that bad news came via telegram, and I bravely picked up the receiver.

"Is this Mrs. Ken Greer?" a male voice inquired.

"Who is this?" I countered.

"I'm a reporter for The Houston Post," the caller explained, "and I have a message for Mrs. Greer."

"I'm Mrs. Greer," I said, kneading the sheets in anxiety.

"Oh, good," he sighed with relief. "I apologize for calling this time of the night, but I wanted to talk to you before you saw the morning paper."

My breath became shallow and I could not speak.

"I am in London and have just talked to your husband," he went on. "There will be a picture in the paper showing his plane shot to pieces. However, I have interviewed him and he is OK. In fact, they didn't lose anyone. I just wanted you to know."

I could not go back to sleep and was awake when the paper boy tossed the paper onto the front sidewalk. I threw on a robe and ran down to retrieve our copy. There on the front page was a photograph of a mangled airplane with four smiling men standing jauntily beside the wreckage. I immediately recognized Ken! I pressed the paper to my chest and laughed out loud.

The article quoted his commander, Tom Brode, as saying, "We're the most fortunate people who ever flew a B17. No one was lost, and we landed safely."

I cut out the picture and kept it beside my bed. Every night I would look into those laughing eyes and imagine he could see me.

Then one day in May 1942 I was getting dressed when the doorbell rang. Mother went to answer it. After I finished my shower, many minutes passed and Mother did not come back upstairs. I was running late, so I finally called down, "Who was that?"

"I'll be up in a minute," she replied. But she did not come.

I finished arranging my hair and grabbed my purse and ran down the stairs. Mother stood in the kitchen by the sink, looking numbly toward the stairs. "What do you have in your hand?" I demanded.

She did not answer and thrust the paper defiantly behind her back. I stomped over and grabbed it from her hand. I staggered when I noticed the three stars in the corner of a yellow telegram. I knew that a telegram from the armed services with one star meant the soldier had been killed; two stars meant "presumed dead," and three stars meant "missing in action." The text confirmed my fears. Ken's plane had been shot down over Germany, and no bodies had been recovered.

"They shouldn't notify you until they are sure!" Mother exploded. That's when I realized that I had dropped the telegram and she had picked it up from the floor and read it. "They shouldn't put you through this until they know for sure!" Her face was red and she was grinding her teeth.

I looked through her and tuned out her shouting. I walked to the telephone and called the bank. "I won't be in today," I told the receptionist. "I just got word that Ken is missing in action."

Just then I remembered Ann, Ken's sister, who was visiting me. She had heard the clamor and had grabbed her robe and was descending the stairs when she heard me tell the receptionist the news.

"Oh, no!" she cried. We fell into each other's arms and sobbed. Finally I let her go and said, "I've got to tell Mom. I don't want anyone but me to tell her."

Ann agreed and called her older brother, Lee, to meet us at the train station in Seaton in two days. In the meantime word spread around the bank about my terrible news. Two coworkers arrived at our house within a short time and spent the day with me. They knew of my strained relationship with Mother and felt they could help me most by being a buffer between us.

Lee was waiting when we stepped onto the portable step the train porter placed for the departing passengers and drove us straight to his mother's house. Mom was cooking when we walked into the house. The measuring cup she was holding slipped from her hands and clattered to the floor, and the color drained from her face when she saw me. "What's happened to Ken?" she cried.

There was no point in trying to soften the blow for her. As a mother, she knew instinctively the fate of her beloved son. I stayed a few days in Illinois, being comforted by Ken's family, but finally had to return to Houston and my life —whatever it would be.

I found Mother just as bitter when I returned as when she first saw the telegram. "He should never have tried to enlist in the first place!" she complained. "Some men still haven't been called up. Maybe he'd still be here if he hadn't been so pig-headed."

"Stop!" I screamed. "He's gone, and you are just making it worse! Never mention his name to me again." I ran into my bedroom and slammed the door, wishing I could bar the angry woman from my life forever. Not only had I lost my beloved husband, I had also lost the barrier between me and Mother's demands. She quickly resumed her position on the throne and did not step down until death took it away from her. I was too tired to fight anymore. Friends soon learned not to mention Ken in Mother's presence because she would launch into a tirade about how stupid he was to have tried to enlist.

The captain of the squadron flying in front of Ken's that fateful day turned out to be a friend of a neighbor of mine. After learning of the connection, he got in touch with me. While I appreciated the glimpses he gave me into Ken's life as a soldier, I wish he had not told me one piece of information. The mission Ken was on was his fifty-second mission. Two days later he would have been coming home on temporary leave that was granted after fifty-two successful missions. The timing was the hardest part of his death to accept. He was so close to returning and yet it was not to be.

The captain also told me what had happened the day Ken died. Again his report raised more questions than it answered. Two squadrons were returning from bombing Kiel and Wilmshaven, ports in Germany through which most supplies for the German army passed. Destroying the ports seriously crippled the German advance. This action was part of the beginning of the end of World War II. I clung to that information proudly.

The captain began, "My squadron was flying in front of Ken's. We were flying through billowy clouds that were flashing big bolts of lightning. I split my squadron to fly around the clouds and thought Brode, Ken's commander, was doing the same. However, they never came out of the clouds. Eleven planes just disappeared and were never found. We assume they were burned up by the lightning. None of the men on board was ever heard from."

He shook his head. "I'll never understand why Brode didn't direct them around those thunderclouds." He said that when his squadron landed, he realized that enough time had passed for the other squadron to be landing also. When no other planes appeared, he gave an alert and other planes were sent to look for them. No planes, no debris, no bodies were found.

The revelation just made it harder for me "God, why did it have to end this way? Why didn't Brode react to the lightning differently? Why couldn't Ken have completed just one more flight and come home to me? He would have been home for two weeks and the war would have been over. Another twenty minutes and he would be alive today!! Why, Lord?" I asked the questions hundreds of times, and the answer was always the same. There were thousands of other families suffering losses as piercing as mine. I had not been singled out. Such was the legacy of war. God was my strength in dealing with the loss, not the cause of it.

Over the next weeks I continued working and saw our mutual friends from time to time, especially the wives of the men in our wedding. Gradually, though, my single status became awkward and the married couples invited me to join them less and less. I began developing a new circle of friends at church. I also became active in the American Institute of Banking, a national organization headquartered in New York and operated under the jurisdiction of the American Bankers Association.

People were more than kind about my loss. The governor of South Dakota who had been such a fan of Ken came to visit me in Houston shortly after I notified her of his being missing. We kept up a warm correspondence even after she retired from her position. Several years later I had a letter from her sister, informing me that she had died from complications of pneumonia. The sister said the ex-governor had mentioned how much she looked forward to visiting me as a "civilian."

After Ken was killed, the Martin-Seymour Company held a banquet to announce its findings and its production of the climatized paint. Ken had been within eight months of completing his five-year paint experiment with Martin-Senour when he joined the Army. A man came from Lincoln, Nebraska, to finish his part of the work. I was touched that they invited me to join them in commemoration of Ken's contribution to the decision.

People ask me all the time how I coped. What else could I do? I held on to the slight hope that Ken would be found alive. Even when the government sent me a telegram fourteen months after he disappeared saying that Ken's body had washed ashore in Holland and he was being buried in a new American cemetery in Belgium, I did not give up hope. Love is like that. It never gives up.

The telegram promised to send me a grave number after the ceremony in case I wanted to visit someday. This time my grief turned to anger, and I wrote a passionate letter to the War Department. How did they know the body was Ken, I asked. In all that time—fourteen months—the body as well as any dog tags would have deteriorated. Why did they keep torturing me with reminders?

I never received a reply. And I never made it to Belgium although Ken's sister-in-law, Aggie, did visit the plot.

Another fourteen months passed, and I heard from the government again. This time they sent me a flag and his pen, billfold, and some letters that he had left in his barracks before the flight. Where they had been for more than two years, I'll never know. I could never bring myself to open the letters. The flag, according to a note in the box, was to be flown in honor of Ken. It was still too painful to accept that he was gone, so I gave the flag to Ken's brother, Boyd. He flew it a few times, but the memories it evoked were too hurtful and he packed it away.

Even if I had been able to suppress the memories of Ken and our life together, life would not let me forget my status. In fact, as the wife of a soldier missing in action, I had no status. I was not a widow nor a wife in the eyes of the law. In 1944 I decided to try to adopt a child. A judge I consulted discouraged me because the law was not clear on how such adoption proceedings should be decided. He said to continue with adoption outside the law could lead to major legal hassles and perhaps heartbreak years later. And so I suffered the heartbreak alone rather than risk putting a child through the trauma of losing its family.

I could not settle Ken's estate because if he were not dead, there was no estate to settle. I could not even buy property. When Mother and I decided to invest in a house in Houston in 1949, she had to purchase it in her name. Later she deeded it to me since I was the major investor. While I was not alone in my no-man's land, the government did very little to assist the families of MIAs, and the law taunted us again and again.

Even forty-two years after receiving the telegram with three stars I was confronted with a new reminder of Ken's absence. I was visiting St. Paul's Cathedral in London in 1985. In the back of the chapel area stands a beautiful altar dedicated by the Queen Mother to all Americans who gave their lives defending England during World War II. Silver vases on either end of the altar hold lovely flowers at all times. Two kneelers wait at the foot of the altar for anyone who desires to kneel and pray. In recessed areas of the marble altar tiny chips of mirrors flicker to create a stunning light play, like the shadows of memories of the men and women listed alphabetically in the handsome book locked in a Baccarat crystal case in the center of the altar area. The names are artistically written in script in India ink along with the date of death or their missing in action, their rank, and the city they were from. Each day a page of the main book is turned so another listing of names is displayed in the case.

The monk who lived at the cathedral kept a copy of the book in his quarters for the public to view. He patiently showed me Ken's name, the last of the G's. I stared at the name as if I could will him to appear off the page. Then I gasped. The monk, who had no doubt witnessed many grief-stricken family members, lifted his hands to be ready to help if I were to faint. I just pointed at the page and shook my head.

He looked puzzled and said, "Madam?"

"Look!" I stammered. "He's on the missing-in-action page, not on the page of the dead. The U.S. government says he is dead."

The monk shifted his weight uncomfortably. "I don't know what to say, madam. Perhaps you could ask the tour guide."

I immediately turned to my tour guide, who was a senior warden of the English Parliament when it was in session. In between sessions he gave tours of the city. I explained the discrepancy in information between the two governments' findings. He said, "All I can tell you is that our government engaged quite a task force of people to research the missing and lost military, and I feel their findings are accurate."

He gave me permission to photograph the page with Ken's name listed as missing in action. I sent it to our War Department, who never answered. Finally I engaged the support of my congressman, Albert Thomas, to try to get some response. He was told in essence to drop the matter, that our government would not accept the English government's conclusion.

For many years I did not give up hope that Ken would return, but finally the day came when I had to let him go. Today the pain is still vivid and my tears come just as readily as they did just after learning of his fate. I will never quit missing him and those precious moments of such divine happiness. He tried and succeeded in making up to me all I had missed as a young girl and a young lady, and that supportive freedom he gave me was one of my life's greatest gifts. He was a jewel and adored by both men and women. I am thankful to God for him and the glorious family I have as a result of our marriage. I am still in touch with the whole family, and they love me as much as when Ken was here. I am so blessed to have such a precious and loving family. I will ever be Mrs. Kenneth Sidney Greer in my heart. Ken will ever be my husband and my sweetheart.

Ken's family included me in all their family celebrations through the years, and I loved being part of the clan. Mom used to tease me about all the spices I cook with. When Ken and I visited her home once, I complained to him in private, "The food had no taste! Is that the way she always cooks?"

Later in that visit Ken and I offered to cook dinner for Mom, Ken's brother, Boze, his wife, Tommy, and his sister, Ann. We cooked a roast seasoned with Worcestershire sauce and soy sauce, herbed new potatoes, string beans seasoned with bacon and buttered almonds, and cornbread, which we knew would be a new taste for the family. We dressed up the routine iceberg lettuce salad with radishes, celery, and romaine lettuce. Ken had asked a friend who lived nearby to make one of his famous raisin pies for dessert.

As everyone took his place at the table, Ken and I winked at each other, anticipating the compliments on the subtle flavors of each dish. After saying a blessing, Ken served the roast while everyone passed the other dishes and helped themselves. I thought the portions placed on each plate were rather meager, but I didn't really think about the reason for the hesitancy.

Mom cut into her roast while Boze delved into his green beans. Ann stabbed a bite of potato and popped it into her mouth. Ken and I watched their faces for approval. Instead we saw deliberate swallowing and grimacing. Boze cleared his throat while Tommy reached for her water glass and took a long drink. Mom patted her mouth daintily with her napkin and smiled weakly at Ken.

Ken and I exchanged glances, not understanding the problem. We continued eating the succulent meat and hearty potatoes. I buttered a tall piece of cornbread and felt uncomfortable in the silence. "So . . . how was work today, Boze?" I asked in an attempt to dispel whatever damper had fallen on our meal.

"Oh, fine," he said, "just fine." He looked helplessly at his wife.

"Would anyone like some salt?" I tried again, puzzled.

They just shook their heads and sat. I realized that Ken and I were the only ones eating. "Is there something wrong?" I asked.

"No!" Mom responded. She picked up her fork, studied the food on her plate, and sighed heavily. "Jackie . . . Ken . . . I don't want to hurt your feelings, but we just don't eat this way. I mean . . . we just can't eat this with all the spices. We appreciate all your effort to fix it, but we just can't eat it."

Ken's face clouded over, but I laughed. "Well, I'm sorry. This is good Texas eatin'! That'll just mean more for Ken and me."

Mom nodded, pushed back her chair, and went into the kitchen. In a few minutes she returned with toast and scrambled eggs, minus salt and pepper, for the other three. They valiantly tested the raisin pie later and managed to eat an entire piece each.

In our bedroom that evening Ken vented his anger. I thought the incident was funny. "Just think what they are missing," I said, trying to soothe Ken's hurt feelings. "Do they ever use spices?" I asked incredulously.

"Not only never, but never!" he barked.

We never cooked for them again.

Before Ken died, Mom came to Houston for a visit and we took her to our favorite Mexican restaurant. Since she didn't know what to order, Ken ordered for her. When the chili was set in front of her and she tasted the first spoonful, she declared, "This is delicious! I wonder what is in it." Ken and I tried not to choke on our contained laughter. On one trip to her house she had announced that she would be cooking "chili" for supper. I was elated because it meant that we would have some seasoned food. I had watched with dismay as she browned cubed stew meat, no salt, no pepper, no garlic, a quarter of a small onion chopped, a scant pinch of chili powder, and a few tablespoons of water. When she finished her cup of real Tex-Mex chili, she looked at me and winked, "You must have laughed at my chili many times."

I smiled and nodded. She well understood the difference the spices could make and always wanted to eat Mexican food when she came to visit even after Ken was gone. She always ate whatever was put before her at the Mexican restaurant and loved it—even though the dishes were generously seasoned.

This very special family is so bonded and caring. They meet as a family for all birthdays, anniversaries, and holidays. In 1997 Aggie and I drove to Ohio for a week-long reunion. Even after seventy-two years they still include me in all family planning and keep in touch with me just as though it were yesterday I came into the family. Dad's prediction came true. I do have a vast extended family and cherish each one. God never leaves us alone, and He has blessed me with an unbelievably wonderful family.

seventeen

chapter 17

HOME AT LAST

For several years after Ken's disappearance, I struggled to live with the void in my life. I threw myself into my work and community activities—anything to keep my mind occupied, keep me away from home, and move toward my future, whatever that would be. I continued my courses with the American Institute of Banking and was elected to a two-year term on the board of the organization. I began meeting bankers from all over the city and nation.

By 1942 I had been at T. J. Bettes Company for six good years. I began to yearn to return to banking and that year accepted a position at First National Bank, the largest bank in Houston and the third largest in the state. I was hired as supervisor of the Analysis Department. Four wonderful ladies worked with me, and we became a closely knit little family.

Soon after I began working at First National Bank, all employees received a memo stating that our chairman of the board, a sixty-year banking veteran, was retiring and the current president would step up as chair. That meant a new president would be arriving. Not long afterwards, everyone gathered in the bank lobby after hours to meet Perkins P. Butler, our new president, who was from Beaumont. I was visiting with coworkers until the meeting was called to order. As soon as Mr. Butler was introduced, I gasped and tears welled in my eyes. With his tall frame, ruddy complexion, curly black hair, and sparkling blue eyes, he was the exact image of my father. Years later I showed him a picture of Dad and told about my first reaction to seeing him. He reached over and squeezed my hand and gave me a smile that was Dad all over again.

I did compose myself enough to hear the announcement of several new senior bank officers. On the way back to my desk, I realized that all the new officers were men. "I wonder when a woman will be allowed to enter that inner sanctum," I said to myself. Entering my office, I chuckled at the absurdity of the possibility and went straight to work.

Just a year later I was thrilled to be named assistant cashier of the bank, the title used for a junior executive. I was the first woman in a major bank in Texas as well as in the nation to be named an officer.

The evening I found out, I practically skipped the thirty-five blocks to our apartment. At the door I remembered that Mother was teaching a piano lesson and would be unhappy to be disturbed. I quietly let myself in. Even then, she turned from the needlepoint chair beside the piano bench to frown at me. I suppressed a giggle and put my finger against my lips. After the student left, she came into the kitchen where I was cooking hamburgers and baked beans for supper and didn't even say, "Hello."

Putting down the spoon I was using to stir the potato salad, I whirled around with a big smile on my face. "Guess what happened to me today!" I shouted.

She looked at me under raised eyebrows and silently opened the silverware drawer to get the knives and forks.

"I was named an assistant cashier!" I crowed. "It's a junior executive position—and I'm the first woman in the country to be named an active officer of a major bank!"

Mother walked into the dining room and began setting the table. Over her shoulder she called back with disdain, "Why didn't they make you a senior executive? You've had several years in banking."

A torrent of angry, hurtful words rushed into my throat, and tears stung my eyes. I jerked off my apron, threw it on the floor, and slammed the door to my bedroom. Falling across my bed, the pent-up words gushed out as huge sobs. "Why, God!" I cried. "Why does she treat me like this?"

Exhausted, I soon fell asleep. The house was dark when I awoke. Mother had gone to bed, thank goodness. I sat heavily on the living room sofa and allowed myself to dream. If Ken had been here, I thought sadly, he would have picked me up, swirled me around the house, and insisted we go out for dinner—to Ye Olde College Inn, not just our favorite Mexican food place. Then he would have insisted that we call Mom when we got home. I would have protested, "No! Long-distance calls are just for emergencies."

"This is an emergency," he would have teased. "I have a famous woman living in my house and I'm afraid she'll get so famous I won't know how to talk to her!"

Just imagining the scene made me feel better. When I finally went to bed that night, I lay awake a very long time, reliving days and nights with Ken. "God, help me learn to live with this woman who is my mother," I prayed. "I know you do not give us more than we can handle. I wish you did not think I was so strong. I can't take much more."

I balled up my pillow and hugged it, trying to feel Ken's strong arms around me. God's promise that He was father to the fatherless gently enveloped me and brought me comfort. Mother never mentioned the promotion again.

Two years later, in 1945, the bank president invited me to attend a seminar at the Humble Oil Conference Center to learn about a new area of business that both large and small companies were endorsing all over the country. The new effort was known as an industrial relations department. This department selected staff for the entire organization, interviewed candidates, researched their background, handled benefits, set salary ranges, obtained information for promotions, handled release of personnel, and in general was the focal point for all matters pertaining to people, their benefits, and policy concerns. The term "industrial relations" was kept until sometime in the 1950s when universities began offering courses in personnel management and personnel administration, and industrial relations departments were renamed personnel departments. Today they are known as human resource departments.

I was to report my findings the next day to our new president. Knowing that getting an appointment with Mr. Butler through Miss Jessie, his secretary and bodyguard, would be a hassle because of my lack of clout, I decided to wait until the afternoon when she always went to the Credit Department to look up information for the Loan Committee on the larger loans to be made by the bank.

When I saw that she was out of range of the telephone, I dialed Mr. Butler. "This is Jackie Greer," I began, "and I wondered if I might come down in a few minutes to visit with you about the personnel department seminar."

"Why, certainly," he responded. "Come right on down. I'll be happy to hear what you learned."

I had summarized the many advantages such a department would bring to the bank and was preparing to launch into my personal agenda when I felt a tap on my shoulder. Startled, I spun around to face Miss Jessie's frown. Without an apology for interrupting our conversation, she demanded, "Just how did you get up here without going through me?"

Before I could answer, Mr. Butler stood up and raised his eyebrows. "Miss Jessie," he said quietly, "Jackie simply called me to ask if she might come down to discuss a meeting I sent her to—which I guess I forgot to mention to you—and I welcomed her down."

Miss Jessie nodded curtly. "I see," she said. With a steely look at me, she retreated to her desk. Our relationship was icy for months after that.

"Please, Jackie," Mr. Butler encouraged me, "continue with your report. This is very interesting."

"Thank you," I went on as if there had been no interruption. "As I have explained, a department such as this has great advantages for the bank. And I'm sure you realize that a department of this magnitude would require an officer to head it."

Mr. Butler pursed his lips and nodded. Then he looked down to review some papers I had handed him from the seminar.

"A department of this kind needs official leadership. I am curious to know why there are no women senior bank officers . . . ," I paused as his head snapped up, "for I want to be the first woman to be named a senior executive—as head of this new department."

Mr. Butler blinked and frowned as if he had not heard me correctly. Finally, he cleared his throat and said limply, "Well, Jackie, banks just don't have senior officers who are women."

I raised my eyebrows and fired my ammunition, "So banking is a gender business and not a business for people who also have brains?"

To his credit, he did not answer me then. Years later he told me he could feel the blood rush into his cheeks because that was not at all what he had expected to hear from me.

"Thank you, Jackie, for your observations and your thorough report. If I have any more questions, I'll let you know." He stood and I realized that I was dismissed. I reached out my hand to shake his. "I appreciate the opportunity to attend the seminar. I learned a lot which I think will benefit the bank. Please let me know how else you would like me to apply what I learned."

"I will," he smiled.

Six months later, in 1946, another memo went out to all First National Bank employees announcing the formation of a Personnel Department to be headed by a newly appointed assistant vice president and department director, Jackie Greer. This promotion meant I was now a senior executive and the first woman to be named personnel director of a major American bank.

Unfortunately my promotion was not accepted kindly by older women who had worked at the bank for decades. Also it was obvious that the other officers, all men, were concerned how I would fit into their comfortable "boys' club." I couldn't blame them. Mine was a title and a position no other woman in banking in the country had ever held. Not only was I the first woman bank officer, but our personnel department would be the first in any bank in Texas.

Knowing the trepidation of my fellow officers, I asked Mr. Butler if I could speak at my first meeting with all the officers of First National Bank. After the old and new business had been tended to, Mr. Butler called on me. "Jackie has asked to say a few words. I am pleased to welcome you to our board meeting as a new officer," he smiled, turning towards me and bowing slightly.

I rose and faced the stern looks of the male, and generally much older, officers I would be working with. Some held their fountain pens poised like daggers. Others sat back in their leather chairs with their arms crossed as if daring me to try to be accepted. After taking a deep breath, I said, "Gentlemen, I realize that having a woman on the Executive Committee is a new beginning. I want to assure you that, just like you, I have a job to do and it is going to be done well. My purposes in life parallel yours. If I can help in any way at any time, I am as close as walking up the stairs or calling me on the telephone. I look forward to working with you, and I hope you will reciprocate."

I sat down to give my wobbly knees a rest. The men visibly relaxed. One began to applaud and quickly all joined in, including Mr. Butler. I smiled and nodded my appreciation. From that day forward I was treated as I should have been, and life moved on smoothly and productively—at work, that is.

Ever since Mother had moved in with me after Ken left for the Army, she had badgered me about buying a house. She had never owned one. She and Dad and I had lived in Grandmother's house. After Dad died, she could not afford one and continued to live with her mother. Now she felt I was on the road to a successful career and could fulfill this dream of hers. For years I told her I could not afford to own a house. Finally by 1949, even though the economy was shaky, I agreed to investigate the market.

After work and my extracurricular activities, I did not have time to look at houses. I told Mother to bring me some listings and I would try to check them out. I suggested some troubled homes that I thought I could afford. Mother did not like any of them.

In frustration I consulted with the Real Estate Department at First National Bank and was surprised to learn that a number of houses were available in my price range. I would go out on my lunch breaks when I did not have banking business and look at houses. Still Mother found something wrong with every one. Mostly she insisted that we live close to Willois and Lee Huebel. Willois's parents had been neighbors and close friends in Palestine. Finally I gave up and told Mother to search and find her dream home. She kept finding ones that were out of my reach.

A realtor seemed the only answer. The man we selected informed me that taxes were lower in a section of town known as West University than in the city itself. The police and fire departments were very responsive, and the neighborhood was extremely well monitored and safe. One day Willois called Mother to come look at a house that was being built just behind their house in West University.

Mother went out to look and called me. "Jackie, when can you come look at this one? It's really very nice—a big corner lot."

"I'll call the builder and see when I can meet with him and discuss the price," I promised wearily.

Later that afternoon I met with the builder, who also owned the 75-by-125-foot lot at 3784 Arnold. After looking at the plans and asking about some changes we would need, I made an offer which he accepted. Several weeks later I transferred my estate to Mother, who bought the house, because I was still having trouble clearing Ken's estate. Four or five years later Mother transferred the house back to me.

When construction started, I showed up at the site with an engineer the bank often used for inspections. I wanted to be sure the foundation was poured according to the contractor's specifications and also met the building code requirements for the City of West University. More than once the engineer questioned the workmen about the amount of rebar on the prints versus the amount they were using and about the depth of the concrete. He stayed until he was satisfied with the work. I stayed until the foundation was completed and the engineer returned for another check.

When work resumed on the house in two days, I dropped by to see the studs placed for the walls. Somehow they did not look right to me, so I retrieved a tape measure from my car and measured the distance between them. Then I interrupted the supervisor and asked to see the plans. "Excuse me," I commented after studying the plans a few minutes. "These call for sixteen inches between studs. I measured twenty-four inches over there," pointing to the north wall.

He feigned surprise and followed me to the wall in question. I handed him the tape measure and watched as he measured the space. "Hmm," he said noncommittally. "I guess we made a mistake."

"I guess you did," I said with irritation. "And I guess you'll have to fix every . . . mistake."

"Er . . . yes, ma'am," he saluted me and turned to go.

"One more question," I called. He halted and turned back to face me. His jaw was tight and he did not speak. He merely looked at me.

"These knotholes . . . ," I began. "There are knotholes falling out of almost every stud. What grade of lumber are you using?" I bent and picked up a circle of wood that had fallen out of the stud beside me. I had watched Dad in his workroom enough to know a little about building material.

"What we always use," he growled, kicking the stud nearest him.

"Please show me proof that the grade is what is called for in my contract," I persisted.

He swore under his breath and led me to the stack of lumber from which the workmen were pulling the studs. The number did not match my contract.

"I guess that's something else you'll have to . . . correct," I commented, putting my hands on my hips for emphasis.

"Well, I'll have to call the contractor," he countered, pulling himself up to his full height, "and that could delay construction for a few days."

"So be it," I shrugged. "I have paid for a certain quality house and I intend to have it."

He glared at me a moment, then raised his voice as he called his crew chief over. I could hear their animated voices. Looks were thrown my way as the men argued. I just stood still. The crew chief finally approached each workman, and within a few minutes all work had ceased and the workmen had left the premises. "You can call me at the bank after you have talked to the builder," I said and set off for the three-mile walk to the office.

Once at the bank I marched straight to the president's office and was granted a few minutes to speak to him. I stepped up onto the raised marble-floored platform of the Senior Officer Banking Section and walked through the walnut and marble fence that separated these officers from the public areas of the bank. Mr. Butler greeted me warmly.

"Mr. Butler, I am sorry to interrupt you, but I have an unusual request to make," I said, still breathing rapidly from the long walk from the building site.

"Of course, Jackie," he replied with concern, pushing a stack of papers away from him so he would not be distracted by it. "Sit down and catch your breath."

"No, thank you," I answered, waving my hand in protest. "I don't have time to sit. You know the house I am having built?"

He nodded as he folded his hands on his desk.

"Well, I've been out at the site just two days and already I've found shoddy workmanship. I'm afraid the builder will cut more corners unless I am there to check his every move. I think he is trying to take advantage of the fact that I'm a woman."

"That's too bad," Mr. Butler commented, taking out a handkerchief and wiping his brow.

"What I am asking is whether you will allow me to adjust my hours so that I can be at the site during construction. I know that will take several months and that it will be quite an imposition." I watched Mr. Butler's face for a reaction. He merely knit his brows together and listened.

"I will come into work before the bank opens and work a few hours, then I would like to be allowed to leave midmorning and return around 4:30. I'll work as late at night as necessary and on the weekends to finish my work. If something comes up during the day that I need to be here for, I'll stay that day. Will you please consider my request?" The telephone rang, but he did not pick it up. He swiveled his chair to look down the line of nine executive desks in this ornately decorated area. I hardly dared to breathe.

In a few moments he turned back to look at me. "Jackie," he said, "you have been a valuable employee for the bank. You always follow through on your commitments and handle your work in a professional manner. I don't see why we can't try this schedule you have proposed and see how it works. I understand that you want to protect your investment."

I smiled and bit my lower lip. "Thank you, Mr. Butler! I won't let you down."

The builder called me later that day and tried to dissuade me from being on the premises during construction. "I've talked with the superintendent and there won't be any more mistakes," he told me. "You can count on that."

I tightened my grip on the telephone receiver and said firmly, "That's right. There will not be any more mistakes. I will be around to see to that."

Every day for the next ten months I sat on the job and compared the materials being used with the specifications. I checked lumber, nails, brick, wiring, piping—and much of what was brought to the site had to be exchanged to meet the contractual provisions. To say I was a lady with many names is an understatement—and none of those names came from a Sunday school book! I don't know who resented my presence more—the superintendent or the workmen. All made it clear that I was not welcome, but that did not deter me. This was my house, probably the only one I would ever own, and I intended it to be what I had agreed to pay for.

After a few months of my supervision, the builder showed up at the lot and confronted me as I sat in my lawn chair reading over bank papers. "You are costing me money!" he complained, making a fist and shaking it at me. "I can't make any money with you constantly switching out material. And the men are complaining about your being here every day. They don't like to be watched so closely by an outsider."

I looked up at the builder and replied calmly, "It seems to me that it is your fault and not mine that you are not making any money on this house. If you had not put in imperfect lumber, tried to pawn chipped and broken bricks off on me, used wiring that was not up to code, and substituted zinc pipes for the copper, I would not have had to upset your days."

His face clouded over and he grumbled, "No one else sits around on the job site the whole time I'm building. It's . . . it's just not right." He slapped the blueprints he held in the other hand.

"You made a commitment which I found you were not keeping. Many others would never have thought you would cheat them, so they have not inspected your work. I just happened to come by to see my house growing and found you were cheating me. You gave me no alternative but to stay in the job with you."

He jutted his chin in the air and turned away without a word. I believe if I had been a man, he would have swung at me.

One of our new neighbors was a contractor. He came over to visit with me one morning about halfway through the project and laughed, "I am glad there were not many like you when I was in the business for I would have starved to death. But let me assure you there is nobody in this city who has a house that is as solid as yours. I applaud you for being able to be such a good supervisor."

I just shrugged because the builder had given me no choice. I was relieved, however, to hear that the house was being well built after all.

An old adage says you have to build three homes before you build the perfect one. Believe me, there will never be a perfect home for me after the one I labored over in 1949. That house has not one piece of lumber with a knothole, not a brick that is not absolutely perfect, the best of copper plumbing, and the latest electrical wiring. That is what my contract called for, and I settled for no less. If I ever wanted to build another house, my work crew would be conspicuous by their absence. They had never had a lady on the premises to inspect their every move, and I am sure they prayed that history would never be repeated.

The house was a semi-red brick with three bedrooms, a bath and a half, a large living room and separate dining room, a reasonably sized kitchen, a long hall off the bedrooms, and a delightful room that Mother used as a music room. That room overlooked our backyard, which was picture perfect with its hedges, roses, tomato plants, and azaleas. The back fence was lined with pyracantha. The house had picture windows on all sides. These were pretty to look at but made it necessary for us to keep the house in perfect order for it was like living in a fish bowl. Everybody passing by on either street could see in because Mother refused to have drapes. She said they defeated the purpose of the picture windows.

Over the ten months the house was being built, we were blessed with virtually no rain. As the completion date neared, I told Mother we needed to have a talk about the use of the house. She grimaced but did listen like a lady through most of the discussion.

We sat at the dining room table in our apartment, and I pulled some sheets of paper out of a folder and pushed them in front of her. "I've figured out our expenses for the house and how we will divide them," I began.

Pointing to the appropriate columns as I talked, I told her, "I will pay the mortgage, taxes, insurance, and utility bills. Your share will be food and paying the maid and yardman."

"Why should I have to pay the yardman?" she demanded.

"Because you don't like to do yard work," I replied. "Someone has to do it and if you are not willing to pay the yardman, there will be no flower beds and no garden, and the neighbors will turn us in to the city for lack of lawn care. I am paying all I can just to get us into the house. You have an income also and will have to help out."

She glared at me but did not argue. If she was going to have her house, then she would have to pay some of the upkeep.

"Do you agree with this breakdown?" I pressed.

"If you insist," she said grudgingly.

"Well, now is the time to protest, if you plan to," I countered. "After tonight this discussion is over and will not be repeated. Is that clear?"

She folded her arms across her chest and sat back in her chair. "It's clear," she growled.

"Good," I smiled and gathered up the papers. "Also I want it understood that this house is mainly yours, but I want to use it when I need to. I plan to entertain a lot, and you are not to protest or interfere with my guests. Do you agree?"

She stiffened and mumbled, "Yes."

A few days before we were to close on the house, I sat on the back steps one afternoon and wept until I could not, for my precious Ken would have adored this house. It lent itself to being beautifully decorated, and the yard offered every opportunity for being a winner of any neighborhood contest. With my arms around my knees, I tried to envision the things he would have liked to see in the yard and decided I would plant them—for him if Mother would keep her promise to pay for a yardman. She did, and I had a picture-book yard at all times. The back glowed with hybrid roses of the rarest kinds, gorgeous hedges, and seasonal azaleas. Two Sago palm trees and variegated pittosporum surrounded the entire house in the front. Mother planted lettuce seeds of several varieties as a border to all the flowerbeds so we had beauty as well as a practical food item, which we gladly shared with our wonderful neighbors.

Along the side of the house grew twelve varieties of hybrid tomatoes, some yellow and some bright red. They were plentiful and succulent, and some weighed more than a pound. These large vegetables were firm and tasty and made a great fried dish. Dinner guests raved over them.

People would stop to admire the tomatoes, and even more would drive slowly by to be refreshed by the fifteen varieties of roses growing on the other side of the chain-link fence. What a mass of beauty they made because they all bloomed at the same time. I spared no expense in having the special beds dug. I saw that the gardener followed the watering and feeding instructions carefully and often tended to the plants myself. The care rewarded us every spring and fall and much of the summer. More than once a passerby stopped and asked if he could buy a stem because the stems were long and sturdy and the exotic fragrance carried from the fence to the sidewalk.

My care routine created quite a concern for my mobile audience. What I did was not the norm. Whereas most people in Houston pruned their roses on Valentines Day, about the twenty-eighth of September I cut the bushes to the height of my waist, dug little trenches around the base of each, then for three days watered in a rose fertilizer that had been highly recommended. In late November I doused the bushes with super phosphate and waited. The week before Christmas I had a giant collection of long-stem roses for my table and those of many friends.

The second September when I was pruning the roses, a well-dressed older man drove by, backed up, and even got out of his car. He ran toward me, flailing his arms and shouting, "Lady! Lady! Please cut that out! You are ruining perfectly beautiful roses!"

I paused with the clippers in my hand and answered patiently, "Sir, I really am a very experienced rose producer. When you drive by the week before Christmas, you will see the most gorgeous long-stem rosebuds you have ever seen that time of year. I realize what I am doing is a departure from what most people do around here, and I also know that it works. Please come back then and see for yourself."

He looked at me in utter disgust as he stomped away, muttering words I could not understand—and probably did not want to hear anyway.

The week before Christmas Houston had a rather warm trend and my rosebuds were bursting all over every bush. I was out spraying when the same man drove up, got out of his car, tipped his hat, and said with a sheepish smile, "Forgive me for my outburst some months ago. I wished your theory would fail so I would be proven right. You have won, and I would not believe what I am seeing if I were not standing right here."

Graciously I introduced myself and asked him if he would like a dozen stems to take home with him. Tears welled in his eyes, and he pulled his handkerchief from his back pocket and wiped his nose. He was grinning as he walked back to his car with a dozen perfect, long-stem red and peach roses. These beauties produced for about two weeks, and many friends had lovely roses, especially the red ones, in their homes for several days before and after Christmas. On the last day of February I cut them down to the ground, fed them on occasion, and then came the summer collection. Their colors were more pastel in the spring and more vibrant in the fall, and always lovely.

I made the disastrous mistake of letting Mother talk me out of central air conditioning in the tropical climate of Houston, Texas. Instead in our new house we had ceiling fans in all the rooms, a window air-conditioning unit in my bedroom, and two units in the dining room, which also helped cool the living room a little on Houston's famous muggy summer days. I never understood her reasons, but then what was new? I had to smile for on a couple of occasions when friends were visiting, she would note they seemed uncomfortably hot. With her best manners she would say to them, "I will be delighted to turn on the air conditioning if you will be more comfortable" Of course they wanted the air on, so she would go flip on the three units around the house. I also noted that when the guests left, the air was never turned off. I loved it that she was, in effect, acknowledging that she had been wrong to economize in that way.

We had no furniture to speak of and no money to buy any. I had a bedroom suite and dining room table and chairs. Mother had a bed, a couple of chairs, a dresser, and a baby grand piano. The rest of the furniture in the apartment belonged to the landlord. Ken and I had received beautiful tableware when we married. Mother and I decided we could survive with what we had and add things as the money came in.

Two weeks after we moved in, a friend came over and told us her family was being transferred to Mexico. "We will not be able to take any of our belongings," she lamented. "We would be honored if you two would come over and take anything you can use. I'd much prefer that it go to someone we know than to strangers."

Feeling like kids in a toy shop, Mother and I were delighted that almost all of the Harrises' furniture would fit beautifully into our new house. What a blessing their gift was for us! Before they moved, we gave a dinner party for them.

Since they were not moving right away, it was several weeks before the furniture was moved to our house. Before we received the furniture, I decided to invite some of my friends over for a housewarming dinner. It was now October and the nights were often cool. I felt I could serve soup, a salad, and pie quite easily even though we had no furniture, so I invited my good friends.The day before the party I was in the grocery store buying last-minute supplies and saw some of the checker boys carrying out some apple boxes. My mind started to spin."Ohoooo!" I thought."What a great idea it would be to get some of those boxes, cover them with pretty paper tablecloths, and seat my guests on the floor like the Orientals." So I asked for the boxes, packed them into the car, and headed for home.

A few months earlier I had finally purchased my first car: a two-year-old, four-door Chrysler Town Car, dark green with black leather upholstery. I loved the freedom it offered. I didn't have to coordinate my life with Mother's anymore.

Mother was away from home when I placed the boxes in a semicircle on the dining room carpet, covered them with the colorful tablecloths, and set the table with my best silver and crystal. Then I added a vase of my prize roses on each table. The room was festive indeed.

Mother did not see the room until the next day after I had gone to work. She called me at the bank and yelled,"What do you mean serving our guests on these ... these tacky boxes! You've been raised better than that!" Indeed my parents and grandparents felt that when company came to eat, you were insulting them if you did not serve a three-course meal and use your best china and linens.

I laughed,"Oh, so you don't approve?" I shifted the phone to my other ear so I could continue the project I was in the middle of."Mother, I really don't have time to talk now. Besides everyone has been invited and I fully intended to have the party."

I interrupted her sputtering with a reminder."I think you will remember our conversation about entertaining. We agreed that because I am paying most of the bills, you would never interfere when I was ready to entertain." I didn't have to finish my reprimand because she slammed the receiver into the cradle.

The day of the party we ate a silent breakfast as she pouted. Just before I got up to take my dishes to the kitchen, she announced,"I will not be home tonight when your guests arrive." She paused as if she expected some reaction from me. I just continued to stack my dishes."I would be too embarrassed to be a part of such a low-class party—or even to help with it."

"Well, Mother," I shrugged,"you have a choice. If that is your choice, who am I try to change your mind?"

She looked a bit disappointed that I did not beg her to attend.

When I arrived home that evening, Mother was not there. I hurried through the remaining preparations. I had done most of the cooking the night before and just had to heat the soup before the guests arrived.

I basked in the compliments about our house and was gratified when some of the men offered to help with chores around the house, even digging more flowerbeds if I decided I needed more. When everyone had arrived, I solicited help to transport the food to the improvised tables. Someone asked me, "Jackie, where is Mama Jack?"

I shrugged, "I have no idea."

"What do you mean you don't know?" she replied, pausing with two soup bowls in her hands.

When I told her exactly what had transpired, she burst out laughing. Soon everyone knew the story. "Since the car is gone, there is no telling where she is. I figure she'll come home eventually."

The party was a success, and guests went back for seconds and thirds of my vegetable soup. By the time I had cleaned up the kitchen, Mother was still not home. I just went on to bed, figuring she would show up eventually.

Mother was not home for breakfast the next morning, but I did not worry about her. I figured she was staying away to be sure I understood the extent of her disapproval of my entertaining style. At supper that night she was home and I gleefully told her about the wonderful time we had. "They ate all the food," I exclaimed, "so I guess they liked it."

Mother blotted her lips with her napkin and replied, "I cannot believe you had people sit on the floor and then served them soup, a salad, and a dessert. That is not a dinner menu and I am glad I was not here!"

"A number of them asked about you," I said, trying to soothe her. She just snorted.

"They were very disappointed you chose to be absent for our very first party." I helped myself to another serving of spaghetti.

She did not answer. Several nights later I overheard her talking to a friend on the telephone. She obviously did not know I could hear her. "I was so embarrassed," she complained. "I hope Jackie will refrain from further entertaining until we get some proper furniture." A few minutes later I heard her say, "Oh, I went to a neighbor's house to spend the night."

I had to go into the bathroom, shut the door, and turn on the faucet so she could not hear me laugh. Several years later I was telling this story to some friends. One of our neighbors spoke up with some hesitation. "Well, murder will out," she said, repeating an idiom of the area. The rest of the group looked at her in anticipation. She smiled mysteriously and continued, "After all these years you need to know that your mother and I went to Galveston for the night and had a marvelous time. Did you know your mother has a way of winning after all?"

What could I do but shrug and say, "Well, good for both of you." Several more times I hosted soup and salad parties. Each time Mother would disappear. Those who knew her tried to guess where she might be hiding this time, but it was a fruitless game.

One of our neighbors also disapproved of a decision I made about my house. The woman felt strongly that I should plant something in the grassy parts of our walkways on the side street to enhance the beauty of our lot. I politely disagreed and said I would prefer to leave the grassy borders for the time being. The neighbor frowned, crossed her arms across her chest, and stomped home.

Shortly after this conversation the bank sent me on a week-long business trip to New York. Mother drove to Palestine for a visit while I was gone. I returned at night and was so tired I thankfully fell into bed without even unpacking my suitcase. The next morning as I was fixing breakfast, I looked out the kitchen window and squeezed my eyes to be sure I was not dreaming. In the median area between the sidewalk and the side street stood four Chinese tallow trees. I dropped the spoon I was stirring oatmeal with and dashed out the door. I hated tallow trees because they dropped berries that stained sidewalks and were stark and ugly in the winter months. I caught a glimpse of a neighbor and called out to him. "Do you know anything about the tallow trees?" I demanded, hurrying across to face him.

He merely smiled and said, "I knew you would erupt when you saw the trees. Yes, you know who planted them. She was determined to have trees on the corner so took it into her hands to have them planted."

He shrugged when he saw my face cloud over and my jaw tighten. "So you have some trees. So what?"

Mother agreed with the neighbor. "What's the big deal?"

After a few days, good sense won out and I dropped plans to retaliate. The trees were still shedding their berries on the walkway in the year 2003.

Another incident did not pass so unobtrusively, however. One day I left the bank early to do some trimming in the yard, work in my rose garden, and rearrange the garage cabinets. As I opened the back door to enter the house, I smelled smoke. Dashing inside, I could see smoke in the music room where Mother was conducting a lesson and noticed the hall was filled with smoke. I did not check any further but ran to Mother to warn her. As I entered the music room, she put her finger against her lips and said to her student, "Run through that line a few more times, please."

She rose from her chair and came to stand beside me. Facing away from her student, she said quietly, "Jackie, the house is on fire, but I cannot leave my student right now. You may call the firemen to come see about the fire, but tell them not to dare sound that siren and upset my student."

In total disbelief I called the Fire Department and rushed to the heater closet, where the smoke seemed to be thickest. That appeared to be the center of the trouble, but because of the vast amount of smoke I could not determine the cause nor what to do. By this time the Fire Department had arrived QUIETLY as instructed. One of the men climbed into the attic and discovered the problem. I had stored some boards up there that I used to hold down the sheets I used to cover my plants when a freeze was predicted. Two of these boards had fallen over and landed against the pipes leading from the heating system. The pipes had gotten hot and caught the wood on fire. With the use of chemicals from hand extinguishers, the fire was out in seconds, there was no damage of any consequence, and Miss Retha never missed a beat in teaching her pupil. Fire or no, the teaching must go on.

The fire chief rang our doorbell later that evening and brought an inspector to be sure all was still well. After their inspection they sat in the living room writing a report. The inspector turned to my mother and said firmly, "Mrs. Matthews, if this ever happens again, I do not want to hear of you continuing your teaching. Get out of the house immediately and take the child or children with you. I hope this is clear."

Mother's stiff neck proved that she had understood the message. As she opened her mouth to explain her priorities, I left the room and went outside where I could giggle to myself. It had been a long time since I had seen the dictator lectured, and I have to admit I enjoyed the scene. I waited outside for the chief and his assistant. When they came out of the house alone, I reached out to shake their hands and express my appreciation. I chuckled, "Chief, you met your match tonight."

He replied, shaking his head, "And then some."

Thank goodness there were no more fires, and Mother's cooperation was never tested.

eighteen

chapter 18

END OF AN ERA

As I adjusted to life as a widow, I still sought out people for whom I could stand in as a mother, aunt, big sister, or friend. One such relationship brought me more joy than I could have imagined when it began. In 1949 some friends introduced me to a fine man named Bill. We enjoyed each other's company and dated for two years. Bill had raised his son, Bill Jr., by himself since infancy. Bill Jr. was then in junior high school. As I spent more time with Bill, my friendship with Bill Jr. also blossomed. One week Bill Jr. telephoned me. "Jackie," he began hesitantly, "can I ask you something?"

"Well, certainly, Bill," I answered. "You know you can talk to me about anything, anything at all. What's on your mind?"

"Well, there is a school dance this weekend and some of the guys were talking. We'd like to do something after the dance 'cause it ends early, but none of us has any money to take the girls out. Do you have any ideas?"

I smiled into the receiver, then answered seriously, "Yes, I have an idea. Why don't you and your friends and dates come to my house after the dance? I'll have Cokes and hot dogs, and you can play games. Now you'll have to go home by midnight. I'm sure the girls have to be in by then anyway. What do you say?"

"Oh, wow, Jackie! Do you mean that?" Bill Jr. shouted.

"Of course, Bill. Just let me know how many to expect."

"Way cool!" Bill exclaimed.

That Friday night a little after nine, a dozen youngsters burst into the house. Mother had wisely chosen to spend the night with a friend. I heated the hot dogs, laid out soft drinks and chips, and provided cards and board games. Mother and I did not own a phonograph, but soon the din of teenage banter filled the house with its own melody. About eleven everyone was engaged in a game or a conversation, except Bill Jr. He wandered into the kitchen and approached me despondently. "What's up?" I asked him.

"Jackie," he began, looking toward the door to be sure no one had followed him. "I've got a problem."

"What's that, Bill?" I asked with concern.

"It's Julie," he answered with a frown. Julie was his date for the evening. "I don't think she likes me any more."

"And what makes you think that?" I asked, suppressing a smile at the age-old dilemma. I stopped drying dishes and gave him my full attention.

"Well, she's been talking to Kevin for the last fifteen minutes and won't even look at me," he said, staring down at his shiny dress shoes that no doubt were hurting after so long a wearing.

"Just because she talks to someone else doesn't mean she doesn't like you any more," I tried to reassure him.

“Well, it’s more than that,” he said, running his hand through his slicked-down hair. “I’m afraid Kevin will ask her to the football game next week, and I want to take her, but I haven’t had a chance to ask her yet.”

“I see,” I nodded, hurting for this boy who had so much to learn about love. I hoped his learning would be less painful than mine had been. He stood looking at me with such hope that I could solve this major problem for him. I didn’t want to let him down.

“I have an idea,” I whispered. “Will you help me set out the dishes for the banana splits?”

“Well, sure, but . . . ,” he stuttered.

“Trust me on this,” I winked at him.

We moved the oblong dishes from the cabinet to the kitchen table and removed the platter with the few remaining hot dogs. I stepped to the door and called into the dining room, “Julie? May I see you a moment?”

“OK,” she replied sweetly. “Excuse me, Kevin. I need to see what Jackie needs.”

She came quickly into the kitchen and I explained, “Can you two help me get everything ready for dessert? I don’t have enough hands by myself.”

Bill Jr. looked at me as a slight smile crossed his lips. “Julie, will you cut up the bananas, please? Bill, will you open the jars of toppings and put serving spoons next to them? Then please get out the ice cream.”

The two went to work beside each other. “I’ll be right back.” I excused myself and joined the other guests in the dining room. I had done my part. Bill Jr. would have to do his.

About ten minutes later Bill and Julie walked into the dining room, holding hands. Bill Jr. said, “Jackie, the ice cream is melting.” He winked and asked, “Are you ready to serve dessert?”

“If you are,” I replied with a quizzical look.

“That’s fine,” he smiled. “Everything’s just fine.”

I smiled back, feeling for a certainty that I was at last a mom because I now had a son. That was only the first of many heart-to-heart talks, happy hours spent together, and sessions of sharing advice. I got to know Bill Jr.’s friends, and they treated me as they would any mom.

When I realized that my friendship with Bill’s dad was one-sided and he had no intention of marrying me, I broke off our relationship, making it very clear that I would never give up Bill Jr.

The next day after Bill Jr. had had enough time to get home from school, I called and asked him to dinner. I didn’t want much time to elapse after the breakup with his dad before I talked to him. His voice was strained when he answered, “Sure. Why not?”

"Are you up for Mexican food?"

"Yeah," he replied simply.

"Good. Then I'll pick you up at 5:30. Okay?"

The ride to the restaurant was awkward for both of us. Finally after we ordered, I told him, "Bill, you probably know by now that I won't be seeing your dad any more. He's a fine man and I respect him a lot." Bill played with the straw in his glass of Coke and didn't look at me. "However, we see our friendship in different ways, so it's better that we stop dating for now. Do you understand?"

I studied his face and was sad to see him struggling not to cry. His lip quivered, so he took a long drink of soda before he answered. "Yeah, I understand. And you brought me here to say goodbye to me too, isn't that right?" He lifted his eyes to meet mine and immediately dropped them to stare at the linoleum tabletop.

"No!" I cried almost too loudly. "That is just the opposite of why I brought you here, my dear."

He looked confused, with his eyebrows furrowed. He shook his head, not understanding me.

"Bill," I said, dropping my voice so only he could hear me, "I love you as a son. You know that. I've told you that many times. Mothers don't run away from sons. I brought you here to assure you that I will never run out on you. I want you in my life forever. I made it very clear to your father that I was terminating my relationship with him—and not with you. Is that OK with you, son?"

Bill swallowed hard and grinned. "Yeah, Jackie! That's OK with me. But . . . ." He hesitated.

"But what if your dad gives you a hard time about seeing me?" I tried to help him phrase his concern.

He just nodded.

"Your dad and I talked about our friendship, and he promised that he has no problem with our seeing each other just like we have been."

"So the gang can still come over Friday after the game?" he asked anxiously.

"You'd better be there!" I laughed. "I can't eat all the spaghetti I've made!"

I was blessed to be his mom all through his marriage, the birth of two precious daughters, the loss of his wife, and then his death. I am fortunate to remain grandmother and now even great-grandmother to his family.

Even Bill Sr.'s family took me into their hearts. When they learned our friendship had ended, I heard from his parents, his sisters, and his brother. They all assured me I would ever be a family member—and they have remained true to their promise.

I mothered one nephew through medical school. In the last few years he has experienced a major tragedy and also lost his brother. This death left him with no root family. I have stepped a little closer so he would not feel alone. How honored I am to be his family. Many of Bill Jr.'s friends still come to visit me, bring their families, and take me out for lunch. God has been so gracious to take me from having no supportive family to having a family that cannot be counted and whose value cannot be measured. What a blessing to be allowed to belong.

I was also grateful that my fellow bank officers allowed me, a woman, to join their circles and participate on an equal footing. I was elated one day in 1952 when some officers of the Houston chapter of the American Institute of Banking invited me to lunch and asked if I would consent to running for president of the chapter.

I told them, "I am flattered and would love to serve in this way."

The men reached out their hands to shake mine. I held up my hand instead. "Wait a minute," I laughed. "I can't just agree to this. If I should be elected, this would be a major step out of the ordinary. Also I know the time involved. My boss needs to agree to this. If you get his permission, I'll be more than happy to run."

They nodded their understanding. I was still the only woman officer of a major bank in Houston or the state. They knew, as I did, that some senior male members of the chapter would not be happy to have a woman president. In fact, some of the members snubbed me and tried to put my abilities into doubt.

One day Miss Jessie telephoned me, "Mr. Butler would like to see you as soon as you can come down."

Rolling my eyes at the stacks of paper on my desk, I sighed, "Tell him I'll be right down." I quickly took the stairs from the mezzanine to his office on the first floor.

He greeted me warmly and asked, "So . . . how is the AIB campaign coming?"

"Well, there really isn't a campaign as such," I told him. "The election is next week, and the winner goes to work in another month." I studied his face to understand what he was leading up to.

"Not everyone sees the election that cleanly," he said, motioning me to have a seat. He plopped into his soft chair and folded his hands on his desk. "Jackie," he began in a fatherly tone, "one of your fellow members has just visited me to protest your running. He says it is . . . unseemly . . . for a woman to run for president of a banking organization. He wanted me to talk you out of running."

My heart began to beat faster and I sat up straighter, remembering to keep my knees together and my feet crossed at the ankles and at an angle under my chair as Mother had taught me.

"I told him that you are a very responsible manager and you will run the chapter wisely," Mr. Butler grinned.

"I appreciate your support, Mr. Butler," I replied, letting out a noticeable sigh.

His smile faded and he leaned back in his chair. "I thought you would also like to know that this ... gentleman ... works for Mr. Jones's bank." Jessie Jones was a successful entrepreneur in Houston, who had connections to many businesses and community efforts. "I thought Mr. Jones would like to know how ungentlemanly one of his officers was behaving, so I called him and told him I thought it would be prudent for your fellow member not to enter our bank again. He agreed and assured me it would never happen."

I laughed out of relief and held my hand out to Mr. Butler. "Thank you, sir. I'm sorry this event is causing you trouble."

"Oh, no trouble, Jackie," he responded, pushing back his chair and standing. "No trouble at all. You have managed our Personnel Department very professionally as I know you will handle the chapter business—and that will reflect very well on our bank."

"Thank you, Mr. Butler. Thank you so much," I said, standing and walking toward the exit. "This is a great honor to run. I appreciate your allowing me the opportunity."

"You've earned it, Jackie," he replied.

I grinned and promised to make the bank proud although I saw no way that a woman would win such a contest in a male-dominated group. I did feel affirmed that the board had nominated me to run. That was victory enough.

When the votes were counted, I had received seventy-eight percent! This landslide almost destroyed some of the men on the board who would have to work with me. In 1953 I was inaugurated as president of the Houston chapter. In the few weeks between the election and the inauguration I prepared a detailed operations manual for the board. It was the first for any chapter in the nation.

At the first board meeting over which I presided, I reviewed the manual in detail. At the end of each specific effort of the board, I read the name of the proposed chair. The board members, now including a few women, sat in stunned silence while I laid out my organizational plan. I did not dare give time for comments until I had finished because I could not read the reaction of those seated around the conference table. They focused all their attention on me and what I was reading.

Finally I reached the last page. I placed my manual on the table and took a deep breath. No one attempted to speak. One man cleared his throat. Several others reached for their coffee cups. I looked deliberately around the conference table and made eye contact with those who would meet my gaze. I smiled and said with as much confidence as I could muster, "Ladies and gentlemen, now it is your turn to tell me that you will accept this policy and your individual assignments—or whether you prefer to resign from the board."

No one moved for an uncomfortably long time. I made myself remain still although my heart was racing. When a chair scraped against the hardwood floor, I tried not to look fearful. Was this the beginning of a revolt?

I relaxed a bit to see that the man pushing his chair back was a good friend of mine. He stood and glanced around at his colleagues. "Folks," he began, "the first thing we need to do is give Jackie a round of applause. I have never seen anything done with such precision and completeness. She has presented a long-overdue plan that all of us should have thought about years ago."

He looked at me and smiled. I nodded my appreciation.

"So what I am asking," he went on, "is that all who will support this stand up and give your new president what she deserves."

The explosion of applause and chairs screeching on the floor startled me and I jumped. I could not help but grin back at the volley of compliments, clapping, and cheers. Then I noticed that my opponent was still seated. Well, I was not going to allow him to ruin my victory party. At last I motioned for the board members to be seated. Before I could resume the meeting, my opponent popped up and said, "Friends and colleagues . . . ." He hesitated and looked directly at me. "I want to apologize for underestimating Jackie and ridiculing her because she is a woman."

I nodded my head slightly in acknowledgment of his comments. He continued, "I could not be more sincere when I say I wish you well." He pointed his palm in my direction and bowed with respect.

I turned to face him squarely and said to the board, "My friend has shown his true colors. I am grateful to him and to all of you. Be assured that we will all have a great two years working together."

And indeed we did. We had a hundred more members enrolled in our educational program than ever before, including many from surrounding towns who had not participated before. The chapter's membership expanded by more than forty percent, and we were the talk of the nation for some of the programs we started. One successful program was sending bankers into Woodrow Wilson Elementary School to mentor first through third graders. Bankers from all over the city volunteered to assist the students once a week with whatever schoolwork they needed help with. The program lasted only a year but greatly benefited the students as well as the volunteers.

The same year I was elected as AIB president, the Houston Chamber of Commerce asked me to serve on a committee to develop a working relationship between business and the high schools in the area. During the chamber's Business/Industry Educational Week program, students chosen by each school would meet in their schools with business and professional people for an hour or two a day. The next month those same students would spend a week in a business or profession of their choice to observe firsthand how the business functioned. I wrote the program for the banks to use to teach these young people. The program lasted about five years. It was a great loss when the chamber decided to cease sponsorship.

Perhaps as a result of my success with AIB, I was named in 1954 to Who's Who in America, a first for a woman officer in a major bank.

In 1955 my new visibility with AIB earned me the position of associate councilman for the national office of the American Institute of Banking, helping organize chapters along the Texas Gulf Coast. At the time I was the only woman who had held this position. In my two-year term I organized three chapters and four study groups—a record for the organization in our part of the country.

The next year I was given additional assignments in the Business Development Department of First National Bank. My job was to travel around the country, making contacts to be the correspondent bank for smaller banks. Each bank designates a large bank in a major city as a depository and borrowing bank. First National was the second largest bank in the state, and we were already the correspondent bank for banks in Los Angeles, New York, and other parts of the country so we could do business outside of Houston with good credit. I also represented First National's Oil Division and Foreign Banking Department. My efforts paid for my expenses and the expenses of setting up the accounts. The only problem was that this was not true for the men who performed my same duties. None of my contemporaries wanted me to be the first to turn in an expense account any month because theirs were always higher. I had to admit that an exact comparison of their expenses and mine was not fair to them. As a woman, I was more often taken out for dinner or entertained, so I had fewer expenses to turn in.

Also my experience at Shell with expense accounts determined how I handled mine. The men who had done the work longer than I had resented that I documented all my expenses with receipts. This was not required of them at the time. The comptroller of the bank finally saw the wisdom of having verification and required everyone to provide supporting documentation for all expenses. Resentments toward me skyrocketed. I was relieved when the Internal Revenue Service finally began requiring documentation of expense account claims a few years later. I was no longer the cause of the unpopular ruling.

As I traveled around the country meeting bankers and businesspeople, I began to see a common denominator among successful people, men or women. I noticed that education, personal ties, or longevity in a business did not have as much impact on a career as a solid, positive attitude. As I began touring the country to develop clients for First National Bank, I began lecturing boards of banks and other businesses about my revelation. I wanted to see people succeed, and this ingredient was available to everyone who would avail him or herself of it. Through my traveling and lecturing I became a household word in the banking world—and still am amazed how many people know my name. Eventually I spoke in every state except the Dakotas.

In April 1957 my world and that of almost 500 people experienced a monumental earthquake when First National Bank merged with the City National Bank to become the First City National Bank, one of the strongest banking institutions in America. From this merger I learned a lesson I preach to this day: Bigger is not the answer. The answer lies in striving to be the best. Better comes first; bigger is the reward. The demise of so many large businesses in 2002 proved that when greed takes over, disaster is not far behind.

Of course the merger meant the release of many employees, including me. The owner of First City National Bank had no interest in benefits programs of any kind, so I notified the companies First National had worked with that the new bank would no longer be engaging their services. One of my visits was to Dr. John Kelsey of the Kelsey Leary Clinic, one of Houston's fastest growing medical clinics and the forerunner of Kelsey-Seybold Clinic. I had begun a program with the clinic under which our top executives and even some junior officers had a mandatory physical every year. The program paid for itself from the start when the first series of exams detected tuberculosis in two of our officers. Early detection precluded any serious illness, and our investment in these two outstanding people was protected.

When I told Dr. Kelsey that the newly organized First City National Bank would no longer do medical exams, I also mentioned that I would be leaving the bank. Dr. Kelsey asked if I would consider being the medical manager and personnel director of the clinic. In due course I accepted his offer. At that time the clinic consisted of four physicians and two psychiatrists. Today the clinic consists of many satellite locations all over the county with well over 250 physicians. To this day I continue serving in an advisory capacity on the board of the Kelsey Research Foundation.

I was to begin working at the clinic in October of 1957. On September 26 Mother was in her bedroom, studying the Iliad and the Odyssey for her class at Rice Institute. The five-year Great Books course was her eighty-second birthday present. As I passed by her room to go to bed, she called me into her room. "Alice Cornelia," she said imperially, "give me your thoughts on the tone of these poems."

"Mother," I yawned, "I read those stories in high school! I made an 'A' on the report, and I don't remember a thing about them."

"You ignorant girl!" she sneered. "Go to your room and stay there until morning. I don't even want to have breakfast with someone who cannot discuss classic literature after I struggled to send you to college!"

Since I was going to bed anyway, I just shrugged and started to leave her room. I happened to glance at her legs and noticed that they were badly swollen and she was breathing quite hard, more so than an angry outburst should have caused. I mentioned my concern and she just yelled again, "I am quite capable of taking care of myself! Go on to your room and stay there." At forty-six I thought this instruction a bit too elementary, but it had always been so between us.

I noticed too that her temples were pulsing. She sat up straighter on her bed and continued, "Besides I have an appointment with the doctor tomorrow afternoon. I don't need any suggestions from you." She shooed me out of her room.

I walked straight to my bedroom and called our doctor, who lived only a few blocks away. Within moments the front doorbell rang and Dr. Kelsey rushed into Mother's bedroom. After one quick look at her legs, he said, "Mrs. Matthews, you need to get to the hospital immediately."

"Alice Cornelia called you, didn't she?" Mother shouted. "She just thinks she knows so much. I told her I was to see you tomorrow."

Dr. Kelsey was digging into his black bag, ignoring her ranting. He pulled out a syringe and ordered her to hold still while he gave her a shot.

"Mrs. Matthews, I'm calling an ambulance for you," he said firmly.

"Oh, no, you are not!" Mother cried, slapping the bedspread. "If you do, it's the last ambulance you will ever call! I will ride in a car, but not in an ambulance."

By this time Willois and her father had come over in answer to my urgent call. It took all of us to hustle Mother into my car. Before she would stop fighting us, she insisted on dressing in her best silk robe, putting on earrings, powdering her face, and retrieving a clean embroidered handkerchief out of her dresser drawer. She never left the house without a clean, ironed handkerchief. She slipped her feet into her black velvet house slippers with a touch of silver running through them. I drove frantically to St. Luke's Hospital, where the staff spent three valiant hours trying to keep her alive. She had suffered a massive heart attack.

I had called several friends, who in turn called our minister, so I was not alone at the hospital. As I stood beside her bed after she was pronounced dead, I thanked the doctors for their efforts. I said, "I am grateful that she never gave up a second of her total independence and she was in command until the last breath." Everyone who knew her rejoiced that she was never deprived of her tight control over life, which would have made her miserable, even as it sometimes made those around her miserable. In my more reflective moments in later years, I couldn't help but wonder if she exercised control over everything around her—except her own happiness.

As the hospital staff was scurrying quietly and efficiently around the small room, I said aloud, not expecting anyone to answer, "This afternoon she had her piano class recital, taught one lesson, and had a quick bite of supper so she could get to her studies for her Great Books class." I rubbed my eyes, aware that I had no tears. "She has gone to a home she has worked hard to gain entrance to all her life. What a magnificent ending for one who always ruled her universe."

The doctors merely went about their duties, tidying up the room and writing reports. I'm sure they had heard everything from family members after a death and didn't bother to try to understand what was being said.

I could not help but think as I entered my house that night that at last I was a free agent. I would never again have to contend with parental interference in my life choices. Willois had insisted that I spend that first night with them, but I protested, "Thank you, but I have to spend the morning canceling all Mother's appointments and classes. I'd better stay at the house in case someone calls who has not heard of her death."

That turned out to be a wise decision. I spent until almost four o'clock the following day making calls to those listed in her appointment book. Some appointments were not listed, so for almost two weeks people appeared at the door or called to inquire why she had missed a meeting or obligation. Although she lacked the skills to be a good mother or wife, she was a talented woman, still active three months short of her eighty-fifth birthday.

Mother drove a 1939 Plymouth Deluxe until she died. I cannot count how many people came to the house wanting to buy the car after her death. It looked like new, and she took as good care of her car as she did herself. I finally sold it to her laundryman for the handsome sum of fifty dollars, which was the Blue Book price. I saw that car almost three years later, and Mr. Tucker told me it ran like a top. A newer model would not have been in such good shape, I surmise.

Several days after Mother's death a very special friend who understood my life told me, "Jackie, I am really interested to know what you felt when you knew your mother was gone."

I had not stopped to think about that and appreciated having the question raised. After a few minutes I looked at my friend sadly and said, "My first thought was 'there will never again be a peach switch behind every picture.'"

I was forty-six when Mother died and there had been no actual switches since my thirteenth birthday, but there had been comments that cut as deeply as the switches. Nothing was ever good enough. There were many firsts in my career, but in her mind they were nothing much when there was something that could have been better. The time came when I never told her about some of my honors and, unless they were reported in the paper, she never knew about them. When something was in the paper and I had not told her and maybe friends had called her about it, she would lay the paper on my bed with the article and/or the picture visible. I would say nothing and would usually take the paper to the office and send it to some of my extended family or a special friend just because I needed some applause.

I am very grateful I had many firsts after she was gone that were honored time and time again and I had the joy of enjoying them and actually basking in their glory. Before Mother was gone and when the hurt got almost beyond me, I would slip out into the yard at night and I would cry and talk to Daddy, for I could always hear him say, "Precious, your daddy is so proud of you—keep up the good work." Then he would squeeze me, kiss me, and smile a smile that is still worth the world to me. Just as God is always my refuge and strength, so is Daddy still there for me.

Not surprisingly Mother exercised her control one last time after she died. I knew she had made arrangements with a local undertaker for her funeral although I did not realize the extent of that until I visited the funeral home the day after she died. I mentioned that I would call Mother's organ teacher, who happened to be in Houston on a visit, and ask him to play at her service. The undertaker squinted and slowly shook his head. "Mrs. Greer," he began apologetically, "I think you need to understand something."

I was expecting some explanation of the funeral home rules and regulations. Instead he said, "When your mother came in to make her arrangements a few months ago, she was very explicit about what she wanted for her funeral—and what she did not want."

I smiled and nodded. "That does not surprise me," I replied.

"Well, I hope you will understand then that she told me that she was sure you or someone else would try to change her preferences and she made me promise that that would not happen." He twisted the top on his fountain pen and looked pleadingly at me.

"Your mother did not want any music at her service," he continued, putting his hands on the desk between us as if to brace himself for a volley of words.

"Did you say, 'No music'?" I asked in disbelief. "Music was her life. Why in the world would she omit it from her funeral service?"

"She didn't say, Mrs. Greer," the poor man answered, his face beginning to twitch. "She just made me promise that I would not change any of her desires regarding her service."

"I see," I said quietly. "Then proceed with her arrangements." This acquiescence to Mother's desires was all too familiar to me. It was her last performance, and I would let her direct this one last moment of my life. After the funeral there would be a new ruler on the throne of my life.

The funeral director sighed with relief, and I departed without another word. The service was very simple—two scriptures including the Twenty-Third Psalm, a few prayers, and a few words by Rev. Rodney Sunday, senior minister at St. Andrews Presbyterian Church, where we attended sometimes. Then her reign was over—with less sorrow than I would have preferred. She was buried in Palestine two days later in the family plot.

The house on Arnold Street that I built for Mother was hers, but when she was gone and it was mine, I had Margaret Frazier, an interior decorator, come and transform it. I lived with the Huebels for six weeks during the work. At night we all went to see her handiwork, which was far beyond what I expected. My friends would stop by the house during the renovation and exclaim to each other, "Come and look here!" for it was all so elegant.

The living room and dining room were papered in an aqua paper with a gold pattern. A gold rug complimented the paper in the living room. The drapes in the living and dining rooms were gold with blue silk tassels to hold the curtains back when opened. At last I would stop living in a fish bowl. The pine panel walls in the adjoining music room were painted a battleship gray and rubbed to look a bit rustic. The furniture was upholstered green to blend with the colorful gardens just outside the picture window. Pictures on the walls accented the room with bright yellows, reds, and blues. The remainder of the house was painted off white. Different colored throw rugs in each bedroom gave each room a different feel. A sand-colored carpet in the hall divided the elegant entertaining areas from the cozier bedrooms. I splurged on little vases, statues, and other accessories that I placed in the living room on a new coffee table made of glass and brass. I loved the luxuriousness of my new home and shared it with others as often as possible. In fact, the house created such a market for the decorator's work that she gave me back $1,000 of what I had paid her!

I learned from some friends several months later that all during the time the decorator was working in the house, many friends came by who did not know I was living elsewhere temporarily. The decorator let them in to admire the renovations. She finally told one couple that she had never seen one person with so many friends. When she found out the kind of life I had lived, she did a lot of things that she never charged me for as she wanted to create a market for me for a new happiness I had never had. She called it "freedom for beauty and fun."

She succeeded. I had four wonderful years in the house after Mother was gone. It was a dream house by the side of the road that was always open and ready for fun or whatever was needed. It was what a home should have been—a real love nest where laughter was the order of the day and night. There were sad moments in the house too for many times when friends did not have close family and sorrow came, I would have them stay with me a few days. It was truly a home, not just a well-appointed house. I often ride by it now and pause for reflections.

I built the house in 1949 for $16,000 and sold it fifteen years later for $17,000 after putting another $10,000 of work into it. A few years ago the new owner sold it for $225,000—ah, inflation! The joy for me is that happiness reigns within its walls, and that is glorious. If we will really look, no matter how dark the hour, we can see a ray of sunshine because we are never left alone. The longer we look and the more we believe, the brighter the rays—that is how God plans it! So life truly began another phase for me in 1957.

A friend from college days came from Austin to live with me after Mother died. Suddenly some years later I received a big promotion at Fannin Bank that required me to travel most of the time. The house and the gardens were too much for me to keep up with and, being gone for long periods, I knew things would suffer so I sold it. My friend who lived with me was furious, but it had to be. Once again I became an apartment dweller, which I have never regretted. Yes, the house was wonderful, but it was also enough!

Not all new beginnings are surprises. Some are necessary and welcome.

nineteen

chapter 19

BACK AND FORTH

A few days after Mother's funeral I began a new venture in a world I knew little about other than infrequent visits to a doctor's office. Life was beginning again in more ways than one, and I was ready for whatever it held.

While I really was not equipped to be a manager in the medical world in all aspects, I did contribute some organization of office procedures and improved collections. I was also privileged to select some outstanding people for the positions that resulted from the clinic's unprecedented growth. While I was with Kelsey Leary Clinic, we expanded our medical staff threefold and moved three times to keep up with our growth.

Shortly after the third move, I realized the clinic would be much better off with an experienced clinic manager. I decided to return to banking and give the clinic this opportunity, so in 1962 I accepted a position as personnel manager and purchasing agent at Fannin Bank, which was in the heart of the Texas Medical Center. Shortly after I joined this fast-growing organization, I told the owner/president of the bank that I wanted to capitalize on my medical experience and contacts and establish some type of banking services that would benefit doctors, dentists, their immediate families, and possibly one key person in their organization who could be their liaison with the bank. He thought the idea had merit and called our advertising agency and made an appointment for us to discuss the idea.

One thing I had noticed at the clinic was that the doctors did not have time to do their banking. I thought that a facility close to them that would open at seven in the morning and remain open until six each evening would be helpful, especially to those practicing in the hospitals. Also the bank needed to have some way to transfer monies for them with a telephone call followed by a written request. The form needed to be designed for their convenience so it could be signed and either delivered or mailed to us as the "on-file authorization for transfer." I also envisioned working with the American Express Company to see if we could develop an authorization for the doctors' liaisons to purchase their travelers checks, take them to the doctors, and let them sign the checks at their convenience while releasing both the bank and American Express from any responsibility for loss for any reason.

All of this took a year of planning, but finally the Medical Express Banking Department was born. A special department was set up in the bank with our own parking areas and entrance; our own stationery and forms; and a staff which included a secretary, teller for both checking and savings accounts, and a loan officer in addition to me as the manager.

The department grew from the start for as our doctor customers used the services, they talked to their colleagues about all the conveniences we provided. Other medical customers set up accounts even before we made calls to invite their business. The express banking concept was well received throughout the city, not just in the Medical Center. We had doctors and dentists in various parts of town who used Fannin Bank as their family bank, and with the advent of this new service many came with their professional accounts in order to benefit from our special services program.

In 1962 I was so pleased to be asked to be a key speaker at the Minnesota Bankers Association meeting in Minneapolis. I was one of the first women to be invited to speak before that group. That year I was on the podium with Mrs. Ivy Baker Priest, the treasurer of the United States, and Dr. Charles Mayo from the well-known Mayo Clinic in Rochester, Minnesota. The invitation was an excellent way to increase the visibility of my bank and of women in executive positions.

When I learned the identity of the other speakers, my heart skipped a beat. Who was I to be in such august company? I should not have worried. After the morning meeting and lunch Mrs. Priest whispered to me, "Jackie, could we go up to your room, take off our shoes, and chat awhile?" I realized that she was a human being with feet that got tired just like anyone else.

Dr. Mayo spoke that afternoon, and I was the last to speak the next morning. I glowed inside when the audience gave me a standing ovation. Dr. Mayo rose from his chair, walked over to me at the podium, and put his arms around me. When the applause lessened, Dr. Mayo leaned into the microphone and laughed, "Folks, Ivy Priest and I are so glad we spoke first."

I closed my eyes to fight back tears of gratitude and humility. I caught a glimpse of Dad, cheering me on. What a gift Dr. Mayo's words were to someone from such an unsupportive background where Mother always questioned why I could not have done something better or done more. What a boost of confidence that remark gave me. Maybe I really did have abilities that were worthwhile. I determined to continue moving forward to wherever those abilities would take me, with God's guidance.

Two years later, in 1964, the Houston Journalists Association named me the outstanding businesswoman of Houston. That same year a friend at the bank suggested we ask one of the loan officers if we could borrow some money each year and pay it back and then start over in order to travel around the globe. He agreed and for fifteen years Vermelle Cathey, my First National Bank friend, and I toured most of the United States and a great part of Europe. Just before we were to leave for Germany, Switzerland, and parts of Austria, Vermelle had a heart attack and died. I worked in trips to Mexico and South America, once for a month. My sister-in-law invited me to be her travel companion to the Orient and the Hawaiian Islands. For about ten years we traveled until I was physically unable to go. I am so grateful to have been privileged to see so many of the countries God has made.

In 1966 I received one of the highest honors I ever received outside the banking world. Her Majesty Queen Elizabeth II of England named me to her Registry of Women of Distinction. She selected a woman every year from another country for the honor. I'm sure that the queen had become familiar with me two years earlier through her representative of England's Educational Department. In 1964 England was considering some banking reforms. The queen was interested in the American banking system, and she had heard about the American Institute of Banking's educational program. Interested in initiating a similar program in England, she contacted AIB about sending her representative to take some of the classes. Since Houston was then world-renowned for its oil business and its busy port, she asked if he could go to Houston.

I was asked to be one of his official hostesses, and I was delighted to oblige. We enjoyed each other's company besides sharing an interest in improving the banking industry. After several visits with him, I recognized a man who longed for home cooking during his two-month stay in the States, so I had him to the house for dinner a number of times. When he left, I sent information through him to the queen. Later that year I joined a tour group to England and was thrilled to be slotted for a personal visit with the queen. Unfortunately my time was changed and the visit never took place.

Two years later I was stunned to be notified that Queen Elizabeth had chosen me for her honoree that year. It was not common in the United Kingdom for a woman to be prominent in banking, so my experience no doubt caught her attention.

After seven fulfilling years at Fannin Bank I decided it was time for a change. In 1969 I resigned and traveled to Hawaii with the intention of staying for awhile. Friends at Great Southern Life Insurance Company heard of my plans and contacted me about a position there. The company owned a bank on the beach and needed a business development person there. They offered me the job.

When I arrived in the islands, I interviewed with the president of the bank. The lobby of the bank looked just like American banks except the tellers wore fragrant leis and the windows opened to a view of the waves lapping the shore. The president and I had a pleasant chat until he asked how I proposed to develop business for his bank. "One of the first things I would do is to call on business groups and individuals and invite them to bank with us," I began innocently. Before I could explain the success of this tactic in other businesses of which I had been a part, the president stood up abruptly and began pacing in front of the picture window. I noticed storm clouds, not on the horizon, but on his face. I could not understand the reason for this reaction.

"No!" he exploded, making a fist in the air for emphasis. He turned to glower at me. "Under no circumstances will an employee of my bank make calls, begging for business," he growled. Regaining control of his emotions, he sat down heavily and continued to lecture me. "Our clients come to us because of our reputation. We are not a retailer that entices customers. We are a respected bank that is ready to serve those who come to us."

The job opening he then described to me was a clerical position. Of course I was not interested. I enjoyed the scenery for a few weeks and returned home to contemplate my next beginning. My friends at Great Southern were furious at his attitude. They tried to reason with him about new approaches and new attitudes, but with no success. In fact, they ended up selling the bank within a year.

Back in Houston, to help out my landlord at the St. Johns Apartments on Richmond, I agreed to act as assistant manager. The manager, a friend from Palestine, needed someone to fill in when she had to be away from the building. The duties fit my schedule at the time. The maintenance manager there, Tommie Jones, also fit my need for someone to help me with housework. As she cleaned my house, I soon realized that she was too smart to be doing manual work. All of her siblings were college graduates with masters degrees. She had had to drop her college plans when her father had a stroke her senior year in high school and she went to work to support her parents. Her father had been the chef at the only restaurant in Athens, Texas, during the oil boom.

Tommie had two precious daughters and needed more income than the apartment job could pay. I got her a job as a maid at Greenway Bank and suggested to the operations manager that she use her to file checks and do clerical work. That opportunity arose soon. Tommie's organizational skills were apparent immediately. Six months later she was moved into Customer Service. By the end of the year she was manager of that department. I enjoyed working with Tommie in a professional capacity as much as I had enjoyed her company at my home.

By the time I was sixty-nine, I realized I would face mandatory retirement in a few years. The possibilities of a bank letting me work out my years until retirement were not promising. One of my former bosses at the First National Bank, Albert Cleere, was now president of Harrisburg Bank, a fast-growing area bank. His administrative assistant was one of my closest friends. We had just returned from a trip to the British Isles when her boss called to ask me to lunch. He informed me, "Jackie, I understand that you are open to a new assignment. I have taken the liberty to confer with the president of another neighborhood bank about a business development department he wants to set up and recommended he talk with you. I hope you don't mind."

Mind? I was grateful for the affirmation. On Mr. Cleere's recommendation, Lanny Goodman, president of Greenway Bank, suggested that I work for him on a two-week contract. After I had a proposal to make, the bank would decide if they wanted me to stay and flesh out the plan. At that point they would negotiate a time frame and fee.

Forms would have to be designed, filing systems developed, and a multiplicity of other details handled. Setting up such a department could consume a mountain of time. I agreed to the two-week contract in March.

During the second week of my stay I asked the president for an appointment of at least an hour so we could look at the designs I had developed for the departmental plan and the forms to support the system. Also, I designed a job description to see if my ideas were parallel to his. We spent a very busy hour, and I left his office with my work cut out for me and with a very positive feeling about the department. As we neared the end of the second week, I asked the president if there was someone who could now take over my designs and be trained.

Mr. Goodman responded, "Jackie, until the department is in tact and the officer-in-charge at the desk, I would like to extend your contract."

I was pleasantly surprised and readily agreed. "This has turned out to be a far more involved experience than any of us could have predicted," he said. We set July as the target date for my work to be completed with a trained officer in place.

I brought many people, both men and women, for this man to interview. Not once did he talk to me about a single person I recruited. Each time I would try to talk with Mr. Goodman in more detail about these candidates, he was either too busy or leaving the bank. One morning near the expiration of my contract, I arrived at the bank very early, hoping to corner him and get something settled. To my surprise when I walked in, he was seated at my desk with coffee and kolaches. I laughed, "What have I done to merit this unexpected honor?"

I accepted the cup of coffee he offered, chose a raspberry kolache, and sat opposite the large mahogany desk. He smiled and announced, "I have found the person for this position and they will start tomorrow."

I stopped chewing my breakfast delicacy and merely stared. Where had he found this rare person when everyone I had recommended had not satisfied his criteria?

Sensing my question, Mr. Goodman broke into a grin, "You are my selection!"

He quoted a salary, a bonus, insurance, and medical benefits. He also gave me a slip to select any car I wanted to be used as my own. How could I refuse?

For six years I enjoyed the challenge of a new department and friendly colleagues. In 1984 my alma mater, now Texas Woman's University (TWU), honored me as a Woman of Distinction. Alumnae are nominated by other alumnae, and the ultimate honorees are selected by the president of the university. Honors such as this are humbling since so many of my colleagues also contribute much to their communities outside the parameters of their employment.

Also this year I celebrated my seventy-fifth birthday. I decided early that year to give myself a birthday party, so I invited 750 guests from Houston, Texas, Mexico,

South America, and all over the United States. The 115 out-of-town guests came from twelve states. Three floors at the Stouffer Hotel housed the guests, and I occupied the bridal suite for an entire week. Some friends from out of town stayed a week, and we had a great time. The birthday party itself was at my church, and the next morning I had a breakfast for all the out-of-towners at our hotel. Like the icing on my big chocolate cake, on the day of the party, my picture and an article about my life in Houston appeared on the front page of the Business Section of The Houston Post.

I had requested no gifts at my party, but some friends insisted on some commemoration of the event. They consulted with each other and finally decided to establish an endowment fund at Texas Woman's University in my honor. An honor it was indeed! After discussions with the president of the university, we designated the funds to be used for scholarships for women in the College of Business Administration at TWU. By the turn of the century, more than 200 women had received financial aid from the fund.

Several years later the university established the "Jackie Greer in Residence Lecture Series," which is run by the College of Business Administration. This program brings an outstanding woman in business to the university yearly for a three-day seminar.

Just when I thought maybe life was beginning to stand still, it burst forth anew for me. One day in 1985 I had trudged wearily into my apartment and sat down to peruse the mail. I perked up when I saw a letter from Marilyn Pharr, a good friend who was assistant marketing director at Republic Bank. The letter informed me that she wanted to nominate me for one of Houston's Outstanding Women on the Move, a program sponsored annually by the Texas Executive Women (TEW), an organization made up of entrepreneurs and top-level executives.

My ego piqued, I read through the requirements and glanced at the questionnaire of information they wanted for their judges. Initially, I laid the letter on the table and opened the rest of the mail. Houston was full of women executives by now, many with much higher positions than I had ever had, plus they were more widely known. Over dinner I picked up the letter again and decided, "What can it hurt?" I carefully filled in the information on my career, included a letter of deep appreciation for the nomination, and went to bed.

Sometime later the TEW committee notified me that I had been selected one of the top twenty candidates for the honor and said I would be invited to meet with the organization's judges for the elimination process. Ten women would be chosen for the final honor. I was delighted but did not have any expectations of being chosen for the final group. On the day of the interview I sat in great humility in a waiting room with one of the first women in the astronaut training program and the president of one of Houston's better known small businesses. We were all dressed in new suits and chatted pleasantly, realizing that everyone seated there had accomplished much although not all could be named for this recognition.

Before I went into the "Lion's Den" as we were calling the room where the selection committee was interviewing candidates, I actually prayed that I would not be asked a question concerning women's liberation. This was a subject I was rabid about, and I knew I would be out the door quickly if this question came up.

My name was called and I entered the austere room in which five judges, four women and one male reporter from The Houston Post, sat around the far perimeter of a circular conference table that was polished to a glow. They smiled to put me at ease. Actually I was not nervous since I did not think there was a chance I would be chosen over such publicly acclaimed women with whom I had been visiting in the waiting room. They began by congratulating me on having made the cut to this level and asking a neutral question about how I chose banking as a career.

When I finished answering, the moderator said, "Thank you, Jackie," and looked at her notes. She met my eyes and asked, "So, Jackie, how do you feel about women's liberation?"

Knowing that the Lord had answered my prayer—because He does answer them—although certainly not in the way I had hoped, I decided quickly to be myself. What was there to lose? After drawing a deep breath and looking around the room at the illustrious group of judges, I answered, "I know nothing about this matter and, moreover, I do not want to know anything about it." Some of the women placed their pens on the table as if to listen more carefully. One wrinkled her nose in disapproval. They knew my career history and could not figure what I could possibly mean. I could hear my voice rising as I launched into my uncommon stance on the topic of great current interest in our country. I continued, "I was born free, and I have gotten to where I am with the help of both men and women. I did not go into business for gender reasons. I went in to use my brains that God gave me. Use them I have and I will continue to do so."

Stepping down off my soapbox, I suppressed a smile as I looked at the group of talented women, most much younger than myself and many of whom had had to fight male dominance to rise to their current positions. I felt good that I had been true to myself and my beliefs, whatever they thought of my opinions.

The moderator thanked me. After a few more questions of a less volatile nature, the judges dismissed me, saying that if I should be chosen, a delivery service would bring the announcement to the bank. I thanked them for their time and went out to a relaxed lunch with another candidate who also was sure she had not made the cut. We briefly discussed the nice experience, and it slipped out of my consciousness.

Years later the reporter told me he was about to explode with laughter, but of course the circumstances did not lend themselves to such a display. He said he would never forget that day.

Three weeks after the interview when I returned from a lunch break, half the bank employees were out in front of the building yelling at me to hurry and get in the bank, that something great had happened. Sure enough, on my desk was a crystal and gold bud vase with a gorgeous yellow rose and a note written in gold ink telling me I had been selected as one of the ten Outstanding Women of Houston. I closed my eyes to absorb the immensity of this honor and saw Dad applauding and Ken standing nearby with a proud grin on his face. I felt blessed beyond words.

Two weeks later the ten honorees attended a wonderful tea at the Ritz Carlton, an elegant hotel, to meet each other as well as the members of TEW. I was in awe of being honored along with the owner of several insurance companies, one of Houston's foremost television news anchors, a notable cancer surgeon, and others of equally outstanding achievements. We were informed that we would be honored at a luncheon in mid November at which time we would be presented to Houston by having our pictures in the Sunday newspaper. We could each invite nine guests.

That decision was excruciating since I had dozens of people in my close family of friends whom I wanted to include in this great day. Well over 500 guests participated in our momentous day. What a thrill it was for me and how I wished Dad and Ken could join in my happiness.

The week after the gala, Karen Cole, another banker and honoree, invited the other nine of us to lunch. She said, "We have had such a wonderful accolade and been the recipient of so many nice meals and congratulations that some of us thought it would be appropriate if we, as a class, did something to give something back to the community."

Soon a committee of three had offered to check with their churches and some women's shelters in the city to find a woman we could adopt and nurture to a better life. When we met again, the decision of the group was unanimous. We decided to help an African-American woman living in one of the missions who was single with five boys. One boy was three, twins were almost two, and another set of twins were nine months old. Another committee searched the possibilities for helping her and recommended that we give her no money, but provide an apartment, a job in the Department of Communications at one of the major hospitals, and clothes.

Within a few weeks the mother had moved out of the mission, she had a job, and one of the class had gotten the children in a day school where she could drop them off on her way to work. She was very smart and in a short while she was one of the department's supervisors. We provided Thanksgiving and Christmas for them as well as gifts for the children on their birthdays. We finally were able to help her move into a three-bedroom house with some help from the children's' father. Then we were able to enroll the children into a Head Start program, where they thrived. The mother continued to advance on her job. Strange as it seemed to us at the time, within a year we began hearing less and less from this ward of ours. Soon we realized that we were no longer needed, and without fanfare or any thanks we lost contact with her. A few years later when the oldest boy was about eight, we heard that our friend was head of communications in the hospital, she had a car and had moved into a very nice house, and the boys were all doing well in school. We were grateful we could plant the seed for a better future even if we did not get to be a part of the harvest. Several years after that I was visiting a patient at her hospital and stopped by her department to see if perhaps she was still employed there. She was and we had a delightful visit. She had received more promotions and her boys were succeeding in their activities.

Also in 1985 the president of Texas Woman's University nominated me for the Texas Women's Hall of Fame. I was not selected for this honor, probably because I have never been active in a political party. I do not believe in parties and have never contributed to either. I support candidates on their individual merits, not on their party affiliation.

Now in my mid-seventies I was beginning to tire and ready for a change. I decided to retire for good this time and do some traveling. When I told Mr. Goodman of my decision, he agreed readily, "By all means, take all the time you want. Travel and come on back where you belong. Your assistant can run the department for a month without any concern from me."

Three more times in the next three months I presented him with written resignations. The first two times he wadded up my letter and threw it into the wastebasket as I stood in his office. The third time I presented my letter of resignation, he grabbed it from my hand, threw it in a desk drawer, and slammed the drawer shut. Without a word he stomped to the corner of his office and grabbed his hat off the hat rack. At the door he yelled back at me, "Since you are so insistent, take the damn car with you and don't have any accidents because you are now responsible for the insurance!"

Sadly he did not speak to me until a few days before he died. His bank was one of the most profitable anywhere, no matter the economic trends. He was a genius of a leader, financial manager, and president. Unfortunately he lacked people skills. I will ever admire him, though, for the success he created around him that worked to everyone's benefit.

After I came back from my first trip after leaving Greenway, I went to talk with my financial advisor at Houston National Bank about my financial status and what I could and could not do now and later. I was toying with the idea of starting my own business although I did not have firm plans for what kind of business it would be.

The advisor reviewed my situation and recommended, "Jackie, I think you should shelve your business idea, skip further travel plans for awhile, and return to work."

I laughed from the shock. "And where do you propose I look for work at my age?" I asked.

"Our bank wants you to contract with us and help us find a woman who would work well as a business development person in our Trust Department," he explained. After considering this idea overnight, I agreed and began the next day combing the markets to find people who would qualify for the job. It would require a lot of training for there were few women in this field of finance yet. After five candidates were rejected by the bank, I was not only exhausted but very frustrated because there was nothing about any of the candidates that pleased even one person on the board. I was beginning to feel that I had lost my knack for people selection.

By the beginning of the third week I knew there was to be an Executive Committee meeting the next morning, so I went in early and left a note on the table where they would be meeting and asked to speak to them before they left their meeting. When I joined the meeting, completely fraught and not a little tired and disgusted, I began citing my concerns only to see smiles on every face. Puzzled, I said, "There is something in the air that makes my eyes burn." They all howled.

Finally the officer with whom I had been working spoke. "Jackie, you won't take the nudge, but you have been the chosen one all the time. We wanted to wear you out so you would say, 'Well, since no one I recommend can please you, would you consider me?'" The circumstances of the job were such a challenge, my interest in beginning a business of my own faded into the background.

So I began another banking career in a totally new environment with great excitement. Besides enjoying the work, I gained two precious family members. A few weeks into my employment at Houston National Bank, an officer knocked on my door to inform me that the mother of another officer had died. He asked if I wanted to contribute to a flower fund, even though I was new. Of course I did.

About a week later I went to the bank early to try to get to the copy machine before everyone else did. Passing one office, I heard grievous crying. I hesitated outside the door of Debbie Hogwood, who had just lost her mother, wondering whether I should stop. I hardly knew her. Even so, her sobs touched my heart. Uncomfortably I continued on to the copy machine and made my copies before others formed a line.

On the way back to my office, I passed Debbie's office again. As before, I heard the sobs, perhaps even more intense than before. Stranger though I was, I could not hear such lamentation and ignore it. Gently, I pushed open the door. Debbie was hunched over her desk with her head on her folded arms. Her entire body convulsed with the tears. Quietly I closed the door and tiptoed beside the grief-stricken young woman. She did not raise her head when I said simply, "Debbie, I am a total stranger to you, but there is no way I am going to hear such evidence of grief and not stop to offer any help to you that I can."

If possible, her sobbing intensified. Thinking I had overstepped my bounds, I turned to leave as quietly as I had come. Suddenly, however, my motherly instinct clicked on inside me. I sat down on the arm of her desk chair, reached over, and pulled her to me. Her blouse was drenched in tears, and before we parted, so was mine. When finally the sobs had subsided to infrequent heaves, I spoke, "Darling girl, you need to talk to someone. I would gladly be that someone, but you hardly know me. Is there someone here I could get for you so you could have that person for a comfort zone?"

She simply lifted her head and raised her left hand in front of my face. On her fourth finger glittered an exquisite diamond engagement ring. "Oh, my," I commented. "It's a beautiful ring!" Debbie did not even smile back at me. She just searched my face and swallowed hard.

"Did your mother know your fiancé?" I asked tenderly.

The sobs began again. Between short breaths she blurted out, "Yes, but I don't have a mother to be with me when I marry!"

I held the shivering young woman until she quieted down. "You do too have a mother, and here I am—if you will have me."

Debbie's head popped up and her eyes sparkled. The tears stopped as if a spigot had been turned off. "You mean you are willing to 'mother' me through this wedding?"

"You bet!" I said, clapping my hands for emphasis. "Can you go to lunch today and get started on the planning?"

The first smile of the morning broke on her face and she nodded.

"I'll come by about 11:45, OK?" I asked.

"Thank you, Jackie," she whispered. "You don't know what this means."

What a glorious time we had before and during the wedding. Debbie had no idea what her acceptance of my help meant to me. At long last I had a daughter!

Two weeks after the wedding my doorbell rang one Saturday morning. My heart sank when I opened the door to find Gary Gibson, Debbie's husband, on my doorstep. "Well, Gary!" I cried. "Do come in. Is anything wrong? I mean, is Debbie OK? Are y'all OK?"

"Oh," he answered distractedly, "everything's fine. It's just that . . . ."

"Here," I interrupted, pointing to the sofa. "Have a seat."

He plopped onto the aqua cushions and still looked as if he were carrying a heavy burden. I opened the blinds on the windows, hoping the sunlight entering the room would brighten his countenance.

"Gary," I encouraged, "what is this all about?"

He twisted his hands together nervously. "I really don't know how to ask you what I've come to ask."

"Just simply ask," I replied. "You don't need to build up to anything with me."

"Well," he said, taking a deep breath, "could you be my mother too?"

I didn't know what to say. "But, darling," I began tentatively, "you already have a wonderful mother." His mother lived nearby.

Gary took several short breaths and said quietly, "Did you hear me? I said, 'Could you be my mother?'"

What a delight to be loved so by someone so much younger than I and to be invited into a special relationship—for life.

I choked back tears and forced a smile. "It's going to be really strange when I tell people that my daughter is married to my son!"

We both laughed and he hugged me. What a blessing that another bond with a very precious child came to me so that I could experience the joys of motherhood. I am so grateful for such an unspeakable gift and continually thank God for my son and daughter.

The rest of my stay at Houston National Bank was very satisfying. I was one of the biggest producers the bank had, and I again traveled all over the country and found every day a day of challenge.

Finally after six years of traveling day in and day out, I asked my two bosses to join me for lunch and told them I had reached burn out and that I wanted to move into administration of accounts. This idea did not coincide with their plans in any way, and our meeting ended with the decision being made that possibly I was really ready to retire this time. The hurt that came with this totally unexpected decision still festers for as I realized my offer was being rejected, so did the rejection I had for a lifetime begin to rear its ugly head again. Those two men are dear to my heart and we still keep in touch and are truly a family that no situation would really ever split to any lasting extent. So my life in the world of business faced another beginning and what would it be this time?

The banking business was my child, my solace, my place for recognition, acceptance, and appreciation, and a place to be loved, to love, and to be praised. It provided me with friends that are today "my family" as well as friends who opened other doors in life for me to be of service to my fellowman.

Through all these many years I have friends all over America even today at ninety-three years of age, and until recent years I have been able to travel, accept speaking engagements, and do some consulting through my banking contacts. I have never lost sight of the importance of a good financial background and helping others to do likewise. Such security gave me the dignity I needed, the acceptance I needed, and the challenge I needed, and I have tried to reciprocate by reaching out to those less fortunate than I and serving as an advisor, a mom, or whatever role I needed to play in life to give stature to someone who is hurting.

God has been so good to provide me with room for love and understanding from many who have honored me with their confidence and so often their love. The freedom of choice to love and be loved is one of God's most precious gifts to me and how humble and how grateful I feel. I will ever strive to be worthy of so great a reward.

twenty

chapter 20

A NEW WORLD IS BORN

After leaving banking in 1986, I knew I wanted to do something useful and beneficial, but what? One day I was having lunch with friends in one of Houston's better restaurants. The white starched tablecloths and tuxedoed waiters spoke of prestige and privilege. I looked at an adjoining table in time to see the president of one of Houston's most aggressive companies hand his business card to his guest, receive the card of his guest, and immediately begin picking his teeth with the card. The guest instinctively wrinkled his nose in disgust and no doubt disappointment. When I got home that day, I decided it was time for someone to stand up and talk about the place for good manners—and that place is EVERYWHERE.

I began scouting for a place I felt would be accessible for classes since my home was not an option. At the same time I began to plan my marketing strategy and identify what markets I could target immediately that would provide income for basic expenses for an etiquette school for young executives and children or anyone else interested in acquiring social graces. After six months of research, I decided to locate in or near River Oaks, an old, established neighborhood of large, expensive houses. The area also housed a number of young families with young children. This would be my first market for individuals, and then I would seek a commercial market.

When I shared my plans with friends, many questioned why I didn't just retire. After all I was seventy-seven. I told them, "My father always told me to do things while you are young because sometime you might get old. I need to do this now because someday I might get old."

My target audience developed differently from my plans however. I approached several banks and presented the idea of a program for their employees who are in contact with the public that would help them polish their manners in all aspects of dress, verbal and physical expressions, and the like. One area bank immediately endorsed the proposal. In less than a month the program began. Fortunately the employees received the teaching well and without resentment, and this opened more doors to other businesses.

My most successful contact, Southwestern Bell Telephone Company, came about because of a family obligation. Several years before I had been more or less adopted by Tillie and Tom McDonald. They had no children, and as their declining years approached, it was obvious that they needed a daughter to help them in many, many ways. I was blessed to be chosen for that role. Several years after Tom passed away, Tillie was notified that an award was going to be made in his memory and she was invited to attend a banquet to accept the award. It was my good fortune to take her. We both donned our "lacy" best and went to this event. Seated at my table were Mr. and Mrs. Robert Campbell, new acquaintances to me.

The evening's conversation and presentation were delightful. Somewhere in the conversation Bob and I exchanged pleasantries on our occupations. He was the marketing director for the local division of Southwestern Bell. When he inquired politely about my work, I explained briefly about my manners program designed for businesses. He listened with no show of particular interest other than normal curiosity.

However when we got downstairs to get our cars, Tillie and I ended up standing in front of the Campbells. Suddenly I felt a hand closing something in mine and heard a voice behind me saying, "I do not usually carry my personal cards in my tux pocket, but this one happened to be there. I want you to call me tomorrow and make an appointment to come in for us to talk."

An appointment was made, a contract was made, and for two and one-half years I traveled from Houston to Tulsa, to Oklahoma City, to San Antonio, El Paso, and back, presenting my program to Southwestern Bell employees. Some of my stays were as long as six weeks, in which case the company provided me an apartment. In each of these towns I had a host of friends from my banking days, so I would cook up a big dinner and invite all of them to join me at my apartment. I thoroughly enjoyed the camaraderie of old friends as well as teaching others things that would add to their success.

With the success of my school with local businesses, I decided to expand into a permanent location so I could offer classes to groups and individuals who did not have an office conference room for the classes. I used my life savings to lease a handsome two-story, white house near the corner of Shepherd Drive and West Dallas near River Oaks and advertised the Jackie Greer School of Social Excellence. I decorated the inside elegantly and began teaching two adult classes and many more classes for elementary school boys and girls mostly between the ages of ten and twelve. Clients could choose among such topics as table manners, public speaking, letter writing, or dressing for success. Young executives might choose classes in introduction to new business clients, motivating people, resolving conflicts, or the art of listening. They particularly enjoyed the role playing of business situations they found awkward on their jobs.

While most of the school children came from homes with professional parents and many attended private schools, they often did not know the proper way to hold a knife and fork. Their parents simply had not taken the time to teach them. The parents said, "They won't listen to us, but they'll listen to you." Indeed one father, who became a friend, told me twenty years after his children were in my classes, "They cannot come to my house even today without commenting on my manners. I'm so tired of hearing, 'Jackie wouldn't approve of that!'"

At the end of one etiquette class for thirteen- to fifteen-year-old girls, I passed out thick ecru note cards for the children to write invitations to their parents to the final banquet. The girls read their notes aloud. If there were any errors, I gave another note card and the girl rewrote hers until it was perfect. One girl handed me her final card and asked if I wanted to read it over one more time. I said, "I'd be happy to." I scanned the paper and looked up at the child's eager face. "Georgiana," I exclaimed, "this is as beautifully written as you are dressed."

She beamed. "That's why I could do it," she explained seriously, ". . . because I am so beautifully dressed." Indeed I required students to wear coat and tie or Sunday dress and socks or stockings to my classes. I found quickly that the children performed as they were dressed. They were more orderly when they were dressed nicely, partly because they had been cautioned about not messing up their "good clothes" and partly because they realized that if they were dressed up, something important was going to happen and they had better listen for it.

Another guiding principle of my school I attribute to young Raymond. When his class of eight young boys and ten girls ate their five-course graduation banquet at the elegant Stouffer Hotel, I asked him if he would come to the front of the room and assist me with a demonstration. He eagerly trotted up, smartly dressed in a blue suit and tie. As I reviewed the proper use of each item on the table, Raymond carefully held up the Gorham sterling silver, Havilland china, and Baccarat crystal. After the luncheon Raymond came up to me, smiling shyly. "Thank you, Mrs. Greer, for letting me help you today."

"You were a marvelous help, Raymond," I said, giving him a hug.

"I couldn't have done it yesterday," he told me matter-of-factly.

I stopped packing up my silver utensils and leaned down to look him in the eye. "And why is that?" I inquired, puzzled.

"Because yesterday I was seven, and today I'm eight," he shrugged.

This adorable little boy led me to see that, in every case, eight was the ideal age for beginning to teach such social skills to children. Seven was indeed too young.

And my school, unfortunately, was indeed too young to weather the economic decline that hit the nation in the mid 1980s. Businesses and families cut back their expenditures, and certainly my classes were not necessities. Partners who had promised to invest in my venture had to back out, and I was stuck with all the bills. I closed the school, giving the leased house back to the owners. I eventually paid off all my debts from my adventure into business, depleting my life savings in the process.

So out of grim necessity, my school venture gave way to a consulting management firm which survived a number of years until the economy again dipped and companies began using in-house expertise again.

By now I was in my late seventies and decided to consider a change of pace from a paid person to a volunteer. I have never made a better decision. Not only is there great satisfaction in knowing I am needed and wanted, but it is such fun to meet so many terrific people with whom to have a common bond. Service organizations would never be able to offer the helpful services they do without a wealth of competent volunteers.

For years I served my church, St. Luke's United Methodist in Houston, as a volunteer in the church office six days a month calling all first-time visitors. I often teach Sunday school and serve on the Welcoming Committee of the church. In the economic downturn of the mid 1980s I helped establish a networking program to help the unemployed in my church find work. I gathered together every angle I could think of to help—including planning menus that cut grocery bills and utilized leftovers. I was humbled in 1999 when the church named me a Distinguished Life Member, an honor I cherish and continually work to deserve.

I also had continued volunteering in the Texas Medical Center since my days at the Kelsey Leary Clinic. While working at the clinic in the late 1950s, I often accompanied doctors on their rounds to explain to patients issues about insurance and expenses that might not be covered. My heart often was touched by tiny patients who seemed so afraid of their surroundings. The parents understandably were distressed when they would have to leave the hospital for a short while and they had no one who could stay with their child. I told many parents, "If you need me, just call me. I'll rearrange my lunch hour if at all possible and come sit with your child." For three years I helped a number of worried parents and got to love on a number of precious children.

After I left the clinic, I served on the board of the Kelsey Seybold Foundation. The infant foundation did not have the funds to hire someone to do their development work, so on Saturday or Sunday or sometimes at night I worked in the office sending out letters soliciting funds from people whose area of interest I had identified.

I was so pleased in 1995 to be named the Volunteer of the Year for the Texas Medical Center Volunteer Program. These and other volunteer positions gave me much satisfaction. While I had spent my career in banking and teaching others how to handle their money, I proved again that one cannot measure one's life by a balance sheet. The people we give to and allow to give to us are the best measure of success. By this definition I knew I was successful beyond description.

twenty-one

chapter 21

PASSING THE BATON

In 1993 one of the members of the Texas Executive Women's Women on the Move (WOM) group invited all eighty past recipients to meet for dinner to talk about what we as a group could give back to the community. That meeting was possibly the most constructive three hours I have ever spent. We decided to begin a mentoring program in one of the Houston Independent School District's high schools. We wanted to begin with a group of sixteen-year-old girls who would be ninth graders and offer a program that would give them an identity we felt they were entitled to possess. I was elected to find the school because I knew the key district superintendent who could guide us to the most appropriate school. We wanted to work with underprivileged girls who would be most likely to need our efforts. Also we desired to work with a school where the support of the faculty and counselors would be evident.

After just a few telephone calls we were meeting with the principal of the Westbury High School, who was ecstatic about having such a program since the school had a comparable program for a similar age group of boys. The school chose sixteen girls, and Texas Executive Women provided sixteen mentors. Each of us spent a minimum of three hours per week with our mentee and more when we could. We made every effort to gain their confidence so they would confide in us. We met their families and visited with their teachers, counselors, and coaches.

About every two months all thirty-two of us would meet in the home of one of the mentors and compare notes. Since this program was new, we had to feel our way along to see what worked and what did not work. By the end of the first ten months we felt we would accomplish more if we changed to a group mentoring program. Many of our mentors found regrettably that last-minute schedule changes sometimes prevented them from meeting their mentoring obligations. We felt that in a group setting, scheduled a year in advance, more girls could be exposed to the finest speakers and resource persons with less possibility for an interruption of support. This was recommended to the principal and accepted.

Shortly afterwards I received a call from the principal of the Aldine Independent School District's Stovall Middle School inviting me to begin a group mentoring program at her school. I went out to the school and talked with her about what I could expect in support, what leeway I would have for planning programs away from the campus, and a number of other issues. After our second visit I agreed to accept the assignment and did so with the blessings of TEW. Other women continued the program at Westbury and eventually added one at HISD's Austin and Milby High Schools.

On my first day at Stovall I met with forty-two eighth-grade girls—a mixture of Hispanics, African-Americans, and Asians—in the library. A tougher group of girls I had never seen. They sneered and jeered all through my presentation. "Yeah, we've heard that before!" they called. "You don't care nothin' about us. You're just lying like all them others. Why don't you quit talking so we can go home?"

I wanted to turn and run out the door, but I was not willing to be dismissed so easily. I finally did dismiss the group and told them I would be seeing them around campus. They merely laughed rudely and booed as they quickly gathered their books and backpacks and left without even a look back at me. I headed for the principal's office.

"I can't believe you are serious," she gasped when I told her my plan. "That's seventy miles a day . . . for girls who just booed you out of the library." She looked at me over her glasses with a quizzical look.

"That's what I want to do," I assured her. "I want your permission to be on campus every day and talk to the girls in class, in the cafeteria, in the hall, on the school grounds. I need to gain their confidence and respect, and that can't happen if we don't communicate with each other."

She shrugged and shook her head. "You know, I believe you'll make this happen for a change."

I said, "Well, all I can do is try. These girls don't have a clue about the possibilities that are theirs. They don't know about the world beyond what they were born into and they don't realize that they can contribute to making the world better for themselves as well as for someone else. I want to expand their horizons—if they will allow me to."

After giving me permission to be on campus, the principal confided the reason for the girls' rude behavior. Others had come to their school and made promises that were not kept. I recognized rejection and knew just what would overcome it.

For the next four weeks I got up at five, drove thirty-five miles out to Aldine, got there by 6:45, and was at the door when the girls came into the cafeteria for their free breakfast, which was provided by the district for underprivileged students. The first week I was completely ignored although I heard several ask, "Who is she?" I heard some answers to the effect that I was "some lady who told us she wanted to start a program for us, 'but she ain't comin' back out here just like all them others.'"

I bravely entered the cafeteria and tried to find as many girls as I could recognize to speak to. Hundreds of students crowded into a large room with grimy walls and long folding tables with attached benches. The smell of greasy sausage and warm donuts hit me as hard as the stares of the students. When the girls saw me coming, they would turn their backs and become deeply involved in a conversation or simply walk away. Undeterred, I met them at their classrooms, in the library or the hall, or wherever I could find them so as to be visible. It was almost two weeks before any of them would carry on any kind of a simple conversation with me, but finally at the beginning of my third week I spoke to the girl who had been the most vocal at the initial presentation. "Hello, Amelia," I smiled. "I hope you had a fun weekend."

She stopped beside me, placed her hand on her hip, and said, "You ain't kiddin', are ya, about comin' out here?"

I so wanted to reach over and pat her on the shoulder, but I knew better. I merely smiled and replied, "I don't kid about things that are dear to my heart. Yes, I am coming for a long, long time, but I had to prove it so you would listen and hopefully want to participate in the program I hope we can establish. I want to give you a better chance at success." She stared at me, fidgeted with her hair, and finally said very quietly, "I'm glad."

After that, things began to improve. By the end of my fourth week of appearing at school every day, some girls would wave at me when they came in the mornings and would speak to me in the halls. I decided it was time to give the program a try. Our first class meeting was on "Attitude, the Key to Success." We took each letter in the word attitude and selected words that began with that letter which increased the meaning of our root word. For example for the letter "a" we selected ability, assurance, and apply. When we had covered all the letters, we talked about how these words applied to us individually. Before the end of that day the girls were excited and had actually made a commitment to try to do better and act better!

For our next class a faculty member who had a beauty shop on the side lectured on the importance of make-up that added to one's beauty. She emphasized that make-up was an enhancement of one's inner beauty, not the focal point of the face. She talked about pride of hair grooming and a dress code. Then she did a complete hair makeover for a lucky girl, and our program was on its way.

By the end of the second year our programs were all set by the time school opened and we had a name for our group, Ladies of the Nineties. Several speakers asked to come back and speak to the group again and again. One was a lady who writes books for teenage girls, especially the underprivileged. She teaches them the art of saying "No" to sex, drugs, or playing hooky from school.

By 1993 the future for our girls began to look brighter, but my health began to decline as I repeated the history of my mother and grandmother of severe hypertension. At the time I started the Aldine program, I was paid by Texas Executive Women to serve as their secretary. One of the members had extra space in her office complete with computer and printer where I was officing when the mentoring program began. Linda Holt was a genius at organization and creativity. She had raised two children and knew what teenagers needed. She could understand where they came from. When I felt it was time for me to switch places from the key mentor to the coordinating mentor, I asked Linda to step in. She has added so much to the program that it has been publicized all over the city and has been copied as well.

In 1994 we dropped the eighth-grade program and began two others, at Aldine Senior High School and at the Ninth Grade School. The ninth graders call themselves Ladies of Excellence. The high schoolers call themselves Ladies of Distinction. Each letter in excellence and distinction was given a meaning by the girls to remind them of their goals. For instance, "e" stands for enthusiasm and inner energy. The "d" stands for dedication and determination.

As of January 2003 we have had almost 1,300 girls in our Aldine program with only five pregnancies, no drugs, and no encounters with the law. The participants' grades have risen dramatically, and we have had many students on the Honor Roll. Soon we began hearing, "When I go to college . . . ." whereas before their participation, they did not even consider a college.

Many of these girls have no idea who their father is or where their mother is. They have no amenities at home. Few have cars; some have no television. They are truly deprived. We had lots of seed to sow, and sow we have. Now we have two in the military taking their college work and more than a dozen in college, including one of our girls going to Rice University to study biomedical engineering! She has received $88,000 in scholarships, some of which are renewable. We are going to make it possible for her to live on campus for she needs this association and there is no home transportation. She is heavily involved in doing community service. We require all the girls to do 50 hours per year and she had done more than 195 hours when there were still two months left in the semester. Many girls work more than their required 50 hours of community service. Last year alone we tracked 5260 hours given by these girls to their communities. The Rice student spoke last year to my church's Women's Society. Before more than 100 women, she told her story about the mentoring program with not one note. When we look at this precious girl and others like her, all the weary hours of meetings and planning seem more than worthwhile.

I had to raise the money for whatever I wanted to accomplish in the mentoring program for we had no income and nowhere to get it from either. Finally I set a budget and raised the money among my colleagues for my needs. All year we apply for grants and are always surprised by generous donors who send from $50 to $5000 for expenses and our endowment funds. Now TEW donates approximately $40,000 a year to the programs. The funds help pay for off-campus trips to businesses and such special events as a five-course meal at the Hotel Sofitel using their newly acquired social skills. This meal follows a seminar with a nationally known presenter.

In 1997 TEW named their endowment fund for me and I established a fund, the Jackie Greer Dollar Club, to sponsor girls to go to our best community college for two years on a full scholarship.

Two years after the mentoring program started, the girls asked if they might be privileged to be givers of Christmas gifts instead of receivers. They did not know what they were asking because they had nothing to give except their hearts. Seeing their need to give back though, we said we would see what we could do.

God worked out the details to give these girls their desire. A friend at church heard me tell of their wish and asked if I could use peck-size baskets. If so, she could get them donated by a manufacturer in Jacksonville, Texas. When this donation was verified, I contacted friends at the local Farmers Market, who agreed to fill the baskets with fresh produce. Wal-Mart furnished ample pieces of cellophane in gold, green, and red to line each basket and construction paper so the girls could make accompanying greeting cards. An organization in our neighborhood made up of Catholic and Methodist congregations delivered the baskets to needy families who would not have had any Christmas other than these gifts of love. This has become an annual giving mission, and each year more people help us expand the giving by furnishing more baskets, fruit, and other supplies. The girls benefit from being the ones to give, and they are encouraged by the number of people who help them accomplish their project.

As I delighted in the successes of our mentees, I also delighted in the honors that continued to come my way. In 1991 the Houston Federation of Professional Women named me a Woman of Distinction. In 1994 I was thrilled to be the first to be named Woman of Distinction by the Texas Woman's University College of Business Administration. In 1997 I was proud to be named a Champion of All Seasons—the Dynamic Aging Honoree by the Medical Center's nursing association and the Houston Chronicle. Four women were so honored for "personal vivacity and community achievement." A luncheon in our honor raised close to $50,000 for nursing scholarships.

My highest national honor came in 1998 when the justices of the United States Supreme Court chose me to receive the coveted George Washington Valley Forge Foundation award for the Outstanding Woman in Mentoring in America. My good friend, Dr. Kate Bell, was instrumental in making them aware of my work with TEW and the Aldine mentoring programs. The next year the Aldine Independent School District was instrumental in my receiving the State Board of Education's Annual Award, "Heroes for Children," for my mentoring work. I cherish this recognition as much as I cherish the memories of the many girls who are fulfilling their potential because of our program.

The girls' achievements remind me of a new hobby I developed as the result of two protégés of mine who invited me to their new house. On the back porch they proudly pointed out a nondescript, little wire cage holding a caterpillar that was almost ready to go into the chrysalis, the hard shell that protects the creature while it is transformed into a butterfly. They offered to give the caterpillar to me. I was so excited I could hardly contain myself because I have collected butterfly accessories for my house for years. As they drove me home, the caterpillar started wildly swinging back and forth inside the cocoon. Suddenly there was a little splat on the bottom of the cage. The furry creature had shed its coat and was drawing itself up to conceal itself inside the chrysalis. Soon a butterfly would emerge from a rather transparent mass that hung at the same spot the caterpillar had attached itself to before "hiding" in the cocoon.

My friends explained to me that in a couple of days I would notice a small black band around the top of the chrysalis. The band would be indicative that the wings of the butterfly were forming. Then several days later a wider dark orange band would form that would indicate the wings were formed. About three days later I saw creases in the outside of the chrysalis. Within a few more days those broke open and the little wings began to emerge. It took all day for the butterfly to leave its covering. At first it was small. As I watched, I could see it elongate to a full-size Monarch butterfly. What a glorious sight this was to see one of God's creatures develop into what He intended. The butterfly then began trying its wings, and by the end of the day the Monarch reached the door of the cage and flew out, heading south for Mexico as it was getting close to the time for the butterflies to arrive at their roosting place.

Because these friends had built a habitat for Monarchs, I was able to get the eggs and food and raise them for about a year. Then in 2001, due to toxic pollution, millions of butterflies died in Mexico and we have not had any Monarchs in Houston since. Whether we ever have them back in Houston is anybody's guess. I guess even for wild creatures, life is a series of beginnings and endings, and there is always a beginning again somewhere.

If we are fortunate, as we hope our mentees are, life is an unfolding of our potential like the butterfly. With God's help and our persistence, even caterpillars can develop into beautiful creatures. I was living proof of the possibility.

twenty-two

chapter 22
REFLECTIONS

People often ask me, "How do you stay so active at ninety-three?"

Not all believe me when I answer that I have always believed in keeping your friends under the age of sixty and continuing the schedule you have always kept. It is not unusual for me to spend ten to twelve hours a day at my computer and desk. Sometimes I hop on the Internet and stay up all night talking to folks all over the world. I figure that if I don't change pace, I won't slow down. So far, that is working.

I continue consulting when the occasion arises, sit on boards when asked, and volunteer with the Aldine girls and often at my church. I have never lost touch with the world at large and never plan to do so. I do a lot of entertaining, with breakfasts and luncheons. In the early 1990s Tommie Jones, my friend from the early 1970s, left banking and became my personal companion and helper. She is a wonderful cook and enjoys hosting parties as much as I do. She also keeps me organized, helps with shopping, and manages my household. With so much to do, the days pass too fast for me.

Some nights when I can't sleep, I wander into the kitchen, search the refrigerator for whatever ingredients I can find, and attempt a culinary creation. It matters not whether it is vegetables, meat, or fruits. I enjoy trying new dishes. While not all of my experiments are worth repeating—or even eating!—I share two of my successes at the end of this chapter.

At ninety-three the same principle applies that has governed my entire life: You can do what you want to do. It may take a little more planning than when you were younger because some days it is a challenge to stay focused. Also I try to follow the advice Dad gave me when I was fourteen: Take time each day to reach out to someone and share a good word. I try not to let a day pass that I don't make a telephone call or send an email or card, cook a dish, or drop by to visit someone. God takes time for me every day, so surely I can do the same.

Age is not a factor in our lives unless we allow it to be. I have a standard answer to the oft-asked question, "How old are you, Jackie?" I answer, "I don't know exactly. All I know is that I have been on this earth long enough to roll up a wealth of experiences." I see age as merely a combination of experiences. Furniture may be old, but people are experienced, some more than others.

When I was a young girl, I vowed never to compare myself to furniture. My grandmother had a house full of German antiques. They were beautiful—to everyone but me. Every week I had to take a paint brush and painstakingly clean the grooves of each of eleven pieces of furniture. Some were elaborately and intricately carved, so my job was tedious and time-consuming. I vowed that when I grew up, I would have no antiques that had to be cleaned with a paint brush, and I have kept my promise. I do have some priceless pieces such as candelabras, cut glass, and a few pieces of silver which I enjoy, but they have no tedious cleaning requirements. I must confess that I often wonder what my grandmother did with all of her antique furniture. The pieces she reluctantly gave to Mother and me were not the antiques. They were disposed of while I was off at college and when I asked about them, I was told very curtly that was not public information. I never disputed that she had the right, as owner, to do with them as she pleased. I just wondered who had agreed to clean them during the next century.

I have learned that the tonic to life's ailments is not the things you possess or your accomplishments, but staying active and being useful. Even with limitations you can do something to brighten someone else's day. We are all needed; we all contribute something different to the wonderful mix of life.

Even my mother, with all her shortcomings as a wife and mother, was a marvel. At eighty-two she registered at Rice University for a five-year course in "The Great Books of Today and Yesterday." The classes were intense, with huge chunks of reading each week of such classic authors as Shakespeare. She drove about ten miles every Monday, Wednesday, and Friday night to Rice and sat in class from seven to ten. Every night as she prepared to leave the campus, she called the West University Police Department and asked them to send an officer to meet her at a nearby intersection and follow her home. The officers delighted in obliging this elderly woman, they admired for her optimism in signing up for anything that lasted for five years. They would wait until she was in the house and the kitchen light came on.

I learned after her death that the police department knew her also because they often stopped her for speeding. They laughed that she was always quick with an excuse for her malfeasance. "Now, officer, I was detained at my last appointment and have a piano student who will be waiting for me at the house. Please follow me home so the child does not have to wait for her lesson," she would say as if she were the one enforcing the law. The fact that she had been speeding was immaterial. All she could see was her schedule.

Of course Mother's main occupation was teaching piano to children between the ages of five and thirteen and organ to students between sixteen and twenty-nine. In addition to lessons at our house, she taught at two other studios in town, to which she drove twice weekly.

Mother remarked to a friend once that she had no intention of having older friends for they surely would die and leave her all alone. She said she intended to die and leave her friends, and that is what she did. Indeed I recall only one of her Houston friends between the ages of fifty and sixty. The rest were close to my age.

We always have a choice about how we view aging. My age has taken me more places and allowed me to do more things in the past forty years than I could have ever imagined. The credit for these wonderful experiences goes to my extended family and my friends in business and socially. Had it not been for people who believed in me, I would have had no reason to perform and nothing I could recognize to give.

In spite of my childhood and early adulthood I have learned to turn all matters over to God and be governed by His decisions. Mother should never have married and certainly there should never have been a child, but it happened. I happened. Even though my childhood and early adulthood were painful, I learned what the apostle Paul meant when he wrote to the people of Philippi, "I can do all things through Christ who gives me strength." God led me through the sorrows to a life full of love and appreciation.

On my ninetieth birthday in 1999 I hosted another party at my church. Since I did not include out-of-town friends, only 426 attended and I did not have the follow-up breakfast. On my ninety-third birthday in 2002 a protégé of mine hosted a lovely party in her home. We invited 180 and were thrilled that 145 attended with no out-of-town guests. When we plan my ninety-fifth birthday party, there will be a list of approximately 1100 and that will be the last party for me to give. When I reach the centennial year, somebody else will have to give my birthday party. I have played hostess in five-year intervals, and I think my time has been served.

However I continue to share some observations I have made over my career and to warn that ignoring them will invite disaster. I readily share the system of career progress that worked for me time and time again. I encourage younger workers to decide what they want to do and tell them to go to the top executives in the organization and ask if they see you in that role. If they think you are not prepared, ask how you can get prepared. Then do what they suggest. If you can't reach your goal in one organization, possibly you can in another. You have to make your own path sometimes. Be graceful as you go about it, but don't hesitate. Being proactive is not the same as being aggressive. It just makes good sense to ask for what you want.

The most obvious observation I point out to people is that, in business particularly, bigger is not always better. I seldom hear executives talk about being better than their competitors or guiding their companies to excel. Instead I hear of plans for growth and expansion, as if they were rights of all businesses. When I hear management talk of getting bigger without first planning for improvement, I lose confidence in that company.

However disappointed I may be looking at some ways of the world, I remember all the wonderful people who have crossed my path and am grateful for each one. I learned early that a loving heart never quits loving. I look forward to each day for the love that will be revealed and I keep focused on the future as I also remember that life always begins.

twenty-three

chapter 23

NO END IN SIGHT

Not too many people want or need to go to work at age ninety-three, but it does happen and so it was with me. As my years outstripped my financial resources, I returned to the workforce as a marketing consultant for The Hall Group and continued consulting as the opportunity arose.

When I was explaining to a group that I had had to return to work, a friend spoke up, "Well, that is really remarkable, but I am going to speak for all your friends. Please just die before you retire this time for eight retirement parties are more than enough."

So I promised to be considerate of my good friends and work until the day I was called to another address.

So life always begins—and, as always, life will come to an end. I want the end of the life of Jackie Greer to be a continuation of God's life through the many people who have filled my life with so much happiness and meaning. My life would be in vain if the blessings of my life did not continue to blossom through my extended family and my special friends who have let me be a part of their lives.

Each day I include time to reflect on all that God has given me. I encourage everyone I meet to make a difference in someone's life on a daily basis. What you do may be small and inconsequential, but the important thing is the fact that you cared and you made your love known.

Before you close this book, I encourage you to thank God for family and friends. Then take time to tell just one person you love him or her, and thank the person for enriching your life and reflecting God's love into your life.

Although I missed many things as I grew up, the pain of those years were erased and replaced with the glorious experience of acceptance that came to me as a part of God's plan. He purposed all along for me to have a wonderful extended family and the best friends a person could possibly have. I am so rich and so grateful for God's promise in Joel 2:25, "I will restore to you the years the swarming locust has eaten .... You shall eat in plenty and be satisfied, and praise the name of the Lord your God, who has dealt wondrously with you."

Friends and family have restored the painful years of my youth. "A friend is your need answered," a wise prophet said. How true that has been in my life, and I have tried to make it true in the lives of others. God did not leave me alone, and I rejoice that He will not leave me alone whenever the time comes for my ultimate new beginning. Life always begins and God is always with us, no matter where those beginnings lead.

the

BEGINNING